Acclaim for Bruce McCall's

THIN ICE

"Known for his fantastical illustrations and sure-shot humor pieces, McCall here proves himself an able memoirist as well." —*The New Yorker*

"Engaging . . . McCall superbly evokes a world in which parents are giants if not gods, and every-thing—events, attitudes, the very notion of what life meant—revolved around them."
                    —*The Washington Post Book World*

"A wondrous and eviscerating memoir. . . . Rich and haunting."   —*Chicago Tribune*

"Peers into the Canadian soul." —*The New York Times*

"A wonderful, bittersweet memoir . . . so funny that I found myself reading passages aloud."
                              —Peter Jennings

"Bruce McCall recounts the exquisite horror of coming of age in Canada when one is not simply a social leper but an extraordinarily lousy ice-hockey player in his comic memoir."   —*Vanity Fair*

Also by Bruce McCall

Zany Afternoons

Bruce McCall's

THIN ICE

Canadian-born New York resident Bruce McCall is a prolific writer and illustrator who got his start in the glory days of the *National Lampoon* and whose unique visions now appear frequently in *The New Yorker*, *Vanity Fair*, and other magazines. A collection of his humor, *Zany Afternoons*, was published in 1982.

THIN ICE

Thin Ice

BRUCE McCALL

Vintage Books
A Division of Random House, Inc.
New York

FIRST VINTAGE BOOKS EDITION, MARCH 1999

Copyright © 1997 by Bruce McCall

The drawing on the title and part-title pages and the illustrations on pages 121-23 are by Bruce McCall. All McCall family photographs are from the collection of Hugh McCall.

The Library of Congress has cataloged the Random House edition as follows:
McCall, Bruce.
Thin ice : coming of age in Canada / Bruce McCall.
p. cm.
ISBN 0-679-44847-0
I. McCall, Bruce—Childhood and youth. 2. Canada—Biography.
3. Simcoe (Ont.)—Biography. 4. Canada—Relations—United States.
5. United States—Relations—Canada. I. Title.
CT310.M245A3 1997
971.063'092—dc21 96-49620
[B]

Vintage ISBN: 0-679-76959-5

Author photograph © Sara Barrett

www.randomhouse.com

Printed in the United States
10 9 8 7 6 5 4 3 2 1

To Mike, Hugh,
Tom, Walt,
and Chris

FOREWORD

It's doubtful that Jim Carrey, k. d. lang, Wayne Gretzky, or any other Canadians of the post-sixties generation who have settled in the USA would understand what the hell much of the huffing and puffing in this book is all about. Over the past thirty years or so, since I slipped away, the distinction between being a Canadian and being an American seems to have blurred to the point where the official border between the two nations seems less a true border than a minor bureaucratic formality indicating that a single culture has merely shifted gears.

It's the animating idea of this book to try to re-create a time when things were very different indeed—a time when a Canadian, certainly this Canadian, felt himself to be about two-thirds American, with the other third composed of a grayish ball of chaff: hockey/plaid/butter tarts/earmuffs/CBC/Mounties/toques/wheat/fish/lumber/God Save the King/Queen. This led the average Canadian to discount automatically his home and native land by about 33.3 percent, especially in the presence of Americans. Aside from the pathos of Canadian smokers forever pining to wrap their lips around a Camel or a Lucky (no Yank was ever reported to have craved a Craven-A or a Sweet Caporal), the sense of not quite measuring up created the world's only national culture nourished by self-effacement. It drove some natives half berserk with America-envy and into reactive fixations on Ed McCurdy, Inuit carvings, or the

Group of Seven, and delivered many of the more suggestible among them, including me, across the ice floes and into the brawny embrace of Uncle Sam.

It will perhaps still the pens of letter writers—and a check of the correspondence columns of virtually any periodical in North America will attest that letters to the editor are a Canadian pastime at least as popular as eating doughnuts—to state up front that in my particular reaction to the Canadian Dilemma I was, well, unique: The confluence of circumstance, environment, and genes that shaped my experience is no likelier to be repeated anytime soon than the anomaly that produced the Dionne quintuplets. And before Fred G. of Carp, Ontario, can race to the post office/*bureau des postes* to argue, I know very well that the Canadian milieu today—separatism and all that apart—is altogether too healthy for the squiggly things that infested my youthful imagination to breed, much less take hold.

Besides, this doesn't claim to be a work of historical research, only a personal memoir. Not necessarily how it was, only how it felt. I wouldn't for a moment presume to horn in on Mordecai Richler or Pierre Berton as explainer of Canada to Canadians and the world. Anyway, mine was exclusively—one might say suffocatingly—the Anglo-Saxon Upper Canada experience. Upper Canada—that is, Ontario—is the most densely populated part of the country and the richest, but even on the decidedly mild Canadian index of spice and ferment it always ranked somewhere above New Zealand and below Belgium. If anyone dared to say that it is representative of the spirit of the whole nation, Canadians from Nova Scotia to British Columbia would rightly protest.

The specific Canadian family at the center of this story—mine— is seen through an even more subjective lens. Our parents are dead, but my five siblings are still alive and alert, and I expect them to be especially alert when they sit down to read this unauthorized version of our joint and individual early lives. The conclusions and observations herein about life under the same roof and parental regime are solely and deliberately my own. To have proceeded via a sibling consensus would for all I know have produced a superior book but a quite different book from the one I felt impelled to write, which was neither an oral family history nor *Rashomon*.

Finally, I resisted whenever I could giving people in this story the fake noses and mustaches of altered names; it seems bizarre to have to set up a witness-protection program in your own book about your own life.

NEW YORK CITY, 1996

ACKNOWLEDGMENTS

Preparing to write this story provided a wonderful excuse to cadge reminiscences from my brothers Mike, Hugh, and Walt and my sister Chris. All of them are fitted with high-powered wide-angle zoom memory lenses that over and over brought dim and fuzzy moments into startling sharp focus, and none of them regards recollection and reminiscence as any reason to suspend their wariness of the mawkish or their knack for detecting the ironic, the ridiculous, and the absurd. All were cheerfully forthcoming, often on matters that couldn't always have been pleasant to recall. Mike not only answered my every question but frequently followed up with thoughtful and witty written amplifications, some of which are quoted in the text.

Hugh, his total recall augmented by forty-nine years' worth of daily diaries, kindly vetted the manuscript for inaccuracies. The distance along Danforth Avenue, in Toronto, from Broadview to Main Street, as he pointed out in his faxed list of offenses and corrections, is not 4 but 3.1 miles. It's Gerrard Street, not Gerard Street, and the restaurant was Bassel's, not Basil's. If an error should have somehow survived Hugh's scrutiny and made it into print, it was my lapse alone, and I apologize to him before he can fax again.

My wife, Polly, more than tolerantly forbore the intrusion of this book on our family life for the better part of a year and a half. My writing regimen was strict: steal every spare minute I could, anytime, anywhere. I stole the better part of idyllic vacations on Nevis, in the

Caribbean, and in France, more country weekends than it's comfortable now to count, and far more time overall than I promised I would, sealed off from Polly and my daughter, Amanda, with my memories and my notepad.

Appreciation is due my agent and friend Liz Darhansoff for retaining a client too muddleheaded to even remember to send her a manuscript. The enthusiasm of Doug Pepper, of Random House Canada, was downright inspiring. Daniel Menaker, of Random House in New York, my editor, made this book happen. He then kept me in a frame of mind about it that fooled me into thinking I could actually pull it off. Thanks to Dan for making this the happiest creative project I ever undertook.

NEW YORK CITY, 1996

CONTENTS

Part I

CANADIAN LIFE, AMERICAN DREAMS

THE SCAVENGER OF HIGHWAY #3

Another spacious summer afternoon in 1946 in Simcoe, Ontario, pop. 6,000. Most local youngsters not off at camp, lolling on the nearby Lake Erie beaches, or picking strawberries in the surrounding farm fields are gallivanting at the municipal swimming pool. Half a mile north, as cars hurtle by, inches away, a lone eleven-year-old boy slowly patrols the shoulder of the two-lane highway that cuts through town. He looks only down. He sporadically scoops this or that small object from the gravel and dirt of the shoulder and inspects it. Most he casts aside after a cursory look, but a few go into a pocket of his short pants, which he then fondly pats each time, as if it were money in there, or jewels.

Provincial Highway #3 is a heavily traveled shortcut between the American Midwest and the northeastern states in these pre-interstate days; and the boy—me—is pocketing a connoisseur's selection of matchbooks, Camel packs, Schlitz bottle tops, and Baby Ruth wrappers flung from passing cars bound from Detroit to Buffalo and vice versa.

To me, they are no mere roadside detritus. They are to be fondled, savored, prized. They are rare and priceless artifacts delivered fresh from a higher civilization. They are American.

Meanwhile, a carton of freshly printed books has arrived at the Eva Brook Donly Museum on Norfolk Street near the center of town: the first copies of *The Genealogy and History of the Norfolk McCall Family and Associate Descendants, 1796–1946*, compiled by Delbert T. McCall, a distant relation.

The dedicatory poem on the first page sets the tone:

> Dear were the homes where they were born,
>   Where slept their honored dead;
> And rich and wide, on every side,
>   Their fruitful acres spread;
> But dearer to their faithful hearts
>   Than home, and gold, and lands,
> Were Britain's laws, and Britain's crown,
>   And grip of British hands.

Delbert's genealogy is mainly a proud and detailed recapitulation of 150 unbroken years' worth of fealty to God and the Crown—not always necessarily in that order—by the generations of Norfolk County McCalls that are his subject matter.

The patriarch was Donald McCall—"Old Donald," "Noble Donald," "Noble Old Donald," as his hagiographer variously exults—late of what is now Basking Ridge in Somerset County, New Jersey; before that, of His Majesty King George III's army; before that, of the Isle of Mull in Scotland. On a July day in 1796 Donald stepped ashore from the boat that had brought him and his family to Lake Erie and a clearing on its northern shore, on the final stage of their long voyage from temporary refuge in Nova Scotia.

Regional history would classify Old Donald as something more than a patriot and a pioneer. He was a prototypical United Empire Loyalist—a kind of inverted but non-gender-specific member of the Canadian version of the Daughters of the American Revolution—and as such a superpatriot and founding Canadian. His was the classic U.E.L. story. He had sailed to America from Scotland in 1756 as an enlistee in the Forty-second Highlanders. He fought the Indians, he fought the French, he fought with General Wolfe at Quebec in the successful battle to raise the Union Jack over Canada and forever lower the Fleur-de-Lis. His enlistment period finally over, Donald—

then in barracks at Philadelphia—did as many other such British Army veterans did upon discharge: Eschewing a return to the old world, he settled in the Colonies to farm and to raise a family.

But not for long. Staunch British loyalties were rapidly becoming more than a social handicap in places like Basking Ridge. They were halfway to treason. Donald took the hint. "The abuse and persecution these old stalwarts were subjected to," fumes Delbert, "was more than they could endure and they finally yielded to the fates, sacrificed their humble and happy homes to share the lot of numerous refugees in the far-away northland, where British laws and assurances restored them to that peace of mind so relished by honorable people."

Donald's reward for his loyalty to the Crown was twofold: a six-hundred-acre land grant in the Long Point Settlement in what is now Norfolk County, Ontario, and immortality—among those who value such things—as a United Empire Loyalist.

Old Donald would be gathered to his ancestors in 1818. His immediate and later descendants largely chose to stay close to the original homestead and spread their roots not wide but deep. Delbert's history records McCalls, generation after generation, clustering there in Norfolk County—farmers working the fertile land, lumbermen, millwrights, storekeepers, innkeepers. Fellow Scots by the hundreds had migrated there in Donald's wake to spread across southwestern Ontario like marmalade; McCalls married almost exclusively within the local Scots immigrant colony and spawned large families. By the mid-nineteenth century, barely fifty years after Donald's advent, the Norfolk McCall family tree was already an impenetrable thicket.

A drunk, profligate, slow-witted, or deviant McCall never appears in Delbert's circumspect family chronicle. They are an unfailingly pious, sober, civic-minded line, these Duncans and Jameses and Daniels and their Phoebes and Charitys and Jemimas. And patriotic. They had but to hear the word *war*, or even *rebellion*, or only *raid*, before the clang of McCalls dropping their adzes and scythes and saws to pick up their muskets reverberated across the county. Delbert proudly recounts in his chronicle the rallying to arms of seven successive McCall generations, beginning eons ago with Noble Old

Donald's father at the Battle of Culloden and up to my own father's
R.C.A.F. service in World War Two. Donald's sons, chips off the old
soldier, made almost an avocation of Yankee-potting in the early
1800s, in the course of defending local settlements from marauding intruders in the skirmishing that preceded the all-out Canadian-
American War of 1812–14. A McCall was there—indeed often
more than one, and one often in charge—at every call to arms
through the nineteenth century. One was a captain in the Home
Guard during the Fenian Raid; another was a boatman on Kitchener's
Sudan expedition of 1883. My own Grandfather Walt sailed off
with the Canadian Army contingent to the Boer War in 1899, to be
captured—shades of young Winston Churchill—then to escape.
The first Norfolk County soldier to be killed in World War One, a
few days after reaching the front in September 1915, was a McCall.

As Delbert's genealogical reconstruction makes vivid, the McCalls
of Norfolk County embraced the British view of events on the
North American continent from the Revolutionary War onward:
The American colonists were seen as an ingrate rabble so infected
with their zeal for independence that they itched to drive the British
not only out of their own colonies but off the map of North America, annexing Canada at the first opportunity as part of the process.
The greedy Yanks had been plotting to do just that until 1812,
when, as every Canadian schoolchild learned in history class, it came
to a head in all-out war. Canada, valiant David against the American
goliath, thereupon (with, er, a little help from the British) trounced
the bastards, and for good measure torched the White House.

Fears of a Yankee takeover subsided somewhat in the aftermath,
but the suspicion that they might try it again sometime lingered with
surprising persistence for much of the rest of the nineteenth century,
especially in places like Norfolk County, within easy raiding distance; and the residue of that suspicion fueled the faint hostility, the
sense of having to always be on guard, that colored Canadian attitudes—certainly McCall attitudes—toward the USA well into the
twentieth. By my father's generation that impulse had metamor-
phosed into a hot but largely dormant little glob of bile lodged
somewhere in the Canadian craw.

• • •

I grew up in a world where the average Canadian would rather be trampled by the R.C.M.P. Musical Ride than be found publicly admitting anything American to be superior, or even much good. Nobody, not even the most rabidly anti-American Canadian nationalist, could or would deny the economic and cultural facts of life that all but swamped our nation in Americana. But that didn't mean Canadians had to like it. That would mean accepting and even liking Americans, and wait just a minute, eh? If the general attitude of Canadians toward their mighty neighbor to the south could be distilled into a single phrase, that phrase would probably be "Oh, shut up." The Americans talked too much, mainly about themselves. Their torrid love affair with their own history and legend exceeded—painfully— the quasi–British Canadian idea of modesty and self-restraint. They were jammed permanently in extroverted high gear, confident to the brink of, if not over the edge of, arrogance; strident, take-charge, can-do—fatiguing. There was about the American style something, indeed plenty, that jarred the Canadian love of calm. Americans spent far too much of their vaunted energy out at the extremes of feeling. They were forever busting their buttons in spasms of insufferable yahoo pride or all too publicly agonizing over their crises.

The patriotic Canadian should keep his distance, then. Snuggle in the warmth and safety of the British institutions and customs and attitudes that have always underpinned Canadian life, lending it dignity and order, helping shield it from the obnoxious blowhards forever yelping and banging and partying next door, way past bedtime.

This was the view of the Americans I had breathed as part of the very air of Simcoe and Canada since infancy. Evidence that ours was a superior civilization was obvious, at least to us: We had the Imperial gallon, two-dollar bills, Mounties, the more scenic part of Niagara Falls, grade thirteen in high school, a governor-general, Eskimos, three downs in football, the Toronto Maple Leafs and the Montreal Canadiens, our Deanna Durbin in Hollywood and our Max Aitken, Lord Beaverbrook, in London, and a permanent private pipeline to Buckingham Palace.

And yet, even by age eleven I was beginning to secretly backslide. I had begun to find myself privately questioning my faith and putting it to the test. I was beginning to wonder if, despite all the evidence, Canada really was so inherently superior and the way of the USA really was so inherently intolerable. I was feeling the first pangs of envy arising from a strong and growing suspicion that not all that far away, over the border, the average eleven-year-old American kid was having lots more fun. From all appearances, indeed, being first in fun was part of the American boy's birthright.

Reminders were as plentiful as the comparisons that inevitably followed. American kids got whistles, rings, glittering prizes in their cereal boxes; all we got was cereal. They could goggle at page after page of color comics—"Prince Valiant," "The Katzenjammer Kids," "Smokey Stover"—in their Sunday papers; we didn't even have Sunday papers. The comic book, that archetypal American expressive form—splashy, loud, rowdy, and manic, boiling with superheroes and supervillains, a TNT charge to the boyish imagination—had only a pallid, pathetic Canadian counterpart. The few Canadian comic books were black-and-white, vapid, and hopelessly wholesome. American kids, as I vicariously feasted along with them via the comic-book ads, guzzled Royal Crown Cola, rode balloon-tired Schwinn bikes with sirens and headlights or deluxe coaster wagons or futuristic scooters. They shot pearl-handled cap guns drawn from tooled-leather holsters or Daisy air rifles, wore aviator goggles, flew gasoline-powered model airplanes. American kids even had their own exclusive boys' mail-order department store in the form of the Johnson & Smith catalog. Rushed to your front door C.O.D. from Racine, Wisconsin—ventriloquism kits, genuine onyx signet rings, whoopee cushions, treasures Made in the USA.

But not for me; not for Canadians. In the fine-print legalese, in the radio announcer's dream-smashing disclaimer, four words would serve to keep every son of the Maple Leaf empty-handed and brokenhearted, with his nose pressed enviously to the glass that separated him from the delirious ongoing American carnival of plenty and fun: "Not Available in Canada."

I was beginning to discern that this bounty showered down upon

American boyhood was a mere by-product of a system so inconceivably rich and generous that it was almost carelessly throwing off wealth in every direction, nonstop.

The American cars swishing through the north of town weren't the dusty old Fords and Chevrolets Simconians drove. They were big Buicks and Packards and Chryslers and Oldsmobiles with whitewall tires and metallic paint jobs, the brightest colors ever seen in Norfolk County. They drove fast—naturally, as brother Mike explained; everybody knew the Americans had better gasoline. The Bakelite model of the Empire State Building on the desk of Dr. Sihler, the family dentist, had transfixed me from about age five; I now realized why. Canada had no Empire State Building, no Hoover Dam, no Golden Gate Bridge; Canada declined to soar in any way.

The Americans had Franklin Delano Roosevelt at the helm. We had a dyspeptic-looking old bachelor, MacKenzie King. Canada lacked the energy to make it through a week without closing down on Wednesday afternoons and all day Sunday to rest. The USA was open twenty-four hours a day, seven days a week, and even that was barely time enough for them to cram in all the things they were up to. The more I pondered it, the more true it seemed to be: Everything exciting, bold, glamorous in life could be traced back to America. To New York, Hollywood, Detroit, and Washington, D.C.

It was probably foreordained, such a view, when the picture of America was obtained exclusively through the peephole of mass media by an eleven-year-old kid whose familiarity with Canada was limited to his small hometown. The duel for affection between America and Canada was rigged from the outset. Canada, its thin population strung out across four thousand miles, one in ten Francophone and thus out of the action, could never generate the cultural combustion that made a country buzz. Canada couldn't afford a domestic movie industry, or even a commercial radio network, and its few national magazines couldn't compete economically or editorially with their giant American counterparts.

It was superficial, but my handful of empirical evidence was all I needed to decide that whatever their failings in the dour Canadian view, the Yanks seemed to be doing things bigger, bolder, better, and reaping the rewards by way of a richer and more exciting life than anybody north of the 49th Parallel could ever hope to live.

And, in fairness, something about my growing disenchantment was real: the growing discrepancy between Simcoe's and Canada's metabolism and mine. Being a true son of the strong, north, brave, and free required a calmer, steadier, more controlled temperament than the one beginning to jell within me. Canadianism seemed to require, beneath everything, contentment with the world as it was. Not so— emphatically not so—down south amid those amber waves of grain. In fact you could take almost any random Canadian trait, invert or reverse it, and—presto!—you had an American trait. And U.E.L. ancestors, generations of proudly anti-American McCalls, "O Canada," and all the sturdy virtues it celebrated notwithstanding, in the American style I was coming to recognize the greater part of myself.

So let them gibe and rant and call me turncoat. Give me the shoulder of Highway #3, any day.

SIMCOE

Niagara Falls and the cities of Toronto, Cleveland, and Buffalo all lie within a hundred miles of Simcoe, Ontario, but in my time there, before superhighways and the accelerating pace of postwar life had devalued distance, a hundred miles meant what a thousand miles does today—particularly to a kid. I may have ventured outside Norfolk County two or three times before the age of twelve; Simcoe itself seemed dense enough with mystery and wonder to make the trip to its south end from the north end, where I lived, a hegira into strange realms where, for all I knew, unicorns pranced.

The roof of the Mason Arena skating rink collapsed in the twenties, and Falls' department store burned down in the thirties. Otherwise, and excepting a royal visit early in the century by the duke of Connaught—his train paused at the Airline Station north of town so the duchess could receive a wreath from a local delegation—nothing more of note had ever happened in Simcoe than in Delhi, Aylmer, Tillsonburg, or any other of the small, middling-prosperous farming centers in the adjoining counties. Norfolk did produce the man who embalmed Rudolph Valentino, and Simcoe gave the world its quota of N.H.L. hockey players, as well as Rick Danko, of The Band.

Simcoe sits eight miles north of Lake Erie at the headwaters of the Lynn River, a tributary of the relatively mighty Grand, on whose banks, about twenty-four miles north, near Brantford, Alexander

Graham Bell dreamed up the telephone in the late 1860s while visiting his parents. (This is a Canadian fact, which, like the Canadian dollar, is seldom accepted in the United States and heavily discounted when it is.) It might be noted that Brantford, named after the great pro-British Iroquois leader Joseph Brant, gave us Wayne Gretzky, and the novelist Thomas B. Costain was once editor of the local paper, the *Expositor*. Between Brantford and Simcoe lies the Six Nations Indian reservation, traversed in my time at speed with the car windows rolled up, to foil scalping parties. I never did see an Indian.

A famously rich thirty inches of loam blankets most of Norfolk County, which is also almost level and largely rock-free. Agriculture was Norfolk's and Simcoe's destiny. The prime crop for decades was tobacco, but cornfields and apple, peach, and cherry orchards also abounded, and the Simcoe air in late summer was always pungent with the aroma of the tons of locally grown tomatoes trucked in, cooked, and canned in factories near the center of town.

Simcoe is named after the first governor of Upper Canada, Colonel John Graves Simcoe (1765–1822), one in a relay of highborn Englishmen dispatched from Whitehall in the late eighteenth and early nineteenth centuries to impose proper British law and table manners on the infant nation while subduing the Indians, evicting the French, and shaking a white-gloved fist at the surly Colonials to the south. A plaque screwed to a rock in what is now Lynwood Park states that the colonel camped there overnight on one or another progress through the region. The plaque fails to mention what my cousin Walter Stewart observes in his lively history of the United Empire Loyalists, *True Blue*—namely, that Colonel John Graves Simcoe was "a perfect fathead," a snob and a martinet and an incompetent administrator. To me, the most interesting fact about him was that he headquartered at York—later Toronto—living in a tent obtained from the estate of the late British naval explorer Captain James Cook. If it hadn't been for the colonel's overnight stop, Simcoe might still be known by its original and infinitely more lyrical name, Bird Town.

Simcoe was founded in the first decade of the nineteenth century, and its population grew steadily over the next hundred years to something like a natural ceiling of six thousand souls, leveled off, and stayed there for decades. If you superimposed an aerial photograph taken in my time over one taken twenty or thirty or even forty years before, Simcoe's downtown and surrounding neighborhoods would look remarkably unchanged. The town was old enough to drowse under ancient shade trees, and just modern enough that the streets beneath them formed a rigid rectangular grid. Most of its redbrick commercial buildings and many of its homes dated from the previous century. There was never the need for any building to rise above three or four stories. The fanciful and the decorative were absent from the heart of town—agriculture being a pursuit that seldom spawns Athenian impulses—but here and there under the canopies of green on the sleepy side streets you would encounter one or another brick fancy in the high Victorian style, flaunting its gingerbread and stained-glass and wrought ironwork. Their owners must have been rich, at least by local standards, but as a kid, all I knew was that these landmarks helped lend the town the timeless atmosphere, the comforting sense of permanence, that struck me then and still does today as among its foremost charms.

Simcoe had its Woolworth's and Esso stations and Ford dealer, but the assumption that it was interchangeable with any midwestern American town of similar age and size would be wrong. From children's Meccano sets and Dinky toys, from boxes of Riley's toffee, to the bottle of H.P. Sauce with its picture of the Houses of Parliament on its label, to the fish-and-chips shop on Robinson Street, to the staunchly Anglophilic Toronto *Mail & Empire* daily newspaper (later the *Globe and Mail*), Simcoe—though four thousand miles west and a self-governing dominion since 1867—still loyally thought and played and bought and ate as British as it could. Peel, Talbot, Norfolk, Metcalfe, Colborne, Windham: The street names were a census of the nineteenth-century British political and military benefactors who had saved us from being Americans. Delhi, London, Waterloo: Within fifty miles lay towns that took their names from the map and the annals of Empire. The heavily German population of nearby

Berlin, Ontario, came to its senses in the nick of time at the outbreak of World War One and changed the town's name to the patriotic if not downright unctuous Kitchener.

I grew up feeling as at home in Simcoe as Prince Charles must have felt growing up in Windsor Castle, and equally privileged. My McCall ancestors having preceded even Bird Town, Simcoe and everything in it felt ours by right of ancient ancestry. There was even a McCall Street, named after my great-great grandfather David McCall. But it was a strictly sentimental interpretation of ownership. The McCall dynasty, on a material level, was close to threadbare. All those solid forebears and all their ceaseless enterprise over a century and a half, and by the 1940s their successors had no family treasure or holdings, no family manse, not so much as a handed-down portrait in oils to show for it. Yet the consolations of some harmless caste snobbery helped offset the stigmas of anonymity and economic underachievement. The McCalls might not own a home, but we had our ancient family coat of arms—a mailed fist raised as if to strike—over a Latin motto that translated into something like "We don't fool around." My father may have been a high school dropout, but as McCalls we were entitled to wear the MacDonald tartan, and most other people weren't. Old Delbert McCall's researches had turned up evidence that through the intersection of the Simpson and McCall lineages early in the nineteenth century, we could claim kinship with none other than Ulysses S. Grant. These proofs of past distinction were heirlooms more valuable than fine china, and more comforting to fondle. It's just as well that nobody had bothered to examine our provenance too closely; as time passed and discrimination grew, the antique silver would prove to be mostly tinplate. What in God's name would a line of illiterate Scottish yeomen need with a coat of arms? That mailed fist and motto came to seem more the product of one of those WE'LL-TRACE-YOUR-ANCESTRY-FOR-$50 ads than real past nobility. What glory was there in having descended from a kind of farm clan of the big-league MacDonalds? And later, more thorough genealogical sleuthing brought the deflating news

Simcoe, 1948. T.C.'s summer project of documenting family history led to the grave of ancient ancestor Colonel Daniel McCall. Grandfather Walt stands behind his namesake grandson, with Hugh at his right. That's me at far left, looking braced for the firing squad.

that we were no more related to Ulysses S. Grant than to Genghis Khan.

Even if our pedigree had been impeccable, it wouldn't have made any difference. Our family dwelled on a socioeconomic rung below the gentry, below even the town's solid middle-class merchants and tradespeople. My parents housed themselves from marriage onward in modest rented quarters—on Dean Street, Queen Street, West Street, and finally in a sturdy, rambling old two-story gray stucco house settling into decrepitude at the corner of Union and Talbot streets, our home from 1942 until we removed to Toronto five years later. It was rented from a purse-lipped old harridan, who arrived annually for a personal survey of the damage wrought by the six young McCall barbarians in the preceding year. She must have left shaking her head. My parents' idea of home improvement amounted to making the beds, and their paltry stock of worn furniture left several rooms looking decidedly underfurnished. The house was roomier than it was elegant, a place of dark hallways and stamped-tin ceilings and scabby linoleum floors, with a nearly moribund coal furnace in the basement and icy drafts in winter, but also a living room fireplace, a sunporch, a side porch, a dining room, a pantry, a playroom, nooks and crannies galore, a long central staircase with a rickety banister built for sliding, and an abandoned livery stable out back full of curling stones and rotting chestnuts and ghosts. The corner lot on which the house stood was vast by Simcoe standards. It was the biggest house our family ever lived in, and no place I ever lived in, before or after, more deeply or sweetly defined the word *home*.

The eight-room North Public School was a ten-minute walk away, and its principal had taught our parents before us. The grade-six teacher was our very own Aunt May. A regulator clock, a portrait of King George VI, and a benevolent female person were fixtures of every classroom, and my classmates were my neighborhood chums. They were named Leatherdale, Pingle, Taggart, Cronkwright, Abbey, Richards, Lawson, Grey, Pipe, Pelling, Mills, Reid, Rogers, Lloyd— and Fiegenbaum, a son of what I believe to have been the town's only Jewish family. There was one black family in Simcoe, and the Italian Bonacorsos and a few immigrant Slavs rounded out the ethnic mosaic. We learned a version of Canadian history that began in the mid-1660s and thereafter followed the British settlement of Upper Canada step by triumphant step. The part of Ontario that our forebears inhabited had been populated and cultivated for eons by Indians, whose flint arrowheads so regularly surfaced in farmers' fields—and even in our own front lawn—as to be commonplace. Of these original inhabitants and their lives, and their role in Canada's and Ontario's and Simcoe's history, we learned nothing. Indians didn't count.

Non–Anglo-Saxons didn't count. The famous Canadian tolerance—famous among Canadians—was not conspicuous in the Simcoe of my time. The migrant French Canadians who appeared every August to harvest the tobacco crop were, without notable affection, known as "Frogs," and widely understood to be thieving marauders. The small local colony of immigrant Poles and Hungarians were en masse branded "Hunkies" and ridiculed for dressing their young boys on Sundays in fedoras and suits and white shirts without neckties. Catholics—especially Italian Catholics—were suspect among my peers, on general principles lightly grasped, and the mick-baiting Loyal Order of Orangemen included many of Simcoe's leading citizens in their annual parade. I found myself one day after school wrestling my classmate Paul Fiegenbaum on our front lawn over some petty dispute; he had gained the upper hand and I was desperate. "Dirty rotten Jew," I screamed. "Dirty rotten Jew!"

The boredom of small-town life is never an issue when you've known no other, and I hadn't. Besides, Simcoe had three movie theaters, including the Capitol (2 SPE IAL FEA URES WORTH SEE NG, the marquee proclaimed, for years), with hard wooden seats unchanged since the days of the silents; two parks, one for sports, the other for picnicking; a municipal outdoor swimming pool; the muddy Lynn River, winding through the middle of town; my Uncle Chick's foundry; a courthouse and jail (rumored to be the scene of almost weekly hangings), with a working horse trough out front at the curb; and the annual Norfolk County Fall Fair with Clyde Beatty's circus, an irresistibly seedy midway, and hell-driving acts at night. Nearby were Houghton Sand Hills, a vast natural wonder of Sahara-like dunes—the wonder of unchecked soil erosion—and the lakeside beach resorts of Port Dover, Port Rowan, Port Ryerse, and Turkey Point. The sinister Lake Unger lay a few miles north, a lake of infinite depths according to leading schoolyard oceanographers, without a bottom. There were the seasonal onslaughts of red ants, those eight-legged Nazis that it was our duty to annihilate by pouring boiling water into their holes, creating a distinctive stink. "Smells like red ants" would work its way into the McCall vernacular forever afterward.

It was not an old-swimming-hole, let's-go-fishin' kind of small-town life—not for me. The McCalls were an urban tribe. I remained a resolute stranger to the natural world, vastly preferring the bustle and hum of downtown to the fields and the woods. Lord Baden-Powell and the Cubs and Boy Scouts he founded were revered institutions, mixed up with Kipling and Empire and muscular Christianity in ways that would cause raised eyebrows if an apparently healthy Simcoe lad declined to join. Peer pressure, and a sneaking admiration for the quasi-military uniforms and regalia, got me into the Cubs. My first meeting in the local den, which required that I squat on my haunches and bark out *Jungle Book*–style mumbo jumbo with my fellow half-boys, half–forest animals, got me right out, for good.

Summers were long, hot, and dusty; winters, Arctic, white, and interminable. There must have been a radical climatological shift since then. The snow came in November and stayed until early April, and for five months or more we lived in a Currier & Ives world of waist-high snowbanks and four-foot icicles hanging from every eave. A snow fort built in December would still be standing in March, its melting ruins still visible in May. Milk was delivered in bottles before sunup via horse-drawn wagons, of the type that also brought our ice and bread; on frigid mornings the milk bottles grew top hats, frozen columns of cream.

Larry Leatherdale was my best friend in Simcoe. He was a classmate and a cheerful companion, who lived five houses away down Talbot Street with his widowed mother and a collection of comic books that in kid currency outdid bars of gold bullion as a sign of wealth. Our first meeting was unpromising; it consisted of ten seconds of pleasantries followed by mutual roundhouse swings. Gary Pingle and his sister, Carol Ann, moved next door shortly after we arrived at Union Street, replacing the family of Holy Rollers who had entertained us weekly with their religious exertions as we peeked through their open windows. Fat Eubanks built gorgeous models of tanks and British Army lorries, and told lies more satisfying than truth. He'd just ridden in a real tank, just flown over town in a Catalina flying boat, he would announce, and embroidered his fictional exploits with a verisimilitude far more exciting than his mendacity was dishonorable.

My career as a ladykiller got off to a bad start with Camille Richards, at age ten; she accepted my invitation and went with me to see *State Fair* at the Strand on my first date. Halfway through she transferred her affections, and left with Larry Bauslaugh.

There was one bike in the family—Mike's—and I didn't get riding time until I was eleven, whereupon my adventurousness was entirely satisfied by a trip around the block. We went to the movies, listened to afternoon serials on the radio, played war games, read and drew, fell under the spell of Monopoly, shivered at the powers of the Ouija board, built card houses, sledded and tobogganed and flailed away at horsebuns in a Canadian version of street hockey in winter, tapped trees for maple syrup in the spring, swam in the municipal pool in summer, and staged nocturnal raids up the alley behind the house to steal sour purple grapes and rhubarb from Mrs. Klein's backyard garden, because there was nothing else to steal. Theft briefly became my favorite participant sport.

It's 8:30 A.M. on another lazy August weekday morning, circa 1945. A flurry of pebbles rattles against the bedroom window; Larry Leatherdale stands on the sidewalk below, hissing those magic words "Let's go hook something at Garten-Holmes!"

I'm downstairs in two minutes and skulking through those empty aisles in ten. Garten-Holmes is a musty, cavernous emporium dating from the late nineteenth century, redolent of yard goods and oilcloth; and other than a small display of Big Little Books it traffics in absolutely nothing of interest or use to a ten-year-old kid. This is neither here nor there to Larry and me. We're in it not for illicit gain but for the sporting thrill. The technique is always the same: browse, spot, then strike, grabbing the chosen object, tucking it into the midsection and doubling over as if in sudden piercing pain, clutching your stomach—and your prize—as you bolt for the exit, obviously en route to the nearest emergency room.

Larry and I never got caught by the elderly ladies clerking at the cashier's desk up front. The loot—glass piggy banks, plaster statuettes, plastic matchbook holders, miniature birchbark canoes—was quickly tossed aside. My crime spree abruptly ended forever one Saturday morning when I made the mistake of lugging in the latest load of hot goods and dumping it on the kitchen table, just as Grandfather Walt dropped by to visit Mother.

"Where did you get all that stuff?"

"Hooked it at Garten-Holmes. Want a piggy bank?"

Whack!

Grown-ups and kids in my Simcoe went about their lives almost as separately as if segregated by law. The postwar definition of family life as the gleeful merging of parents and children into one indivisible, interactive unit of togetherness was still a long way off. If Simcoe dads and lads ever conjoined at Wellington Park for an after-supper game of catch or went hiking and camping on weekends or strolled downtown after supper for a soda at Austin's drugstore, they did it behind my back. The vast gulf between us and the adults who ran the place kept their doings a vague stirring as viewed from a distant shore. They enjoyed the grown-up luxuries of smoking cigarettes and driving cars and staying up late, but from what I ever saw of their lives, they seldom seemed to be having fun; they had migrated to a state of such leaden routine and tedium that there couldn't possibly be anything surprising or even irregular in their circumstances.

Only years later, on receipt of a reminiscent letter from Mike, did

I grasp that those good gray Simconians of my early years were living far more interesting lives than we kids ever knew.

There was love [wrote Mike], and damn little of it unrequited. [Pseudo-initialized] N.P. and M.H., teachers of math and physics respectively, set up housekeeping together in the thirties and lived quiet lives taking care of each other until they passed on. If anyone in town ever knew the word *lesbian*, they never linked it with N. and M. Mr. G. was a tall, rugged swordsman who enjoyed the favors of many. G.'s wife, T., was a true lush, the depth of whose unhappiness was unknown until she and a female lover were surprised, partially clad in an outdoor coupling. C.C., glamorpuss wife of vertically challenged, harmless H., spent many evenings on K.T.'s examination table. (K.T.'s wife, the victim of a hair disease, wore a wig, which often got airborne.) People loved it when the T.s' failings were exposed; they were old family, had lots of money, a big house, and K. was arrogant as hell. He had some sort of comeuppance when, like C.B., he got caught on income tax evasion.

Poor D.M., the car dealer, blew his brains out. Very messy. This lamentable act was repeated by young T.O., a driving, vigorous man, who I recall delivering crushing forehand strokes and bruising comments to his kids on the country club tennis courts. M.L.H., recently retired principal of the North Public School, who found himself doing a laborer's job in a canning factory after retirement, gave his wife a wake-up treat by hanging himself in his basement early one morning. My school chum and close friend J.D. died naked, cold, and probably drunk in the garage of his parents' temporarily unoccupied home. The father of my friend X., having been caught out at income tax evasion, one day walked out of his house beside the fifth tee of the local golf course, put a shotgun in his mouth, and pulled the trigger, thereby saying farewell to his young wife and three children of a second marriage. Judge I. was fatally creamed by a freight train at a notorious level crossing at the north end of town, en route to his happy home from a rendezvous with his main extracurricular squeeze.

For me and for my siblings, Simcoe life was a snug cocoon. Nothing bad ever happened. It became obvious, as uneventful year followed uneventful year, that I had been born into a family exempted from illness, hard times, death. Tragedy was something that only struck characters in books or movies, or families at the far end of town. This freedom from disaster was simply part of the order of things, like being born rich, and like a rich kid, I wasted no time in questioning destiny.

FAMILY

We now see, receding as in the rearview mirror of a moving car, that carefree lad waving to us from his idyllic Simcoe world. The sense of living in a benign universe that had cushioned my first twelve and a half years abruptly ended in November 1947. The McCalls left Simcoe for the big city. The trauma of suddenly exchanging everything familiar and secure for bewildering anonymity and loneliness in a gray urban nowhere was profound; but the move also brought a radical change in the family's way of life, its balance, its emotional climate, virtually from one day to the next. And that's what ruined everything.

I had a father again. He had left Simcoe to pursue his career in Toronto when I was three, and for the next nine years was at best a weekend commuter to his nominal home and hearth. Now, at last, we'd all be together under one roof. It would quickly prove to be the worst idea in McCall family history. This man I barely knew had not been an absentee parent by accident. I soon found out why he had bolted home and Simcoe almost the minute he could: Family life and kids—particularly his own kids—bored, irritated, and depressed him. Finally cornered at age thirty-eight into living amongst us on a permanent basis, he did so grudgingly, from the other side of a self-declared cordon sanitaire, eschewing fatherhood with all its messy entanglements and intrusions, less dad to six than star boarder

pestered by aliens, baffled and enraged to find his privacy and his
freedom all shot to hell.

Meanwhile, unbeknownst to me in my blissful childish ignorance,
the toll of being left behind in Simcoe by an absent husband for
twelve long years to care for six kids, almost alone and in chronic financial hardship, was not only telling on my mother. It had ravaged
her spirit, and something in her seemed finally to collapse with the
move to Toronto. She more or less dematerialized. She became a kind
of hologram of a mother, a shimmering but aloof maternal figure,
always just out of reach and out of touch. She read *The New Yorker*,
chain-smoked, and increasingly dabbled in alcoholic spirits. Later reconstruction of her decline has dated the onset of the drinking
problem as far back as the mid-forties, long before we left Simcoe,
but it could be better concealed in a big, roomy house than in the intimate quarters of the tiny apartment that was our new Toronto
home. And in Toronto the disease rapidly advanced, until she had
perfected the technique of achieving a private oblivion that gradually
came to last from mid-afternoon, when we kids got home from
school, until it was time for bed.

More baffling than their individual demons was my parents' joint
conspiracy against the very idea of a normal, wholesome family life.
What I didn't yet know—what none of us knew at the time, perhaps
mercifully—was that with a gathering bitterness from early on until
the very end, Tom and Peg McCall felt themselves trapped in the
wrong life. They regarded their production of six children in twelve
years as nothing but an injustice and an affront, a dirty trick. Six kids!
It wasn't supposed to have turned out this way. It was as if Beelzebub
had impregnated Mother while she slept or the stork had been a
hireling in some malign collusion, or nobody had told them (they
were a small-town couple born and bred, after all, and young) that
sex minus birth control equals babies.

The more they had to live with it, the angrier it seemed to make
them. Well, goddammit, they wouldn't take it lying down. My parents increasingly seemed to exercise a form of personal exemption
from responsibility, loosely based on victims' rights. They were stuck
with us and had to go through the motions; but parenthood's weight-

ier and more ticklish burdens, they decided, were not theirs to bear.

A mother indifferent at best to the challenges of motherhood, a father carrying his fatherhood like a cross, the two united in a family-raising policy based on resentment. Between them, in those little ways that even kids can't help but notice—avoiding physical contact, ensuring that requests for parental succor would get about what Oliver Twist's requests for more gruel got him—they soon enough managed to convey the unmistakable impression that we were being punished for ruining their lives. Synthesized and fed to laboratory rats, the air of tense melancholy that settled permanently over McCall family life after we left Simcoe would have triggered a rodent Jonestown.

By the time I was old enough to connect this state of affairs with my own considerable misery and that of my siblings, to realize it was a bum rap and to demand the whys and wherefores, both Tom and Peg were dead, and so too most of their close contemporaries. Elusive right up to and over the boundary line of death, they never provided an explanation. None of your goddamn business anyway, I can almost hear my father bark.

Flashback to the McCall living room at 101 Union Street in Simcoe, circa 1944, and a huddle of battered old books on a shelf—so familiar a part of the household that even now I can see their colors and sizes and recite most of their titles: *archie & mehitabel*, by Don Marquis; Michael Arlen's *The Green Hat; The Benchley Roundup; The Conning Tower*, the collected columns of Franklin P. Adams; *Salt Water Taffy*, by Corey Ford; *Porgy and Bess*, the novel; *All Quiet on the Western Front*, by Erich Maria Remarque. An unremarkable little library if encountered in most households of the time. A startling catalogue of intellectual curiosity and erudition for people of my parents' circumstances. These were working-class kids, in a working-class town. Neither had even come close to the halls of ivy; my father, indeed, had dropped out of high school. Nothing in their individual ancestries or domestic environments—where the presence of any book save an old family Bible would have been as unlikely as a bust of Seneca—could have naturally led either to the life of the mind. But there they were, in their late teens and early twenties, feeding their imaginations with the same smart literary fare consumed by the sophisticates in New York. Almost as prized as these books were tattered copies, laboriously typed and hand-bound, of the high school newspapers—*The Ratcatcher* and *The Mudslinger*—that Tom McCall and Peg Gilbertson had, respectively, founded and edited to vent their teenage ideas of cosmopolitan wit.

Family album photos of flappers in rumble seats and sports in golfing knickers; tales of madcap times with Simcoe's version of a smart set and visits to New York City and Broadway shows: no small-town yokels, Tom and Peg. Nascent Jazz Babies they were, bright young things, flaming youth headed out of torpid Simcoe to find their destiny in the larger world, where they belonged.

Fate would choose otherwise. Fate and one kid after another, born in the midst of the Great Depression to a small-town couple without worldly access or a spare dollar to jump-start their escape. The day their firstborn son and responsibility arrived to stay, in 1931, must have made it seem as if a line had been drawn across their lives—a line that marked an abrupt end to their carefree ways, their precocious dreams, youth and optimism and happiness itself.

It would be almost two decades before they could even break away from Simcoe. By then, with six kids in tow, with the passion of flaming youth long since exhausted and their living standard seemingly stalled forever just this side of the poverty line, the irrepressible *Mudslinger* and *Ratcatcher* spirit of the Roaring Twenties was no more. Scant wonder that they clung to those shabby old books for the rest of their lives as to relics of the cross. Those books were reminders of halcyon days, of that lost moment when anything seemed possible. And we kids were the reminders of how and why it had all gone so miserably, so completely and forever, wrong.

It might be flip but not wholly inaccurate to say that Tom and Peg's tragedy was my rich gain.

Flashback once again to circa 1944 and the McCall household— to the rear of the living room closet, past miscellaneous unstrung badminton rackets, hibernating snowshoes, and off-duty galoshes, to a half-buried bundle of magazines between homemade cardboard covers, each cover bearing the pasted-on image of a twit in a top hat regarding a butterfly through a monocle: lovingly preserved bundles of *The New Yorker* from the late twenties and early thirties, testimony to the handiwork and devotion of Tom C. McCall.

Even to a nine-year-old Simcoe kid—perhaps especially to a nine-year-old Simcoe kid—the sensibility radiating from those musty pages was at first incomprehensible, but soon enough, through the auspices of Messrs. Thurber and Arno and Addams and Ms. Hokinson, it was thrilling, because it was exotic, because something was going on here that I'd never encountered before. Adults were talking to other adults about things I seldom fully understood, but with a subversive playfulness and wit that seemed to kick aside the barrier between the grown-up world and mine and invite me in. "It's broccoli, dear." "I say it's spinach, and I say the hell with it!" I had stumbled upon the outskirts of a strange but clearly advanced civilization.

It took no more than perhaps a hundred wisecracking cartoons before I leapt to the conclusion that if the pictures in *The New Yorker* were this entertaining, the words might be too. I plunged in, to a profile of the late legendary gangster Legs Diamond. What epiphanies I managed to extract from a forgotten piece of reportage, written long before I was born about someone I'd never heard of, I don't recall. But it was enough. In fact, it led me directly from Legs Diamond to insatiability; from plundering those back copies to grabbing every freshly arrived issue of the magazine. And to exploring, outward from *The New Yorker* in successive steps, the world of reading beyond, to any and every available magazine or book that might—even in watered-down form—be up to something of the same heady stuff. Magazines and books were not only available; they constituted the one surplus of any kind in the McCall family's worldly inventory. What their hoard of ancient *New Yorkers* had stirred in me, my parents' lifelong mutual reading compulsion nourished.

No memory survives of our parents ever extolling the joys of reading to their children. It was a selfish pleasure of theirs that I appropriated more by chance than by design, at a receptive age. Indirectly linked as it may have been to the underlying tragedy of their lives, it was the one shining parental legacy of Tom and Peg McCall, and I could kiss them for it. Well, a nice firm handshake; let's not get carried away.

T. C.

Dead and gone almost forty years, my father returns often enough in my dreams that he might as well be living down the street or across town and dropping by for visits. In dreams as in life, I press for his attention, his permission, or his approval. In dreams as in life, he is testy and he yields not. Never.

Thomas Cameron McCall (called T.C. even by his kids, who sensed that this better described the relationship than the presumptuously intimate "Dad") was a formidable man and a dominant presence, so dominant over his wife and six children that we lay low, mushrooms in his shadow, for as long as he cast it, so dominant over me that only with his passing did my own life begin taking shape.

He was in emotional turmoil every waking moment of his life and ran on four speeds: ebullience, anger, tantrum, and brooding rage. I don't think he ever put together two successive contented days in all the time I knew him. Knew him? I flatter myself. He dreaded intimacy; you dared not cross his moat. He was a selfish husband, a tyrannical father, an unsolved riddle of a man. Yet among those of us over whom he held absolute sway he is remembered with the vividness and awe accorded a great man. Tom C. McCall was too singular to forget, and almost too vital to die. The Grim Reaper wouldn't dare. He must still be banging around somewhere in the cosmos. I can hear his voice, see his walk, smell his Chesterfield, feel his aura. I wouldn't be all that surprised if he were to walk into this room any minute and ask what the hell I was wasting my time on now.

Circa 1915. T.C., at age six, and his father pose in matching Royal Canadian Army uniforms.

. . .

He was born in 1909 in a room above Jim's Grill in Port Dover, Ontario, eight miles south of Simcoe, the second child and only son of Walter Sidney McCall and Ethel Cameron. I realize in setting down this account that these are among the appallingly few facts I know about my father's first twenty-five years. Either he didn't care, didn't think we cared, or—more likely, because it is more consistent with his attitude toward his offspring—didn't think us particularly entitled to be let in on the details of his personal life.

I do know that he grew up in Simcoe in modest circumstances and by mid-adolescence was something of an athlete and something more of a smart-ass. Evidently considering himself smarter than his teachers, among others, he dropped out of high school short of the finish line.

Here his saga takes a sharp left turn away from that of the usual small-town high school dropout. He might well have quietly sunk into the life of a small-town haberdasher that was his first paying job, but young Tom McCall had intelligence and wit and an itch, and selling neckties soon paled. It was fortunate for him that lack of higher education wasn't the deterrent to white-collar employment it would later become. He found a new job, and his calling, in journalism. In no time he was the editorial spark plug of the local *Simcoe Reformer* newspaper (my namesake was his boss, publisher, and friend Bruce Pearce), an ace reporter, and ultimately a sports columnist of some area renown.

Small-town newspapering apparently chafed as ambition grew. He next parlayed his contacts and experience into a job in Toronto as private secretary to Eric Cross, a Simcoe judge and friend who had been made a provincial cabinet minister. He would gradually rise in the Ontario civil service—his ascent interrupted by four years of military duty—to become deputy minister of the Department of Travel and Publicity. After fifteen years, wearied of meager pay and egregious political meddling, he resigned to join Chrysler of Canada in Windsor as its public relations manager, a post he kept until his death.

Before the fall: T.C. at twenty-one.

He had married his high school sweetheart, Helen Margaret "Peg" Gilbertson, on her twenty-second birthday, in 1930, and six children followed, the first born in 1931 and the last—and only girl—a surprise bonus twelve years later in 1943.

Knowing this much is to know next to nothing, of course. I'm reduced, even now, to staring at old snapshots, peering yet again at brief, jerky sequences from forty-year-old home movies, looking for clues that might help decode the enigma. He could suspend it in an evening's burst of conviviality with friends, listening to a ball game on the radio, cackling over some Thurber or Perelman nonsense in *The New Yorker*; but he was a profoundly disappointed man, so disap-

pointed that he came to live in the sure expectation of disappointment, convinced—as gradually, inevitably, he convinced everyone
around him—that good times were only a respite from life's ongoing, remorseless raw deal.

Why? He was barely into his forties by the time hopeless pes-
simism came to stay, and he was still vigorous, deeply engaged in interesting if not richly remunerative work, with a devoted wife and
six—count 'em, six—healthy kids and a slew of absorbing hobbies.

For some while, my foremost theory was that T.C. had been a casualty of war.

World War Two. King and Country called; and as had McCalls
for generations, Tom C. McCall responded. On July 18, 1943, having waived his exemption from service as sole support of a wife and
large family and wangled a commission as a pilot officer in the Royal
Canadian Air Force, he sailed for England on the converted troop-
ship *Queen Elizabeth*, posted to the Canadian Sixth Bomber Group in
Yorkshire as press relations officer.

The perils of idealism: The splendid blending of British and
Canadian air forces in common cause against Hitler was a sour joke.
They more or less despised each other. The R.A.F. had wanted to ab-
sorb all R.C.A.F. activities in England under its tight control. The
Canadians—mainly for domestic morale reasons—demanded that
they keep their own distinct identity. The Canadians won, but it was
a Pyrrhic victory. Their R.A.F. partners did everything within their
power to make the Canucks pay for their insolence, and their power
was formidable.

The Canadians were given worn-out or obsolete aircraft to fly on
their bombing missions, and ill-trained ground crews to maintain
them. Their bases were sited in the far north of England, adding
hours of time and human fatigue to every run. They were treated by
the British at every level as amateurs of war, bumbling colonials, and
condescended to by what T.C.'s private journal describes as "the dep-
recating superiority of their modesty." The Canadian bombing contingent did make a stumbling start. Staffed by inexperienced officers,
with air crews that had been rushed through training and made to fly

inferior aircraft, the R.C.A.F. bomber group suffered ghastly initial loss rates and dismal morale.

Out of this tragic fiasco T.C. was charged with generating upbeat, heartwarming, pride-inducing, morale-boosting human interest stories about our boys in R.C.A.F. blue for consumption by the folks back home. It would break his heart. Well over four thousand Canadian bomber pilots and crew members died on missions over Europe in World War Two. Most of these "lads," as T.C. always called them, were in fact just that—boys and young men under twenty-two, the cream of Canadian youth.

From Squadron Leader T. C. McCall's personal journal:

August 17, 1943:
Sent out 60 aircraft from the Group on the big Peenemünde show last night and lost 12, which is very very bad. Included in the losses was Wing Commander Crooks and his crew, who were on their first operation on Lancasters. Am afraid that Pete Marsh was among them, which was most depressing.

September 23, 1943:
The Green crew didn't come back this morning, including young Heaney. Had quite a chat with him before takeoff and he was very keen; felt good over his promotion to WO2 and over his skipper hurdling No. 13. Have felt badly all day and had to send a signal to London asking that the several stories I've done around him be killed.

Saturday, October 23, 1943:
Covered ops on Kassel, the boys being due back at 11:40, but five crews failing to return, among them four from 434 Group and including Bill Thomson. Really felt sick about it.

Over and over, as the journal progresses through 1943 and into 1944, the story he had written the night before had to be spiked the next morning. The cheerful lad he had breakfasted with just yesterday was dead today. The funny drunk leading aircraftsman he had driven back to base from a party in town last weekend had gone down Monday night over Stuttgart.

And all T.C. could do was watch and keep writing his stories and suffer inside. He couldn't even publicly claim much sympathy, because it wasn't he who was risking his life every night. He must have roiled with guilt at having been spared that risk, going about his safe, routine duties while magnificent young men by the score were being killed.

On the night of June 13–14, 1944, over Arras, Wing Commander Chris Bartlett's Halifax was hit. He ordered his crew to bail out shortly before the plane exploded, and was listed as killed in action. Chris Bartlett was T.C.'s closest friend, namesake of his daughter, a handsome bachelor from Saskatchewan not yet thirty years old.

T.C. had jotted his final journal entry exactly a week before. His comments had become increasingly noncommittal, mere summaries of daily routine. I think his heart had gone out of it by then, and much of his belief, and he could no longer bear to keep recording the toll Canada's glorious air war was taking on his friends, on his fellow countrymen, and on him.

Shortly afterward, he cracked. They sent him to Ireland to play golf and recuperate, but he'd had enough, and now pulled strings to free himself from service to King and Country as vigorously as he had to enter it three years before. By November 1944 he was back in Canada. By the next spring, he was officially discharged from the R.C.A.F. and sufficiently restored to return to the Department of Travel and Publicity as director.

I'm no longer convinced that T.C.'s psychic war wounds entirely explain his later bitterness and depression, or that they at all explain why these effects should be so conspicuously concentrated on his relationship with his kids.

He wore the mantle of paterfamilias like an ermine cape, but almost entirely for the prestige of it. The job of raising the kids was Mother's. The day-to-day responsibilities and obligations of fatherhood and family life seemed to clash with, if not insult, his essential sense of himself as a man of urgent and lofty affairs who limped home evenings and weekends only to recuperate. This was an equally urgent business, requiring that the household be instantly converted into his personal intensive-care unit the moment he barged through the front door: martini, sofa, silence.

T.C. stormed through his life and work and household in a state of perpetually agitated high energy. He was a lip biter, a fidgeter, a room pacer. Floorboards reverberated under his feet. He had anxious hands, and his restless fingers usually held a cigarette. His touch was not gentle. Should I botch the job of tying my necktie and he take over, that simple act in his hands took on the desperate jerking urgency of a hangman tying a noose. FATHER CHOKES SON WITH OWN NECKTIE. Waiting for anything or anyone, even for a minute, he died a thousand deaths. He was an indignant waiter-baiter, a road hog, a golf club thrower, a door and phone and plate and cup slammer. Even his wardrobe was semi-violent, featuring fire-engine-red waistcoats and loud checked caps. He favored march music on Sunday mornings, at full volume.

When the idea of making Sunday breakfast occasionally seized him, the household panicked. After half an hour of frenzied utensil banging, what landed on the table in the smoke-wreathed kitchen were hotel volumes of eggs and toast and bacon and sausage, enough to stuff the entire Canadian senate, and his disgust with us was palpable when we failed—and we always failed—to down the third or fourth helpings that were the only way to amortize his overscale repast.

Mike adored Dixieland, and Hugh's love of classical music was early and deep. T.C. also harbored musical passion. One good indicator that his rage was in temporary remission came whenever the record player was turned on to peak volume and the glasses rattled on the tabletops as all resident McCalldom swooned—or were expected to—to his carefully chosen musical menu.

Dominant therein were the oleaginous strains of Guy Lombardo and His Royal Canadians. We McCall boys were unique among our peers, if not most of mankind, in our ability to distinguish Guy from brothers Lebert and Victor and Carmen and sister Mary Ann, on sight. T.C. had acquired eight-by-ten publicity stills of the Lombardo clan from somewhere. In fact, our home was a kind of Lombardo headquarters. We knew that the band's vocalist, Kenny

Gardner, was Mary Ann's husband, and everybody knew that Guy's rise to fame began just forty miles west of Simcoe, in London, Ontario. None of this meant that anybody had to like Guy Lombardo's music, and I didn't. It turned T.C.'s cocktail-hour concerts into musical slivers under the fingernails.

Guy Lombardo's renditions of "Boo Hoo" and "Alice Blue Gown," however, were Mahler's Ninth compared with Basil Fomeen. It was some sadist's notion, in the late forties, to slap together albums of "Greatest Hits" from every individual year of the twenties and thirties—but not by repressing original recordings. Enter the Basil Fomeen band, playing Muzak-quality arrangements in the same ricky-ticky dogtrot style behind anonymous vocalists. Every Fomeen disc packed in its twenty or thirty vintage hits by playing only a snatch of each. Insipid, banal, flavorless, excruciating, these cheapjack knockoffs. And T.C. played them nonstop.

Later came something even worse, because you had to not only listen but also look at it: Lawrence Welk and His Champagne Music Makers, endorsed not only by T.C. but by his employers at Chrysler, sponsors of the Saturday-night ABC-TV massacre of musical wit that had him knee slapping and singing along with America's happiest dolts in their benighted millions, week after week after week. Not even my provocatively insulting cracks seemed to penetrate the daze of T.C.'s adulation. I think I knew then for certain that the gulf between us would never be bridged.

He was fond of grandly quoting Voltaire's line "I disagree with what you say, but I will defend to the death your right to say it," but his idea of domestic conversation was a monologue verging on a harangue, during which, if one presumed to raise a question or to differ, came a spat followed by a snit. "I see," he would mutter whenever thus crossed—meaning the opposite; meaning that he was blind with rage and now more concerned with devising appropriate later punishment than with the merits of the debate. My conversations with T.C. were in any event seldom edifying. Opinion, as long as it was his, flattened fact. His natural intelligence had to contend with his rigidity of mind, his arrogance, and his prejudices, and what a set of manglers. Not only was the cause of reasoned discourse thus stymied, but sooner or later he would say something so grotesquely unfair or so incendiary to common sense or so breathtakingly wrong or stupid that I wanted to haul off and deck him by way of retort.

George VI, the New York Yankees, and his employer of the moment aside, he was a man without heroes. His world seemed to consist almost entirely of horse's asses and fatheads and phonies. Feuds—internecine, interoffice, interpersonal—erupted so suddenly and so often that updating the Tom C. McCall enemies list was an almost daily task. He disliked sloth, small children, pets, sissies, politicians, intellectuals, affectation, all snobbery other than his own, and any open expressions of affection. He hated Germans. With particular venom did he hate the professional classes, especially doctors. His mouth was a ruined graveyard of dead brown teeth as the legacy of his lifelong aversion to dentists, fellow travelers of the medical profession, a conspiracy of bloodsuckers and quacks. He was his own doctor, a specialist in hypochondria. Barely a week seemed to pass without his offhand announcement to a hushed dinner table that he was a doomed man: cancer of the skin or throat or lungs, a brain tumor, malaria. He spurned the sadistic probings and useless nostrums of doctors from youth until his sudden death from previously undiagnosed heart disease.

He had somehow determined that his own fragile security depended on keeping his dependents in the dark. We were excluded from matters of family urgency. When he carried the phone into the kitchen and slammed the door behind him, we knew the balloon had gone up—and also that whatever the crisis, it was none of our goddamn business. "I'm nursing vipers at my breast," he would often mock-lament. Half the time I think he believed it. As he grew older, his distrust came to verge on paranoia. His knack for divining plots against him was almost occult. The plotters—inevitably one of us, forever stealing his typewriter, guzzling the last of his ginger ale, hiding his copy of *The New Yorker*—were dealt with briskly in impromptu courts-martial.

Our ranking far down on his priority list—after his job, his wife, his friends, his golf, and his other hobbies—was so ingrained among us kids that it was not he but we who felt the guilt whenever our needs intruded on him. We learned to pester him as little as possible with our petty concerns; it seemed only normal and fair that he seldom knew or asked what was up in our lives. Bare summaries would suffice. The school report card might have been invented by T. C. McCall. What a time-saver—a terse bottom-line document compressing a year of each of his kids' lives into a three-minute read that told him all he needed or cared to know.

Those rare occasions when the longed-for proximity to the Great Man was achieved could be a decidedly mixed blessing. During the offhand moments of access he granted—on a Saturday-morning run to the Brewers' Warehouse, say—his tense aloofness sometimes gave way to an almost reckless garrulity, whereupon he would observe, as if commenting on the weather, that Hugh was probably a homosexual; Walt was clearly retarded; Mother was going insane and might have to be committed. Such horrific revelations provided me with something brand-new to agonize about for days and weeks afterward, until gradually it dawned on me that not only was there never any follow-up but that T.C. himself seemed to have forgotten all about them within minutes.

It should not have been a complete surprise that T.C. regarded me without conspicuous enthusiasm from around the time my voice changed and thereafter. I must have been a pain in the ass to a father who preferred his offspring to be compliant; my character as it formed came as close as anyone's to matching his, and this could be frictive in a family unit designed to revolve around him alone. We gave each other a wide berth. Indeed, T.C. and I spent a total of three days alone together over the course of his life. (Not that this was an exceptionally meager amount of access; the count for Tom and Walt, for example, was zero.) He took me along on a business trip to Sarnia and Windsor in 1950 as a fifteenth-birthday present, and the weekday-afternoon Tigers–White Sox game we took in at Briggs Stadium in Detroit—my first, intoxicating, unforgettable taste of major league baseball, my dad beside me and all to myself—marked a moment of camaraderie between us never equaled before or after.

Had I missed something in the fine print of the father-son contract? Growing up was a process of being at first mystified and later incensed by T.C.'s indifference. I was shut out of his life, and he seldom deigned to enter mine. I wanted to be an athlete like him, a writer like him, worldly like him, and he wanted only to be spared my cloying attentions. As he wanted to be spared all family burdens.

His hobbies were his own private pleasures and not ours to share. Golf, photography, woodworking, a lifetime absorption in philately belonged strictly to him. He felt no urge to imbue any of us with his passions, to the point that even intruding on his pursuit of these pastimes was a glaring offense. He taught me how to hate golf by dragooning me as his usually unpaid caddy on weekend marathons but never allowing me to swing a club, then killing an hour or so with his cronies at the nineteenth hole while I sat steaming on the car bumper in the parking lot.

His selfishness was close to breathtaking. Letter from Mother to her naval officer son Mike, stationed at the Shearwater naval base near Halifax, Nova Scotia, in the summer of 1957:

> I would dearly love to come down and visit you, but T.C. says flatly that we can't afford it. . . . He can pay five hundred bucks to join Beach Grove Golf Club, buy new golf shoes, bag etc., but can't afford to have the living room painted or let me go to Halifax. I'd give anything to see you both and the children but unless I can beg, borrow or steal $147 I am afraid it is impossible.

The idea of his lending a hand in domestic chores was unthinkable. Maintaining a lordly distance from such tedium helped to underscore his commandership, his freedom from involvement in the distasteful grind of household life. Let his ninety-pound wife haul the groceries, do the wash, scrub the floors. Here was a man who had shaken hands with King George VI and Ronald Colman, regularly rubbed elbows with captains of industry, had a framed imitation-parchment certificate right there on the living room wall proclaiming him an Admiral of the American Airlines Flagship Fleet.

And yet T.C. could never be written off as an unalloyed bastard, and that was what gave life among those who depended upon him its piquant charge. His sudden bursts of hilarity, his flashes of generosity, could wipe away days of bleakness in an instant and lure us into thinking, this was the *real* T.C. To his innumerable friends and business colleagues he was an endearing figure: witty, companionable, a bon vivant. He was well read and comfortable among the sophisticated. His worldview had entirely outgrown his provincial origins. He was earnestly and entirely honorable, and bound himself to a code of probity famous among his peers. That he toiled so hard all his working life, to such relatively lean reward, is a mystery explained in part by considering the retardant effect on a professional career of absolute honesty, fair dealing, loyalty, and responsibility.

As memorable as his pettiness in small things was his tolerance and generosity when the stakes were high. He'd throw a fit over one of us taking his stamp ruler without permission, but one day—without permission, before I even had a license—I took his brand-new Plymouth for a drive and promptly crashed it. He shrugged off the incident with a joke and fixed it so there were no charges. A few years later, heading from Windsor to Toronto one winter afternoon in my brand-new Triumph TR-3, I almost killed myself when it spun out on a patch of ice and was belted into a field by an oncoming car. Yet T.C.'s reaction to the news—the same T.C. who exploded in rage and panic if the family cat suddenly jumped into his lap—was "Well, these things happen."

All of a sudden his air of gravitas would disappear entirely, revealing a born clown amazingly gifted at making a comic fool of himself. To his wondering family, it was as if Hitler had stuck a lampshade on his head and gone prancing around the Reich Chancellery. "Where was you at Vimy?" he would begin, launching into the drunken ravings of a dim-witted Canadian Legionnaire, rambling on for half an hour and displaying an ear for beer-hall wisdom and the self-delusion of the loser that made me laugh until it hurt.

He once lavished countless after-dinner hours on the creation of a family album like none before. It was a blackly satirical genealogy of the McCalls of 2377 Danforth, complete with invented family tree, depicting us as the latest in a line of congenital Kallikaks and Snopeses. He mobilized costumes and props and even Mother as a

cast member in his surreal photographic record of morons and de-
generates of all ages and styles. His text was as zany and strange as
his pictures. It was funny, but also rather frightening in its relentlessly
squalid theme. Even T.C. realized this once the fever of creativity
subsided, and the book was quietly withdrawn from circulation.

Such tantalizing glimpses of a loveable T.C. were all I ever got. I
was jealous of them. And they couldn't and never will offset his
transgressions. I wanted to, still want to, love the man; so did we all.
But his ruthless denial of himself to his offspring barred even understanding, and what is left is the bitter memory of the fool who
spawned a family of six and then proceeded methodically, deliberately to squander his treasure.

PEG

That six bouncing babies could have issued from Peg McCall's tiny body was almost worthy of Ripley's *Believe It or Not!* She was thin and light almost to the point of semi-transparency and as gentle of gesture and movement as her husband was coarse. She never raised her voice. She floated noiselessly on her tiny feet and folded into a chair like a cat. There in her chair is where I most clearly remember her, a Player's in one hand and a book or a copy of *The New Yorker* in the other, a puff of Kleenex tucked into the left sleeve of her sweater, Tambo the cat in her lap.

By the time she had reached her forties her white hair was already thinning, her face already sagging, her eyes sunken and moist, and she looked sixty-five. She had been an alcoholic for at least ten years and a chain smoker forever, but the harshest ravages came from the heart. She was trapped in a kind of solitary confinement in the wrong life, from which there was now no escape and against which she saw little point in struggling. She was simply playing out the string.

Helen Margaret Gilbertson was born in 1908 near Simcoe to a Scots immigrant apple grower and his Scots-descended wife, and was the last by several years of five children. She and T.C. met and fell in together in public school, from which point their eventual marriage seems to have been all but foreordained. Both were bright, verbal, sharp-witted, and iconoclastic, and in the generational tug-of-war between the staid small-town Simcoe of their parents and the Jazz Age just then combusting all around them, it was no contest.

A pretty girl of ten in a party dress smiling for the studio cameraman; a flapper with intelligent, mischievous eyes reclining against a tree: Early photographs suggest a person so different from the woman I knew as my mother as to be someone else entirely. The tantalizing, infuriating truth is that I grew up living under the same roof but never knew and still don't know who this gentle, elusive creature really was. She herself preferred to reveal as little as possible; as far as her kids were concerned, her life before marriage was a mystery behind a door she shut and sealed before we were born. An alternative Peg Gilbertson profile offered in a letter from brother Mike, long after her death, jolted my lifelong image of the shy Scots farmer's daughter making her quiet way through life:

> I know that Peg did not want to be married, but with my arrival she was trapped. She once confessed to me that she couldn't imagine why she ever married. The best time she ever had, she said, was when she came back to Simcoe (after a year of what we would call domestic science at MacDonald Hall at the Ontario Agricultural College in Guelph) and was working in the office of McKie and Farrer, an insurance agency on Peel Street in Simcoe.
>
> I think we have to face the strong possibility that Peg was a "party girl" and that she might have had a bit of a reputation. This is based on remembered conversation with Aunts Eva and Netta, who recalled her as being full of life, always happy, tremendously gregarious. Her imprint is all over a hilarious precursor to the *National Lampoon*—*The Ratcatcher,* a Simcoe high school humor magazine, which she and some chums put together. I once saw a copy—carbon copies with a stitched binding—but have no idea of what became of it. And when I was about fourteen or fifteen and belonged very briefly to a circle of north-end boys and girls of my own age, one of them allowed as how her mother had told her that my mother was drunk at the high school graduation dance, or whatever function was held to mark significant events in the progress of Simcoe scholars.
>
> So, even assuming not one of these things is totally true, put them all together and you come up with a picture of someone who came from a stern Scots Presbyterian family with all the hang-ups which go with that territory, was the youngest, prettiest, and most doted

upon of her siblings, who (I suspect) was sent to MacDonald Hall for a year to get her out of town after the high school graduation event, and who "went all the way" and got caught.

The Jazz Age curdled into the Great Depression at almost the moment Peg married Tom and adult life began in earnest. She was a mother at twenty-three, and whatever career ambitions she might have nurtured died then and there; in the Simcoe of 1931, a mother's place was in the home. He made less money than he'd expected; they had more kids than they'd expected; they'd expected Simcoe to be only the starting point but soon found themselves ever more entangled and ever more firmly anchored there.

By 1938 the long, lean years of the Depression were coming to an end at last. Peg's reward was to be effectively abandoned, left in Simcoe to tend their brood of five while T.C. scaled the career ladder in faraway Toronto and commuted home on weekends. The lopsided parental partnership was to last for the next ten years, and the drudgery and boredom and loneliness of it withered her. Her inner collapse showed in her neglected teeth and an indifference about her appearance—and gradually about her housekeeping, her kids, her life. It was all an empty shell, more often than not empty even of a husband.

Some carryover from her upbringing among the self-abnegating Scots, the fate of women in that unenlightened time, the Canadian curse of diffidence? Whatever, it was beyond Peg McCall's nature to demand that her needs be met. Perhaps she felt her pain to be too deep and too massive to be treated or even understood, even by her husband. It could only be numbed. She picked up a bottle and retreated into herself.

For the balance of her life she went through the motions of motherhood and housekeeping and family life while making herself increasingly unreachable by the outside world. It was no part of her heart or her temperament to be like other mothers and draw nourishment and pleasure from motherhood and family life. Her young daughter excepted, she could find scant comfort or even interest in her kids. Her response was a guffaw when I once suggested she join the P.T.A.; it was akin, I later realized, to suggesting to Dorothy Parker that she join the Girl Scouts. She had few friends, no hobbies, no outside activities. She never learned to drive, perhaps because there was nowhere she wanted to go.

She was a perfunctory chatelaine. Ours was not a poverty-stricken household, but it looked and felt like one. From Simcoe to Toronto to Windsor, the serial McCall households exuded the same dispirited musk of dinginess, of worn carpets, bulb-burned lampshades, dust kittens, and tattered furniture. T.C. co-conspired by refusing to release funds for new furniture or decoration; the same set of shabby possessions, most dating back to the thirties and dead relatives, were recycled from one new home to the next until they disintegrated.

Peg was modest and delicate but also entirely self-reliant—and too self-contained to be drawn into relationships even with her own

Peg in her late teens.

children. She asked few favors and never spoke up, never intruded. She was more intelligent than T.C.—subtler of mind, more thoughtful, more tolerant. Perhaps just because she never, ever asked for it, she had our sympathy. The remnants of girlishness and warmth and a subversive wit still flickered just enough from within that ruined soul to suggest, tantalizingly, the Peg and the mother who might have been. But the DO NOT DISTURB and DO NOT TOUCH signs posted all around her were respected. That her loyalty belonged to T.C. first and always, and that he possessively demanded as much, also had to be accepted.

Summer 1950. T.C. is off on a business trip and one sultry afternoon, on a whim, Mike packs Mother and the rest of us into his 1932 Pontiac for a picnic outing a few miles east of the city at Frenchman's Bay, a mite of beachfront on Lake Ontario. Released from her dead routine, Peg seems to revert to some former self. She

1957. Mother in the last year of her life. She was all of forty-nine.

comes to life. It's the happiest and most relaxed we've ever seen her, a golden afternoon. We clown and caper all the way home—to find T.C., back unexpectedly early from his trip, enraged that his wife has gone AWOL and dinner isn't on the table. She'd better not make that mistake again. And she didn't.

The sense that she was as much a casualty of T.C.'s tyranny and selfishness as we were evoked a protective urge as much as it did resentment at our exclusion from intimacy. Young brother Walt's Christmas present to Mother in 1950 came with a card. He signed it "Your Friend." The experience of her motherly love had eluded him, as in large measure it eluded us all. The nearest I could ever come was the ache to trespass those boundaries of hers, the longing to somehow get close. It would never happen; and I forgive her.

SIBLINGS

Naming his issue was one paternal duty that T.C. embraced with zeal. Michael Scott Cameron McCall. Thomas Hugh Gilbertson McCall. Walter Miller Pearce McCall. Thomas (this second Tom honoring someone other than himself, I like to think) Joseph Keith McCall. Ethel Christine McCall. I was Robert Bruce Eugene McCall—or so I'd always been told—but thank goodness I hadn't invested heavily in monogrammed handkerchiefs, because at age fifteen, when I received my birth certificate, I found that T.C. had apparently forgotten all about a change of mind en route to the registry office fifteen years before. There I was in official black and white, the new, real me: Bruce Paul Gordon McCall.

Mike

Mike secured a lifetime pass to his parents' affections by the clever stratagem of arriving first. Their very own baby boy clearly thrilled the Tom and Peg of 1931. T.C. had yet to become an absentee father. Grandfather Walt, still vigorous, doted on his son's son; it was Mike's privilege to become Grandfather Walt's close companion and co-conspirator in the chicken thievery and other minor mischief that served as his version of hobbies. Mike's head start, as he was led through Simcoe life with T.C. holding one hand and Grandfather Walt the other, gave him a familiarity with and a knowledge of the place, its people and its customs and scandals, that would make him our unofficial ambassador to the town's and family's past for the rest of our lives.

For his younger siblings, until he left home at age twenty-two, big brother Mike would serve as junior officer detached from parental H.Q. to discipline and lead our bewildered little motley group of noncommissioned draftees. I think of him in those early years as crouching up on the trench step with a periscope, sending down early intelligence on what was out there to the rest of us trembling below, screaming, "Duck!" in crisis, bandaging our occasional wounds. His seniority alone was invaluable; because of it, Mike knew everything we didn't about the terrain and the battle plan. We eagerly followed wherever he led.

That he himself might be struggling to plot out his own destiny and gain his own foothold never occurred to me. Big brother Mike, with all his power and authority, must have it made. In fact, his privileged position seldom brought him much more of a taste of normal boyhood and adolescent life than did ours. He had no more privacy in that household than we did; no dates. His extracurricular life was funneled almost exclusively into the then déclassé sport of cycling, with his sole close friend, Charlie Chinchen.

Mike did find part-time jobs during his high school years that got him out of the apartment and into real life, which in my eyes increased his worldliness no end. He was only a gas station attendant and then a kitchen helper in a greasy spoon, but he might as well have been a test pilot. He knew how the world worked.

Mike the leader, Mike the counselor, Mike the easy touch for cadging dimes, Mike the court of last resort for resolving disputes and dispensing justice and ordering life in our bedroom. He could have spurned the role we forced on him; our needs, plopped in his lap, were a burden no normal teenager could have welcomed. But cheerful, responsible, resourceful Mike was as loyal to us as we were dependent on him.

Four years' seniority, in boyhood and adolescence, is a profound age gap. Mike was developmentally and socially already breasting waters still far out to sea for me. He and I could never be pals. But that

Circa 1937. Hughie, age four, peers out from inside a millstone.

Big brother Mike in his late teens.

he was my leader, the leader of us all, I never questioned. He was bigger, better-looking, smarter, worldlier than me and always would be. It would be helpful if he were also invulnerable, without flaw or weakness, ever in command—and he usually was.

But not always. We're in our accustomed sleeping places in our tiny bedroom in the tiny family apartment in Toronto in 1949, Mike and Hugh and me. Hugh had recently obtained a vial of radium paint. Astronomically inclined, he used it to painstakingly cover the bedroom ceiling with hundreds of tiny dots: our own planetarium, glowing overhead in the dark with hundreds of distant planets and galaxies. That particular night it got Mike to thinking, pondering the universe, the riddle of life itself, until suddenly he jumped out of bed and dashed from the room in terror. "It's no use!" he wailed. "We're all going to die!" Thanks, Mike. I didn't need that. Certainly not from my big brother and spiritual guide.

Hugh

There is good reason why "Hugh and I" appears more frequently in these pages than any other phrase. Hugh and I were seldom out of each other's sight for a quarter of a century. From earliest life until I split off from Windsor to Toronto in 1960, we shared more than the same family. We shared clothes, bedrooms, schools, classrooms, friends, interests, first jobs—day-by-day lives. Superimposed over mine, a chart of Hugh's high and low moments, successes and failures over that period would match up almost exactly.

Thomas Hugh Gilbertson McCall was born in 1933, a year and four months before me, putting us close enough in age to be paired up almost from the outset. Whenever bedrooms were being assigned, clothes purchased, haircuts needed, errands run, as naturally as it was "Tom and Walt" for my twin younger brothers, it was "Hugh and Bruce" for us. The same environment, the same stimuli, the same experiences encountered at the same time—vinelike, our two lives intertwined.

Our two selves never did. Mutt and Jeff, Abbott and Costello, Hugh and Bruce. Genes were to prove a stronger force than environment. Hugh was a Gilbertson, for one thing, and I was a McCall. Hugh inherited ruling Gilbertson traits of calmness, mildness of temperament bordering on the passive, and congenital modesty bordering on the self-effacing that could only have come from his mother's line. My willfulness and tantrums and tendency toward being "high-strung" marked me as pure McCall. It was our differing natures that made us a complementary pair, that kept cool what relentless tight proximity could so easily have made a whetstone for fraternal conflict.

Tots to boys to adolescents to young adults, we liked each other. We never even had to work at it. Jealousy, rivalry, the myriad other textbook upshots when two siblings find themselves in enforced harness never shot up to unsettle our effortless rapport. Pushed too far too often by my teasing, Hugh once up and floored me with a punch to the nose. I was thirteen; I can remember no other such incident, even such an instinct, between us, before or after.

This was just as well. As our parents increasingly withdrew even a sense of protection and the isolation of life in alien Toronto began closing in, bringing terrors large and small to bedevil our lives, Hugh and I came to desperately need each other. We huddled together against confusion, hostility, loneliness. We propped each other up. The accident of our brotherhood and closeness in age became the bond that provided most of whatever emotional refuge either of us found. If we had no friends, we had each other. By necessity as well as by choice, Hugh and I became inseparable, and inseparability became a habit.

Ideally, for the long-term health of both of us, the bond would have better been pried apart early. We became *too* close. The presence of a perfectly attuned companion right there in our own bedroom blunted our urgency, and even our desire, to strike out as individuals into the wider world. Crucial skills were atrophied or stifled at crucial developmental points. Preference for each other's company induced social claustrophobia. We recycled the same ideas, thoughts, and beliefs between ourselves. The lack of conflict or even challenge may have soothed us, but it also softened us, and too often it turned exposure to the world beyond our bedroom into a brutal shock.

Nor did it do passive, easygoing Hughie a world of good to be so tightly shackled to me. I took advantage of his pliant nature. He was older, but I was the one most often calling the shots; and when push came to shove, it was always my needs that prevailed. I was cynically certain that he would uncomplainingly go along. The retroactive guilt is enough to last me a lifetime.

But circumstances were not ideal, and in that emotional family snakepit, psychic survival trumped the psychological niceties, even if I'd been aware of them. Had Hugh and I been pried apart in those bleak years and our lives separately channeled, I'm by no means certain that both or either of us could have survived.

Hugh was ingenuousness incarnate. It left him a sitting duck. The radar that bullies carry always showed a big blip when Hugh came within range; suckered into some mild dispute one day by one of the class thugs at Danforth Tech, he was mercilessly set upon and pummeled for his effrontery. And never understood why. He was selfless; lacking ego enough to be ambitious for himself, he cheered every success of everybody else. He had Mother's gentleness of manner and a studious nature. From where it came I will never know, but he would take the blows with a dignity and good humor that shamed his old man's selfish petulance and my own sweaty wheedling. When the traits were being divvied up, I got all the self-pity and Hugh got all the class.

The Brats

It's a Saturday afternoon in Simcoe in July 1948. The family has fled the sweltering crackerbox apartment on Danforth Avenue in Toronto for a few rent-free weeks in the house of a vacationing aunt. Tom and Walt will be elsewhere. At the moment they're teetering along with a couple of dozen other kids ten years old or under in the back of a stake-bed truck as it pulls away and rattles off down Norfolk Street and out of town.

They're bound for the forced exile of a month's stay at a five-dollar-a-week camp for underprivileged Simcoe boys down near Lake

Erie. I'm the official send-off delegation. Mother has better things to do, and T.C., as usual, is on the golf course. Tom and Walt have never been away from home before, and the look in their helpless, frightened eyes as I wave goodbye summons a pang that will stay with me the rest of my life.

The parental hearts, arms, and doors were closed to Tom and Walt McCall from birth. They were fated to suffer every day of their young lives from a withholding of parental love and care so consistent, so implacable, as to denote not mere apathy but some deeply rooted animus. A punishment. A vendetta.

I was three when they were born, and as with most McCall family crises, a Calvinist version of *omertà* smothered my understanding of events for years afterward. But subsequent reconstruction of events suggests a plausible, if still inexcusable, explanation. Mother had contracted serious pneumonia in the final weeks of her pregnancy with the twins. Birth was medically precarious for mother and babies both. As it subsequently came out, she veered close to death, and the twins' first fragile weeks of life were spent in an incubator, followed by a long, slow uphill climb to health for all three. Mother remained ill for some time afterward, during which period T.C.'s stepmother, Anne, a registered nurse, filled in as surrogate mother to the newborns.

Murmured hints persist to this day that my parents were in no particular hurry to get the twins back, that their stint with Anne stretched to a year or so, and that when finally they were recalled to the family embrace, it was grudgingly at best. They had, after all, almost killed their mother. Neither Mother nor T.C. seemed able to ever forgive them. Adding to their crimes, Tom and Walt represented two more mouths to feed in a family already scrambling to make ends meet, and with three other McCall sons already in the fold, not even the novelty of twinship could relieve their parents' feeling that they were less two little bundles from heaven than the last goddamn straw.

Photographs of the brats from the toddler through teenage years portray a pair of refugees, dirty-faced, shabbily dressed and shod, apprehensive. They lived in a squalid room seldom visited by either parent for reasons other than punitive. I don't think, after the age of six or seven, they ever felt their mother's touch.

It wasn't just their parents; the whole family's psychic angst somehow got displaced onto the brats in a human variation of kicking the dog. Life got you down? Take a whack at Walt. Smarting from some failure? Give Tom a passing clip. One of the more grotesque vignettes in an all too full mental album is Mother, drunker than she usually got, standing in the doorway of that foul hole of a room of theirs one night, teasing and mocking them in response to the request for some small favor. Other than rounding them up to pose for obligatory happy-family photographs and at mealtimes, when their presence at the table was tolerated but not welcomed, their father's attentions to his fourth- and fifth-born sons was almost exclusively disciplinary. It was entirely in character that he returned home late from some local poker game and rousted Walt from sleep to demand that he confess to some playground crime that he was alleged to have committed. The flimsiest such charge always weighed heavily enough on T.C.'s scales of justice to convict on the spot, without the formality of hearing arguments from the defense.

Parental curiosity about their twin sons was sufficiently modest that they were barely recognized as having separate identities; they might as well have been a single four-legged, four-armed, two-headed monster—the Brat. It also simplified life: Their clothes and their Christmas and birthday presents, for instance, needn't be individualized. Two of the same thing would do.

It was a reign of neglect and emotional abuse that lasted as long as my parents and the brats shared the same household. Other kids, of course, have suffered infinitely worse by their own parents. What set the case of Tom and Walt apart, lent their situation so singular a nastiness, was that these parents weren't half-wit backwoods cretins abusing their own flesh and blood. Tom and Peg McCall were people who prided themselves on their sensitivity and intelligence, who saw themselves as members of society's more enlightened ranks. Who knew better.

Toronto, 1949. Tom (left) and Walt (right), freshly scrubbed and photographed for another of T.C.'s family albums. Had T.C. spent half the time being a real father to them as he did in contriving his artificial images of domestic cheer, the twins might really have had something to smile about.

Tom was gentle, dreamy, shy as a deer, and all but defenseless. His parents called him stupid, and willfully contrary, and I think his confusion and sense of rejection escalated until he must have felt excluded, even by Hugh and Walt and me. He wasn't verbal like us, he had no artistic inclinations, and it shut him out.

He flirted halfheartedly with open rebellion by consorting with some local would-be hoods in his middle teenage years and by daring to admit—in a household whose musical tastes were ruled by the twin deities of Lombardo and Welk—that he preferred Laverne Baker and Elvis. But being a rebel wasn't in his nature. He just wanted to find a place where he belonged, and he knew it would never be at home. Tom joined the Navy as soon as he was eighteen and eligible, in 1956, and slipped out of our family's life as unobtrusively as he had shared it. Or tried to.

Here comes Walt, at his usual half trot, a ski cap sideways on his head, jacket flapping open in the freezing cold, snot pouring from his nose. He's been down by the C.N.R. tracks watching the trains go by;

he's got five railroad spikes in one hand and his notebook in the other, crammed with more on-the-spot sketches of train wheels, pistons, machinery. He's half an hour late for dinner and will pay for it, but he's burbling with pleasure and delight at his informational yield.

Walt seemed to have intuited in the incubator that life would be an uphill fight and that his survival depended on energy, a strong will, self-reliance, and good cheer. Walt, from infancy, was the smallest of a smallish brood. How misleading. Into that compact body were packed a thousand mental and a million physical horsepower. Walt was born with the metabolism of a woodchuck. As an infant and kid and adolescent, his body and his imagination were never ever at rest. His siblings might succumb in varying degrees to self-pity and despair and depression. Not Walt. He had determined to outrun them.

He caught on early to the cheap and handy form of creative escape that Hugh and I were pursuing at our bedroom desk with our drawing. But no idle fantasy for him. By age twelve Walt was an autodidact of fierce, almost frightening intensity. His drive to know about the things that caught his interest was insatiable. Everything caught his interest. He drew and wrote information. With a talent for observation and an appetite for knowledge so beyond his years as to be freakish, he filled notebook after notebook as fast as he could scrawl with detailed studies, sketches, diagrams, and attendant text—homemade, hand-penciled personal mini-encyclopedias. Volume one was trains; the next, dinosaurs; the next, the moon. And he was barely warming up.

Weather, distance, physical risk meant nothing to him in his quests. By age fifteen he had shifted his focus to the technology and installation of television antennas. Nobody taught him anything; he taught himself. Collecting piles of scrap tubing and wiring on forays through the junk piles of the East End of Toronto, he started building his own experimental antennas in the alleyway behind the apartment, and then—with a blithe disregard for the danger of great heights that would have done a high-steel Mohawk proud—was performing acrobatic feats high above the Toronto rooftops, erecting professional-quality working TV antennas for the sheer pleasure of it. Years later, on tours of the old neighborhood, he could proudly point out antennas he had installed decades before—still standing tall and intact.

Walt's phenomenal thirst for knowledge and his knack for retaining, synthesizing, and applying it were to T.C. only a sign of mental aberration and a source of shame. He'd have far rather fathered a football-heaving dullard than this peripatetic little pack rat with his furtive obsessions.

The next and most flaming obsession, Walt's Holy Grail for the rest of his life, was fire trucks. What it was about those lumbering mobile hardware and plumbing exhibits that so ignited his imagination I never knew, and I don't think he has ever bothered to ask himself. But while other kids played ball or sat at the movies, he roamed the city on foot in his customary dogtrot to visit firehouses, chat up firemen, and vacuum up information, until within months his knowledge not only of fire trucks but of fire-fighting equipment and tactics and lingo would embarrass a working fire marshal.

He started by cobbling together crude model fire trucks, from memory—out of cardboard and shoelaces and drinking straws and whatever else he could scrounge. Soon, Walt being Walt, he couldn't stop. He didn't give a damn about school, friends, sports, social life. It was as if he were racing against the end of the world to record in miniature every fire truck that had ever existed—not only in Toronto, but in North America. He no sooner finished one model than he dived into building the next. The collection eventually ballooned into the hundreds, squirreled away under his bed, in his and Tom's clothes closet, into every crevice he could find.

It takes no Freudian to divine that these obsessions served practical psychic purposes through the long, barren ordeal of growing up an outcast in his own home. They were escape, comfort, subliminal outlet, among other things. And they probably saved his sanity, if not his life.

But try as Walt might to make them do so, they couldn't answer all his unmet needs. By late 1957, in the shattering aftermath of Mother's death, Walt was more of a pariah in his father's household than ever. He was nineteen and idle and useless—a high school graduate without a job or a clue about what to do with his life. He picked up occasional odd jobs and hid out upstairs in his room, avoiding a father who could by now barely abide the sight of him.

Something had to give before something awful transpired, and in January 1958, it did. An old family friend (the Hugh in brother Hugh's name) ran a newspaper in the dreary railroad town of St. Thomas, a hundred miles away, and by way of a personal favor was willing to take Walt on, sight unseen, as a cub reporter. It was not only an opportunity; as far as T.C. was concerned, it was an order. With his borrowed clothes and borrowed luggage and borrowed grubstake, Walt climbed aboard a train one rainy Sunday night and disappeared from T.C.'s life for good.

Chris

Ethel Christine McCall was a shoo-in for parental doting. She was a girl after five males.

The novelty of a daughter seemed to revive whatever feeble parental instincts Tom and Peg had. If Tom and Walt had been consigned to the dungeon at birth, Chris was the princess in the tower suite. Having a baby girl in our midst delighted us boys as much as it did our parents. We competed to tend to her needs. She must have been close to the most fussed-over McCall in history, and her early months and years marked a high point—the high point—of good feeling in our beleaguered family's annals.

By the time she had graduated to curly-haired moppethood, Chris was beloved of her brothers for another reason: She refused the all but irresistible opportunity to be the kid apart, privileged and spoiled. From inside the cocoon of preference her parents spun around her, she seemed to be giving the rest of us a sly wink: Hey, guys, I have to go along with this stuff for now, but don't worry—I'm not going to take advantage. And, against all temptations, she never did.

But in time that family nest of anger, tension, alcohol, repression, and depression would blight her childhood too. Worse, her arrival late in the psychodrama of a deteriorating family meant that she found herself struggling with it at a cruelly tender age. That this acted to mature her emotionally before her time, arming her with a toughness of spirit and a clear-eyed realism that would help her endure later trials, seems small recompense.

She suffered as much as she gained from her closeness to Mother, sharing all too intimately the confusions and betrayals that alcoholics inflict on the ones who love them the most. Repelled by T.C.'s abuse of the twins and his whole suicidal program for family misery, she squirmed in his possessive embrace.

I still don't know quite how my kid sister managed to raise herself, to grow into the bright, steadfast girl she became. She was effectively alone for most of her formative years. On school days, at age nine or ten, she'd come home for lunch to find Mother still in bed, hangover-dazed, and be told to take a quarter from her purse to buy a malted milkshake at Acme Farmers Dairy for her lunch. At night she'd often have to put herself to bed. There was no chance for girl talk, advice,

Chris at age six, with storybook. A couple of years later she was trilling, from memory, "Hey, Jack, which way to Mecca?," "Let's go down to the Trans-Lux and hiss Roosevelt!," and every other caption in a fat book of Peter Arno's racy prewar *New Yorker* cartoons.

a motherly ear when her mother was non compos mentis by dinner-time.

Chris had little chance not to grow up to be a tomboy. I didn't help. I conscripted her, well before the age of consent, into after-supper servitude as the designated victim of my thwarted drive to baseball mastery. It had come to this: My kid sister was the only person on earth upon whom I could impose my baseball sagacity, enthusiasm, and will. Demanding of her far more dedication, discipline, courage, and talent than I had ever mustered on my own behalf, I ran the poor girl ragged evening after evening, a flinty John McGraw belting out grounders and fly balls and stinging liners, brusquely dismissing her pain and tears when a bad hop got her in the kisser. A medical exam later showed a rib cage grotesquely distended from all the hard pegs to home I'd forced her to throw. But one helluva short-stop, that Chris.

Having inherited, or perhaps emulated, her mother's shy and private nature and the aversion to emotional exposure that underlay it, Chris evidently decided early that trust was dangerous; self-reliance, vital. At age fourteen she faced the crisis that would test her nature to its limit and seal it in place forever. Her mother died.

Chris endured the overnight loss of the central person in her life and the family's plunge into emotional limbo almost as if she had half expected it all along and was braced. As, given the life of the preceding ten years or so, she almost was. Black trees, black figures, black despair in the November sleet. I see that fourteen-year-old girl beside me at Oakwood Cemetery in Simcoe the day they buried her mother, a kid, alone as a fourteen-year-old could ever be, facing more loneliness and a future uncertain at best, and stoically refusing to crack.

Another brutal ordeal followed shortly. T.C. had fixed on the idea that the only proper place for a motherless teenage girl was boarding school, and in September 1958—by unilateral parental decision—Chris was duly delivered to Bishop Strachan in Toronto. She gamely tried to fit in and make it work, but it didn't. She and the rest of us would remember it as a miscarriage of justice akin to imprisonment for some crime she hadn't committed. Life in that blockhouse of Anglican rectitude and English institutional aloofness, among rich kids, was an empty hell. She was lost, cut off, lonelier than ever, starved for emotional solace while still trying to cope with the loss of her mother.

She spent the summer of 1959 in quiet dread at the prospect of returning. In August, T.C. announced that the two of them would embark on a driving vacation to Quebec—an order, not an offer, however much Chris preferred home and the comfort of her siblings. They spent their first night doubling up in a room at the Benvenuto Inn in Toronto. It was as far as they got. In the middle of the night T.C. bolted upright, groaned, and died of a massive heart attack as his fifteen-year-old daughter watched.

Chris never did return to Bishop Strachan. She lived first with Hugh and me at Byng Road and later with me in Toronto—cook, housekeeper, high school student, and world's least self-pitying orphan. In the fall of 1962 she took up quarters in the freshmen dorm and began higher education at the University of Toronto. She was nineteen going on forty.

OVERTIME IN THE
TANTRUM FACTORY

Who's that dreamy kid sprawled on the living room carpet, absorbed in scrawling flights of fancy in vivid Crayola hues? Not me. At about age six, my eye collided with Mike's inept warplane sketches on the inside cover of his fifth-grade reader. No, no, like *this!* I knew a Supermarine Spitfire in profile didn't look like a stubby-winged banana with a stick figure inside a blob on top. A Spitfire was a specific, unique thing. The world was nothing but specific, unique things. If you didn't recognize and record their differences and particularities, what was the point of having eyes?

I winced to see my kindergarten peers slopping about with their poster paints and brushes, rendering rainbows and mountains that didn't exist. The point and pleasure in drawing was in getting it right, trapping the truth on paper, demystifying another piece of the world. Even if the shutter kept jamming, my eye was a camera. The shortfall between the curves of a Spitfire wing, say, was precisely registered in my mind's eye, and my effort to duplicate it in pencil line at first baffled and enraged me. I'd spend a goodly chunk of the next few years straining to close the gap, wrestling with my own recalcitrant small-motor skills and led on just enough by the occasional miracle of accuracy to tolerate my hand's endless betrayals, its mulish refusal to set down on paper the high-resolution pictures being transmitted by my brain.

I knew the shape of a '41 Ford by heart, saw the nose of a DC-3 as clearly as I saw Mike's blond-wood X-Acto knife kit on the desk before me. But crumpled paper zinged around the bedroom like snowballs, hot tears blinded me, and the floorboards thundered under my pounding feet when once again—and again and again—I tried, and failed, to capture them on the page. Vows to abandon drawing inevitably followed, always broken after an hour or two of sulking. I couldn't stop.

Ours was an unaesthetically inclined family on all sides. If a framed painting existed in the town of Simcoe, I'd never seen it. The notion that my struggles might have anything to do with Art only gradually dawned. The lightbulb over my head finally clicked on with the realization that the comics, cartoons, and illustrations in the newspapers, magazines, and books all around me in that media-saturated household had begun, before they were printed, as drawings. Well, I drew too; ergo, I had been trying to be . . . an artist! Thus unblinkered, I almost immediately moved from drawing things to drawing scenes, and to even higher states of rage and frustration when my timid little tableaux so pitifully mocked every attempt to emulate the masters'.

The mealy-mouthed apologist inside me whined that no ten-year-old could expect to match the smooth fluency of Alex Raymond's penstrokes in "Flash Gordon" or the great Canadian historical artist C. W. Jefferies's ink-line panoramas, richer than paintings, or Norman Rockwell's way with worn shoe leather, dusty windows, almost everything. Shut up, I replied; if I could see it exactly, I should be able to draw it exactly.

I began searching for a shortcut, a Northwest Passage from ineptitude to proficiency, and quickly discovered it: tissue paper. I started tracing every picture I wished I'd drawn. What my copying had wrought was as innocently thrilling as if it were my own creation. Only ignoramuses would call it cheating; it was learning. Following the hand of an adept disciplined my own wobbly hand, sharpened my eye, brought home the astonishing difference in the end result between mere approximation and precise observation. After a few months, having served its purpose, the tracing phase petered out. I was eager to test my newfound sophistication in freehand drawings all my own. My horses came out looking like dogs, and my dogs, like rats; but by age twelve I was otherwise a human pantograph, able to lay down on paper a more or less convincing depiction of anything I chose.

Kind fate had surrounded me with friends and classmates who couldn't draw and wasted no time trying, so among them, the knack of jiggling a pencil until something recognizable emerged became my claim to fame, and a popular parlor trick.

"Hey, do two cowboys in a gunfight!"

"Draw Mutt and Jeff!"

"Can you make a hockey player?"

"He can make anything he wants. Watch."

"Wow, a hockey player!"

"See?"

Thus emboldened, and smug in the belief that I had the field to myself, I decided at age thirteen to flaunt my talents beyond the classroom and the family circle. The art contest, junior division, at the up-coming annual Norfolk County Fair was the chosen venue, because I didn't know of any other. My favored medium was now watercolor on typing paper; since all the other cakes of color in my twelve-piece paint set were either used up or long gone, I worked with a restricted palette of violet and browns. My submission was a set of brown autumnal studies: a rowboat and its reflection (shameless cheap trick, that) on a still autumn lake; misty autumn hills, to amortize the violet; for variety, the decaying autumn-colored corpse of a Japanese soldier mysteriously transferred from the South Pacific to a forest clearing.

A large envelope arrived in the mail a couple of weeks after the close of the fair, bearing a sheaf of red and blue first- and second-prize certificates. I wasn't just an artist. I was a famous artist.

I still have the letter I received in 1946 from my idol Norman Rockwell, politely acknowledging—with exactly the tone of avuncular encouragement and kindness to be expected of that beloved humanist—the wad of pencil drawings I had sent to him, in hopes of precisely that response.

Poor Norman would have bitten his famous pipe in two trying to conjure his patented vignettes of family warmth from among the Simcoe McCalls and their kin. Perhaps never in the course of familial affairs have so many lived so close for so long to so little emotional effect. The principal tribes of the McCalls, the Gilbertsons, and the Camerons and their issue and in-laws formed a local network of blood relations united mainly in their resolute aloofness from one another.

Even the intertwining of the McCall and Gilbertson bonds through my parents' marriage was slack and halfhearted. Perhaps it was a cultural estrangement: the restless, relatively urbane McCalls; the settled, agricultural Gilbertsons. I suspect it had more to do with my father's uncanny gift for ticking people off. Netta and Eva and May—my mother's three older sisters—clearly felt for their younger sibling and her travails as a mother of six too often left to fend for herself; but they had just as clearly long since identified T.C. as a self-centered jerk with airs, and steered wide of him. He, in turn, seemed to regard them as nattering fusspots to be borne only out of husbandly obligation. I don't think Mother herself felt much in common with her sisters. What bored and frustrated her about small-town life obviously contented them. Her loyalties, for better or worse, lay with the man she had married and his more adventurous view of life.

The affinity gap largely escaped our notice as kids. Eva and May, who lived only a few blocks away, kindly took Hugh and me or Tom and Walt into their homes on countless weekends, to help briefly take some of the load off Mother. It certainly wasn't out of any enthusiasm for the company of kids. Gilbertson-style hospitality precluded any invitations to run amok. Eva and May alike seemed dedicated to hammering home to their temporary wards the lessons that idle hands breed mischief, cleanliness is next to godliness, and children should be seen and not heard. Long lists of yard chores awaited us on arrival and hounded us until departure. The rules included frequent hot baths, no running or shouting, formality at meals, and no personal questions asked or answered.

Eva seemed to have made a point of discovering every food I most

loathed—lima beans, parsnips, cooked carrots, scalloped pota-
toes—and heaped them on my plate with the jolly threat that not
until every last glutinous glob was downed could I ever hope to stand
up again. Desperation, father of stealth: I quickly learned how to
sweep the stuff off my plate by the palmful whenever Eva's eye was
elsewhere and mush it into my pants pockets, to be later dumped in
the bushes outside.

May's household smelled of floor wax and glycerine soap and
spinsterhood. She lived in a kind of hospital hush that smothered
even the desire to make mischief, and she doled out the food at mealtimes in portions that might choke a gerbil but made little headway
in satisfying the hunger of a kid.

Aunt Netta, down on the farm at Lynn Valley, was different. Eldest of the Gilbertson sisters, Netta was plump and jolly and the one
unabashedly loving soul of the lot. She never spoke an unkind word
and never had one spoken of her. She was to us an inexplicable fount
of warmth and kindness amid that bony dynasty of pinched Presby-
terians. Ironically, Netta had the hardest life of them all. She and Ed,
her rawboned, taciturn, perfectly tooth-free husband, barely scraped
out a living on their tiny farm outside town; she seldom knew a day
of idleness, and for most of her life electricity and indoor plumbing
were luxuries. She would come into Simcoe from the farm to cover
for Mother when our parents were off on some weekend trip or were
otherwise absent, and those were special times—cocoa with little
marshmallows floating in it; big, generous farm-style dinners; the
freedom to do whatever we felt like. Netta actually listened to us, co-
conspirator more than baby-sitter. Chuckling and clucking, she sat
for hours, a living feast of maternal benignity, as amazed at the six-
teenth drawing I presented for her approbation as at the first.

I would have much more often availed myself of Netta's soothing
presence but for one unfortunate obstacle: The country gave me the
creeps. Lynn Valley, for me, was too still, too silent; with its bedroom
chamber pots and gaslight and ancient well-worn furniture, it seemed
to be slumbering in the previous century. The grandfather clock in
the parlor, loudly ticking away the hours and days, made me itchy. It
all undid me around bedtime, when I inevitably succumbed to the

first queasy stirrings of homesickness, as if I weren't three miles but three thousand away from my own bed.

I seldom made it all the way to bedtime on a Lynn Valley visit. Usually, it would be late afternoon when the yearning for home overpowered me and I slipped away like an escaping prisoner, back up the dusty road that led to civilization.

Grandfather Walt, my father's father, was a man surrounded by a legend so complex and rich, and by my time so ancient, that I never got much more than a fleeting glimpse of the person within and what he might be about.

His only son was a biased source. The entertaining legend of Walter Sidney McCall—mischievous scamp from Huck Finn boyhood through wild adolescence to restless adulthood, with a thousand yarns to tell and still a rapscallion's wink in his late seventies—did not entertain T.C. It disgusted him. His father's lifelong impulsiveness and incorrigible wanderlust, T.C. felt—the childishness and selfishness and irresponsibility behind those colorful tales—had thrown his early life and that of his beloved mother into chaos. He had barely had a father or a settled home; Walt's didoes may have brought him the fun he craved, but they didn't bring much money, and when age finally forced him to give up the adventurous life and settle down, he had had to settle for managing his mother-in-law's small downtown Simcoe hotel, the Melbourne, in exchange for family living space. There my father had grown up, a downscale male version of Eloise at the Plaza, and had not enjoyed it. It was one more way his old man had cheated him of a normal upbringing.

Walt's temperament even in late age was more attuned to kids than to sobersides like his son. Like a kid, he had believed in living the unexamined life, preferably out of doors and away from home. I suppose he could read and write, but any undertaking without the prospect of action, fireworks, and plenty of movement clearly bored him. Insofar as we could ever get at him—T.C. did little to encourage the bond, and Grandfather Walt was always a man of many and mysterious errands, hard to pin down—we reveled in his company. He was a big, stooped bearish man who probably scowled even in his sleep, but around kids he opened up. His huge hands played the most dexterous coin tricks, often involving his even huger ears. His low, husky voice and conspiratorial style drew us in as he began another rollicking anecdote. "Well now, once I met this fella, and he was a son of a bitch . . ."

Hugh and I would often stop by the Melbourne for visits en route home from school. There was always another wild tale to be told, wild enough to be told as it happened, without embellishment, because in his long and checkered life Walt had been everywhere, seen everything, and done most of it. By the turn of the century he'd worked the Great Lakes ore boats, ridden the rails down to Texas and followed the cockfighting circuit, sailed to South Africa as a soldier in the Boer War, been captured, escaped. I suspect this benign old man spinning stories in his living room had once been a roughneck sort of character, maybe even something of a desperado. A kid could hardly ask more of a grandfather than that.

Aunt Margaret, T.C.'s older sister and only sibling, left Simcoe early and remained a peripheral figure in our family life. Too bad. Margaret was as precocious as her brother in her itch for a richer life, and not only found it but also managed to raise four sons as rambunctious and outgoing as their McCall cousins were wan and repressed. We flinched when the Stewart boys came thundering into the house. They talked at the top of their voices, relished argument, the more outspoken the better, and seemed to maintain a cheerful running feud with authority of all kinds. One of them, Walter Stewart, would become one of Canada's best-known muckraking journalists and political columnists. It figured.

I surmise that T.C. regarded it as yet another of his lumberyard of crosses to bear that his sister had gravitated to the contemporary Ontario equivalent of radical politics; she was an active member of the provincial branch of the C.C.F.—the Canadian Commonwealth Federation on the hustings, the Convention of Crazy Farmers to unbending Tories such as my old man: mildly socialist, scathingly critical of the established political order, and forever a distant third behind the Liberals and Progressive Conservatives in provincial elections.

Margaret's infrequent visits to our home over the years always followed the same pattern: innocuous small talk before and during dinner, followed by escalating political debate that by midnight had climaxed in a shouting match that we kids, cowering in bed, half expected to end in gunplay or knifework. I never knew what the hell she and T.C. were arguing about. I did know that whatever it was, I was on Aunt Margaret's side.

CHILD OF WAR, LUCKY KID

World War Two and conscious thought arrived almost simultaneously for me. Primordial memory retains atmospherics more lasting than images: a change in the familiar household tone; a sense of imminence heavy in the air. Memory does replay the few speckled, sepia-brown feet left on the reel marked "September '39." A Buffalo Sunday paper on the living room floor, opened to a spread of war photos. McCalls huddled around the radio, father hissing, "Shhh, here's the King!" Me, kneeling on the chesterfield and staring out the front window of our little frame house on Queen Street at the dark, scudding autumn clouds, wondering if they're smoke drifting in from the battles raging in Europe—whatever Europe is.

But budding awareness of the Armageddon beginning to unfold before me had to jostle for mental space with budding awareness of the Armageddon lurking just behind. The First World War still cast a ghostly shadow that fell over and mingled with the Second in my mind, as it does even today. It was barely twenty years past and had yet to be eclipsed in popular consciousness by its successor bloodbath. A cataclysm that has long since receded into distant history, one more neglected, weed-grown headstone in the cemetery of war, was still an almost palpable presence in the Simcoe of my time, as in virtually every Canadian city and town and village.

Canada had paid a bloody price for its fealty to the British Crown in 1914–18, with sixty thousand of her sons killed and a like number wounded or gassed. Twenty-one years later the trauma still reverberated through that placid and famously unmartial nation. It was not a hope but a duty: The Great War and its sacrifices must never be forgotten.

Not a chance. Simcoe's principal landmark was, and remains today, the Carillon Tower, a limestone rectangle erected in 1925 to commemorate the local fallen of Vimy, the Somme, Passchendaele, and Ypres with bronze plaques, and with twenty-three bells, eternally tinged with mourning, pealing the hours.

My own Uncle Ed—cavalryman, officer, hero—had lost a big toe at Passchendaele. It was worth the three-mile hike down to Lynn Valley, and Ed and Aunt Netta's farm, to climb the attic stairs and paw through the cache of German military souvenirs he had scooped straight off the battlefield twenty-five years before. It was like pulling World War One out into the daylight again. The Luger pistol was to look at but not touch. I was allowed to slide the German officer's field binoculars from their leather case, sling the strap around my neck, and go scanning the surrounding hayfields for Tommies.

But the gray-green steel helmet, the familiar and forever sinister "coal scuttle" of the Feldwehr—that was the prize. No other artifact on earth so powerfully barked "German," "soldier," "war." The helmet was far too big. I felt whenever I wore it as if I were carrying a bell on my head. Let them laugh; I'd wear it until I had to go home. From its stiff leather lining I learned what the Great War smelled like. It smelled like damp earth, like the grave. And, magically, the act of balancing that heavy bucket of German metal on the top of my skull always wrought the same transformation. The Heinie pig, the Kraut brute that I and everybody knew the German soldier to be, had gone off for a smoke or something; I now felt myself a soldat of the Kaiser, defender of the Fatherland, really a quite reasonable guy. Restoring proper Germanophobia after a session under that helmet could sometimes take hours.

There was Armistice Day every November eleventh to snap us back to sense, lest I or any of us forget. The day seemed always to be appropriately bleak, often wet; Flanders weather. Every schoolkid in Simcoe had been mustered before the ceremony at the Carillon

Tower, joining what seemed to be half the town's population. There were wreaths, flags, men in uniform, men of the cloth, one-legged men, one-armed men. Everybody wore the red cloth poppies (". . . in Flanders Fields the poppies grow . . .") sold on every street corner by the Canadian Legion on behalf of veterans' relief.

At exactly eleven minutes past 11:00 A.M. the world fell silent, as if all six thousand Simcoe souls had started holding their breath on cue. Eyes closed. Think Flanders Fields. Deserted trenches; a lone swallow flits across no-man's-land, crosses row on row. Then, boom, a volley of gunfire and its stirring echo. Then the carillon bells, ringing out "O God Our Help in Ages Past," and the departure of the funereal parade of veterans, in their red Canadian Legion berets and blue blazers with ribbons and medals over the hearts, four abreast down Norfolk Street in the drizzle, marching to services at the First Anglican Church.

I revered World War One, but I wallowed in World War Two. Subtract it from my first ten years of life, in fact, and what little remained would barely constitute a life. When it was over at last, I felt not exultation but hollowness. God, it was fun.

Not least because from where I sat it was a triple-header—three wars in one. Thanks to the news and propaganda streaming into Simcoe from Ottawa and Washington and London, you could take your pick of protagonists in the righteous cause: Canada, the United States, Great Britain. How lucky, how luxurious, to compare, like an informed consumer comparing cars, war against war.

This consumer quickly grasped that each nation's individual war followed its own unique narrative, bore its own distinctive look and style, and he would come to know each by heart: British phlegm; American swagger; Canadian steadfastness. But discrimination cried to be exercised, because amid the thick froth of claims and boasts whipped up, in their patriotic frenzy, by all nations at war, even a kid knew that much guff obtained. Somebody's soldiers had to be the bravest and somebody's the yellowest. Somebody's fighter plane had to be the deadliest and somebody's the dud. Somebody's uniforms had to be the smartest and somebody's the crummiest. It was no measly part of my personal war effort to nail such truths, let the chips fall where they may.

Chips showered down on the Americans. Some facts were too insistent, too obvious to be ignored. Dad said it, Mike said it, the poolroom sages and drugstore savants sneered it—even the schoolyard at recess hummed it. Bombast and braggadocio outside, crybabies and quitters inside; that's the Yanks for you.

Wake any Canadian at 3:00 A.M. and out would come the same litany of grievances: into World War One three years later, and the Yanks honked on as if they'd won it single-handed. Canadian Billy Bishop had shot down more Germans than Eddie Rickenbacker ever saw, but it was Rickenbacker who got the glory. Late again into World War Two, the Yanks, and they're already acting as if they'd invented it, as if British and Canadian soldiers hadn't been grappling with the Axis unaided for two bitter and costly years.

And such cream puffs! The Americans shelled out medals like so many Monopoly bills. A shaving cut got you a Purple Heart, we snorted. It went on. Americans surrendered too easily, and—you could look it up—never even tried to escape, while Brits and Canucks were pouring out of P.O.W. camps. Home of the brave? They had to draft their boys to fight. Stalwart Canadian lads saw their duty and volunteered.

The Americans were addicted to flash. A fighter plane was a fighter plane, but the Yanks called it an "all-metal high-speed pursuit ship." Then they gave planes names that sent them bucking into the air as if they were advertising claims. Liberator. Devastator. Vindicator. Vulgar! Refer to British bombers for that model tone of dignified patriotism whose strength lay in its very reserve. The Hampden. The Wellington. The Halifax. The Blenheim.

They pronounced *khaki* "kacky," not the correct—because British—"karky." Their officers in their dress "pinks" looked like doormen. Even their patriotic anthems set us off. Compare Tin Pan Alley piffle like "Coming in on a Wing and a Prayer" and "Praise the Lord and Pass the Ammunition," we huffed, with "There'll Always Be an England" or "There'll Be Bluebirds over the White Cliffs of Dover." T.C., for one, had yet to recover from the invidious old tearjerker "My Buddy." Sissy? It was, he sputtered, a fairy song!

Putting the obnoxious Yanks in their place was almost a patriotic duty, and it shunted my emerging pro-American sympathies aside for the duration. Canada was at war, Dad and several of my cousins were at war, and blood was thicker than Royal Crown Cola.

Beneath it all, every American transgression derived from the same core flaw: The Americans were guilty of the sin of not being British. The game was lopsided from the start. The Americans were our neighbors, but the Empire was our family; Britain, the ancestral hearth; George VI, our King. Ours were after all his Royal Canadian Army, Royal Canadian Navy, Royal Canadian Air Force. England and England's peril were ours. So was England's military style. Not exactly, to be sure—too crisp, too confident, too senior in war, the British, for us Canadians to pretend to be their equal. But compared with the example of the Yanks, it was a perfect fit.

Only the British example would do. Conveniently, it was everywhere. In cinematic epics of the stiff upper lip like *Target for Tonight* and *In Which We Serve*, during which I un-Britishly bawled; in Churchill's ringing radio orations (one of which, "We Shall Never Surrender," I think, I crawled into a mock radio in my grade-four classroom to deliver again); in the classroom, under King George's lambent gaze, every feat of English arms from Agincourt to Mafeking to Dunkirk was pulled from history's musty trunk and shaken out again before our admiring eyes.

Canadian fighting men were the next best thing to being British. They were practically brothers, had fought side by side in wars dating back to the nineteenth century. They wore the same uniforms, flew the same planes, drove the same tanks, smoked the same Player's cigarettes.

It was not lost on me or my contemporaries that the Canadian war effort lacked relative glamour. We played mainly a supporting role, Britain's loyal sidekick, and seldom made world headlines. But then there was no domestic movie industry to fan Canadian fighting pride and manufacture myths. Our top generals came off as postal clerks against the Montgomerys and Eisenhowers at center stage. Even such Canadian heroes as the flying ace Buzz Beurling remained unknown beyond our borders.

But so be it. It wasn't in the Canadian character to be otherwise. Indeed, that was precisely what separated us from the Americans.

Wings over Simcoe

I spent as much of World War Two as I could in the air, figuratively speaking. Hardly uncommon for boys my age, especially boys with fathers in the air force, boys living close to where real warplanes flew, boys awash in comics and movies and picture books that could hardly have more vividly glorified aerial combat if they'd been paid henchmen of the aviation industry. But warplanes and I bonded with a vengeance (Vultee Vengeance, single-engine torpedo bomber, obsolete before World War Two).

What war releases in boys—the sanctioned freedom to break through obscenity's last taboo and find out how men kill other men, sometimes even to watch—aerial combat distilled to an almost exotically pure essence. Men kill each other with weapons. No contest: the Spitfires, ME-109s, Zeros, and P-51s flown by lone hunter-killers across the empyrean, where there was no place to hide, were the sexiest weapons of all. On the shelf next to me as this is written squat a Hawker Hurricane, a Fairey Battle, a Westland Lysander, a Westland Whirlwind, and a Bristol Beaufighter in their authentic war paint, in perfect miniature—old friends.

"They're dying like flies in Jarvis" got a guaranteed cackle in McCall family circles circa 1940. Jarvis was a village nine miles east of Simcoe, and burying the retired farmers who had gone there to die was its busiest industry. That abruptly changed around 1941, when an air base—one of the hundred or more such installations Canada would build as the chosen instrument of the Commonwealth Air Training Plan—materialized out of the nearby tobacco fields. How thoughtful of Ottawa! They must have heard of the plane-crazed lad in Simcoe.

Bright-yellow Harvard and Yale trainers soon became as common overhead as starlings. The roar of their big radial engines never failed to send McCalls tumbling out of the house like the Keystone Kops, pointing and shouting until the noise became a distant drone. Jarvis

Air Base itself was off-limits to kids. If we tried setting foot in it, they'd shoot us on sight. Yet behind its fences lay the answers to life's most enthralling and urgent mysteries. What did warplanes look like up close? How big was a Harvard in real life? How did a cockpit feel? I had to know. But what power on earth could propel a kid through His Majesty's guarded gates and into that forbidden wonderland?

American power—what else? Mother's brother, Gib, had sought his fortune south of the border long ago; now, returning on a visit in the uniform of a U.S. Air Force surgeon, kindly Uncle Gib offered his prestige to intercede on my behalf.

It worked, and for a couple of hours one unforgettable sunny Sunday, Jarvis was mine. Warplanes, it turned out, looked scabby, worn, oil-smeared and exhaust-burned up close. Even Harvards were huge on the ground, topmost prop tip seeming to soar two stories high. Cockpits felt cramped and nasty, jammed full of tubes and levers and junk, and from in there you could barely see out. I devoured it. Authenticity, at last!

More than even the sights and sounds and sheer, shiver-inducing presence of actual warplanes, I would carry away their smell. It mingled the odors of wood, oil, dope, fabric, and the olive-drab matte paint slathered on every nonmoving part inside every airplane. Nothing on earth ever smelled anything like it, and it lingers still in olfactory memory, a kind of homesickness, to this day.

The Home Front

Relayed down through the Allied chain of command from Churchill to Mrs. Coombs, our fifth grade teacher, the message was urgent. If Britain didn't receive Simcoe's complete cache of useless household junk, and soon, the entire war effort would sputter and Erich von Stroheim would be dining off the Buckingham Palace china.

The edict must have made Simcoe a tidier place than it had ever been before. Armies of schoolkids were mobilized to pick the town clean of scrap paper, tinfoil, exhausted pots and pans, and dead appliances and haul it all off by the coaster-wagonful to be mulched into the matériel needed to vanquish the Axis.

Myself, I could never quite visualize how a bale of old *Globe and Mails* and a busted baby carriage were to be transmogrified into guns. Sure, it could get you into a war movie free or earn you a tiny Union Jack badge, but it was all too abstract, and as a result I was an indifferent scrap-collecting subcontractor.

War bonds, on the other hand, rendered instant gratification for the prepubescent patriot. Every postage-stamp-size twenty-five-cent fraction of a bond you bought you pasted into your war stamps booklet, smack atop the cartoon kisser of Hitler, Mussolini, or Tojo. Take that, Axis rat!

The hardships of a nation at war imposed few burdens on the lives of its kids, certainly not the kids of Simcoe, and perhaps that explains my inability to see it all as it happened—except for fleeting dark moments—as more than a gaudy entertainment. A decent show of sadness was in order the few times war's horrible reality hit close to home and penetrated my boyish fantasies—when Simcoe servicemen had been killed or went missing, the day word came that T.C.'s best friend, Chris Bartlett, my sister's namesake, who had once stood in our very own living room, was dead in the explosion of his R.C.A.F. bomber over Cologne.

Not that we were entirely strangers to suffering. I had to eat Soya Spread instead of peanut butter, after all. Soya Spread must have been perfected in some Nazi lab and smuggled into Canada to sabotage the tastebuds of the civilian populace. It was a viscous yet gravelly sludge that oozed from jar to bread, clung to the palate like wet cement, and left an aftertaste of beans, oil, and unknown chemicals so vile that I have never been able to fully rid it from my mouth. We had to do with a measly ration of sugar. Real candy went overseas; the clumps of ersatz offered in their stead went stale for want of buyers. Meat was too often a greasy disc of Spam.

Arms and the Boy

The property at 101 Union Street required little modification to serve the McCall boys and their friends in our after-school, weekend, and summer-long war exercises. Theater of war? It was, by miraculous accident of nature, a whole back lot: jungle, desert, open terrain, even a French farmhouse infested with SS men in the form of a decrepit two-story former livery barn.

The plot was always the same: to shoot each other and, if shot, to die with feeling. Poor military discipline was a vexation.

"You're dead!"

"No I'm not!"

It could bring D-Day itself to a squabbling halt.

The entire household and its goods were mobilized for war. The dented green potato bowl in the pantry, a serendipitously perfect replica of the regulation-issue Imperial Japanese Army steel helmet, was drafted for constant service. Whoever wore it—usually, obliging Hugh—took on the assignment of skulking in the bushes with malign Nipponese intent; then, when flushed and raked by machine-gun fire emanating from somebody's mouth a few feet away, staggering forth into the clear and, after one or two protracted minutes of gruesome throes, dying.

War exacts a savage toll on the innocent. I think of sister Chris's dolls. They were already battered and unfrocked down to their excelsior-stuffed diapers—just as I wanted, because such a doll in such deshabille happened to be the spitting image of a nearly naked Japanese soldier, as regularly portrayed in *Life* and the newsreels being driven out of jungle pillboxes by flamethrower and grenade. I knew what you did with a Japanese soldier. You showed him no mercy. You flung him down the front hallway stairs; pitched him off the side porch; drowned him in the bathtub; bayoneted him with a peeling knife. It was a mutilated and filthy-dirty doll that poor little Chris found on her counterpane that night. The kid was too young to know that war is hell.

S p o i l s   o f   W a r

Having an R.C.A.F. press officer for a father brought us kids certain perks, some of them wearable.

T.C. even managed to get hold of a genuine Mae West. The Mae

West, standard R.A.F. and R.C.A.F. air-crew issue, was a butter-yellow rubber bladder that blew up into a set of giant waterwings buoyant enough to keep any downed Spitfire pilot afloat in the Channel for hours. Mike and Hugh and I tussled for the privilege of puffing air into its capacious bosoms until our cheeks tingled and our lungs burned; the lucky victor got to truss himself up in its various straps and ties and waddle out to flop about awaiting rescue in the heaving English Channel that had so recently been our front lawn.

We couldn't resist showing off our prize. The Mae West was soon being dragged around to wherever it could be admired and we envied. But for the genetic McCall inability to cash in on moneymaking opportunities, we might have charged for Mae West rides at the mu-

1940. Mother stands dutiful attendance as Mike (left), Hugh (right), and I model our new military-style outfits for T.C.'s camera.

nicipal swimming pool and kept ourselves in Orange Crush and B-B-Bats for the duration. Once its prestige value and novelty had been exhausted, the Mae West was retired to the backyard supply dump where faded enthusiasms were stored and where, one day not much later, it turned up missing. We'd evidently done too good a promotion job.

Navy-blue flannel wedge caps like R.C.A.F. noncoms wore, emblazoned with CAPTAINS OF THE CLOUDS, stamped in gold—were we McCall boys not uniquely blessed? *Captains of the Clouds* was another morale-lifting Hollywood war epic, starring Jimmy Cagney and shot in part at Jarvis, and T.C. had drawn the assignment of liaison between the R.C.A.F. and Hollywood. It gave us kids a blue-chip reason to preen. How many Simcoe lads' dads had attended a world motion picture premiere in New York City, a party at the Waldorf-Astoria Hotel later, met Miss Merle Oberon (bad skin, T.C. confided), and got so tight with the moviemakers that they shrugged and said, "Sure, Tom, take all the *Captains of the Clouds* wedge caps you want"?

Mike and Hugh and I wore ours to the special Simcoe showing— to school, at play, and in bed, until the gold lettering had all flaked away. To this day we can still render the stirring *Captains of the Clouds* theme song. In fact, I'm humming it now.

Mae Wests and *Captains of the Clouds* caps helped offset the war-toy gap. Canadian kids had to make do with few and usually crude toys and improvise everything else, while it was known that our American counterparts wallowed in neat stuff.

Dick Hillicker arrives on one of his family's periodic visits from Detroit, Michigan, USA, to visit relatives across the street from our place. He has something in his pocket to show me, and as I watch he might as well be pulling out the Hope diamond. It's better than any diamond. It's a palm-size, olive-drab plastic B-17 that God intended I should have, or certainly would if He had any idea how obviously it had been made for me. Unfortunately, Dick doesn't so intend. The B-17 goes back in his pocket, back to the USA, where such riches belong.

The Haunted Hurricane

Why did some kids warm to Roy Rogers and others ride only with Hopalong Cassidy? Such ineffable preferences extended to one's taste in warplanes: P-51 versus P-38, for example; ME-109 versus FW-190. And Supermarine Spitfire versus Hawker Hurricane.

I was a Hurricanist. If the Spit was a rapier, the Hurricane was a broadsword. It was bigger, older, slower, and homelier, more durable than dashing. But it had been instrumental in winning the Battle of Britain, and it was the fighter I most often flew in my daydreams.

A feature of the Norfolk County landscape in the immediate postwar era was half-dismantled airplanes—bright yellow Avro Ansons and Harvards that appeared to have crash-landed en masse in farmers' yards the night before. No sooner had Germany capitulated than the Canadian government undertook to unload its suddenly surplus military hardware, including planes, at salvage prices—ten dollars apiece, or so said the grapevine. Evidently because they saw in an airplane a ready-made chicken coop or a handy, nearly limitless source of everything from baling wire to scrap metal, farmers became prime customers.

Tame workaday training aircraft barely raised even my eyebrow at this late date. But one summer day in 1946, while meandering past George Culver's farm on Highway #3 outside town, I was stopped in my tracks. There in the pasture sat the first Hawker Hurricane I had ever seen.

It was no less startling a sight than if, say, I'd walked into our living room to find Winston Churchill relaxing on the chesterfield. That familiar, slightly humpbacked fuselage, that dull green-and-brown camouflage paint, the cockpit canopy slid back in open position awaiting the pilot—a Hawker Hurricane, no more than two miles from 101 Union Street! George Culver might own it in the narrow legal sense, but that Hurricane was mine. And thus from late summer of 1946 and every Sunday morning for months afterward we bonded, boy and machine.

This particular Hurricane, granted, had been stripped of most of its wings and its gun sight and instruments, but to my eyes it sat armed and ready to scramble at Biggin Hill. Up onto the port wing empennage I would climb, as I'd seen Douglas Bader do a thousand times in the photos and newsreels, and fold myself over the cockpit edge to plunk deep down into the pilot's bare metal seat. I was too short even to see forward through the windscreen looming ahead but too transported to care. Cold metal, reek of oil and dope, snarls of tubes and wires, the joystick with its center FIRE button, the big square rudder pedals: SIMCOE LAD DOWNS 6 NAZI PLANES IN FIERCE DOGFIGHT!

But never underestimate your adversary. Sooner or later overconfidence would leave me vulnerable and I'd suddenly feel the slugs hitting home and my Hurricane shudder. Glycol fumes! Red light flashing—engine fire! Bail out, bail out! Bang, the starboard escape hatch fell open and I tumbled out onto the wing to be swept away in the slipstream. SHOT DOWN OVER CHANNEL, SIMCOE LAD BACK FLYING MINUTES LATER!

I must have tumbled out onto that starboard wing a thousand times in my career as a Hurricane pilot, until George Culver's need for materials superseded my quest for confirmed kills. It wasn't when the last Japanese straggler was rooted out of an Okinawa cave that World War Two ended for all time. It was when that moldering old Hurricane was no more. And that carcass-become-skeleton-become-random-pile-of-bits-and-pieces lingered in George Culver's pasture for years.

FLYING SAUCERS
OVER SIMCOE

I had to admit World War Two was finally, completely, thoroughly
over when I opened the newest issue of *Life* in late October 1946.
Ribbentrop and Jodl and Keitel and the rest of the last of the Nazi
warlords were shown, fresh from the gallows, laid in their rough
wooden coffins on the floor of a gymnasium in Nuremberg. Twist-
ing my head to get a better look at their faces, I had to agree: They
were dead as doornails. That was that at last. Things could hardly be
more final.

I'd held on as long as I possibly could. It hadn't been just a war; it
had been my environment since kindergarten. I was left feeling a
touch queasy and not a little irked. Now that the good guys had flattened the rats, what was next? What would, what could, possibly follow Carry On, Canada and V for Victory as ideas to live by? How
could the newspapers even keep publishing now, with only bank rob-
beries and the occasional earthquake to report? What in hell would
peacetime movies, comics, radio shows be about? And 90 percent of
the contents of my brain, all that patriotically accumulated war lore
and data, those billions of images—Pearl Harbor and Bataan and
Stalingrad and Iwo Jima and D-Day—had been reduced overnight
to war surplus. What was there left to love? To hate? To believe in?

On behalf of the tank, plane, ball bearing, and widget makers of
democracy's arsenal, advertising illustrators of World War Two had
perforce severely darkened their palettes. Their visions made Goya

look like Walt Disney. Our warships at sea could never be depicted otherwise than battling a force-ten gale. Our warplanes thundered across malignant skies of purple and black, seamed with scarlet. The world portrayed for us beneath those angry clouds was one continuous shattered landscape of blasted trees and roofless houses and billowing black smoke, inevitably populated only by hapless womenfolk in babushkas, huddling babies to their bosoms, evidently too brave to cry but too scared, or too tired, to collect their wits and get the hell out of there.

Other than belief in a better tomorrow, nobody was selling anything. Everybody was too busy working night and day to turn those skies to blue again and to make the world safe for mothers and babies everywhere.

Advertising to the rescue in 1947. Suddenly those advertising illustrators saw the sun again. It was as if America had crept out from a cave into a joyous green and yellow and sky-blue Maytime. Almost before the ashes of Hitler's bunker had cooled, before my psyche had converted to a peacetime footing, life as American advertising chronicled it had been pitched headlong into a strange and wonderful new world. American industry no longer hectored us with calls for sacrifice and duty and fighting spirit. Strike the blasted tree stumps and the mother in the babushka. Now they begged our attention to and approval of things: things to buy, things suddenly being shaken out of a postwar cornucopia to cascade new wonders and pleasures all around us, everywhere.

Including things to drive. Especially things to drive. From those same folks who had been patriotically cranking out the tanks and planes and ships—and the ads that reminded us of their patriotic exertions—now came the first new cars in my conscious lifetime. "There's a Ford in your future!" I didn't know at the time that steel shortages and labor strife were strangling Detroit's ability to produce new cars for more than a handful of all those who wanted them. All I knew was that every fresh issue of *Life* and *Fortune* and *The Saturday Evening Post* and *The New Yorker* teemed with ads for brand-new, dramatically new, spectacularly new cars, and that life from now on would bring an annual thunderclap of automotive progress, innovation, and excitement.

With the advent of peacetime, I could look forward for the rest of my life to those messages from tomorrow in steel and chrome—to moms and dads, guys and gals, entire families and their cocker spaniels waving hi as they hurtled along over summery highways under cerulean skies toward the happiest future in the history of humankind. I knew it, because the car ads told me so. Now it was war that seemed boring, one-dimensional, cramped. Bring on peacetime—and the miracles that came with it.

From the magazine ads that I had always relied upon to interpret the Zeitgeist, I saw that postwar life was catching America up in a delirious swirl of highballs, Luckies, Stetson hats, Florsheim shoes, bridge parties and swimming parties and housewarming parties, decorating and homebuilding and clothes-buying and vacationing. And from all accounts—at least the accounts I was reading in *Popular Mechanics*, among other unimpeachable sources—America presently stood only on the threshold of wonders to come. Soon, double-decker Boeing Stratocruisers with cocktail lounges would be flying down to Rio in twenty hours. Standard transportation for Everyman was about to be a car you could fly, a plane you could drive. Not that—with individual rocketpacks shooting Dad off to the plant and Mom to the super-mart and the kids off to school—the family would really need a plane or car for long. Well, maybe for vacations: Hey, Dad, circle the Pyramids just once more!

We'd soon be watching our favorite radio shows on a home television set. Dick Tracy's mythical wrist radio, sober scientists assured us, could well become reality in our lifetime. Ditto for the ballpoint pen, 3-D movies, home air-conditioning, and even rockets to the moon.

World War Two was well and truly behind me. I could return full-time to gorging my imagination on Made in America dreams. That gush of technological and consumer bounty was, after all, all-American. Even the atomic bomb was one more typically oversize American idea. America: Official Innovator to the World.

Such propaganda was all I really knew of the United States; I'd never been there, and wouldn't cross the border—on a half-hour dash into Niagara Falls, New York—until I was fourteen. But it was all I needed to know. Particularly because, by contrast, Canada in that same effulgent era seemed to be slogging along in its usual torpid way. The Yanks were retooling, redesigning, and renewing the postwar world. Our gaudiest postwar gesture seemed to be Operation Musk Ox, a mechanized sub-Arctic expedition.

This may help to explain why the shift from wartime life to postwar life in Simcoe was seldom easy for an eleven-year-old to detect. The town seemed in no hurry to shed its distinctly prewar state of being. While life south of the border streaked toward a new utopia of push-button ease, where I lived horse-drawn wagons still delivered milk, ice, and bread. A mile or two from town in almost any direction was outhouse and gaslight country, where the water was still pumped from the well and animals still did much of the field work.

And Simcoe didn't yet have even a postwar flying-saucer craze. Reported sightings of silver discs from outer space had revealed a virtual celestial traffic jam of the things in the night skies over civilization's more advanced outposts, such as the USA. This tore at Hugh's and my civic spirit. It was shortly afterward that a succession of cardboard picnic plates, painted silver and covered with the hieroglyphics of an invented Venusian language, could be glimpsed—in broad daylight—cartwheeling across the sky in the immediate vicinity of 101 Union Street.

We must have launched two dozen a day for a week, certain that at least one would be discovered, triggering awe—and maybe even panic—in the community. Somehow, Simcoe ignored this irrefutable evidence of extraterrestrial visitations—doubtless, we assured ourselves, to forestall outbreaks of mass hysteria. Reluctantly, sadly, the bedroom flying-saucer factory ceased production.

If not flying saucers, at least there was new optimism in the air, and it occasionally buoyed even T.C. Never more expansive than after dinner on Sunday, perched on the side porch steps with his cigarette and coffee, he breezily disclosed his plans to shake a few blessings out of the new cornucopia for the benefit of the McCall clan.

One Sunday it would be the little Grumman Seabee amphibian plane he was going to buy; the next, a mighty new DeSoto with Fluid Drive; a week later, a phonograph with an automatic record changer was practically due for delivery to 101 Union Street. We'd get a movie camera and projector, showing color film. All the bounty of postwar technology was heading our way. Part of T.C.'s airy postwar plan was that Hugh and I would be home only occasionally to wallow in it; in one of his more extravagant visionary seizures, he proclaimed that in the not too distant future his second- and third-born sons would be privileged to attend Royal Roads, a private and properly elite military academy in British Columbia, three thousand miles west.

The truth was, of course, that T.C.'s six-thousand-dollar annual salary as a medium-level Ontario civil servant barely covered the basic costs of food and shelter and clothing for his brood and that he couldn't afford a week's vacation or a used car, much less an airplane or a movie camera. McCall family life was not about to be revolutionized anytime soon. Save for the postwar scientific breakthrough of plastic bubbles you could blow and keep, like balloons, life would go on much as before. He knew it and so did I, but I forgave him and his fantasies. It was, after all, 1947.

Part II

THE PRISONER OF
DANFORTH AVENUE

"HOW ARE THINGS

IN GLOCCA MORRA?"

Some inexplicable family-minded impulse led T.C. to pluck Mother, Hugh, and me from the summer routine at 101 Union Street and take us on a three-day whirl around Toronto in the late summer of 1946. Exclusive access to both parents was in itself a thrill; for an eleven-year-old who had ventured outside Norfolk County once in his life, tasting it against the backdrop of the big city colored it like a dream. We put up at the Royal Alexandria Hotel on University Avenue, where you rode in an elevator and they made your bed for you. We dined in restaurants, toured the Canadian National Exhibition, and in the soft blue evenings window-shopped along Bloor Street and in the arcade at Union Station, as grand and elegant as a high-society movie set. I returned home to Simcoe in a daze, and for the first time in my life felt the stirrings of dissatisfaction with my home-town.

A year later, via the family communications line that ran from T.C. to Mother to Mike to the rest of us, the inconceivable was announced as fact: The McCall family would shortly move—not to another house in another neighborhood in Simcoe, but to Toronto.

It was never formally explained why, after a lifetime in Simcoe and after T.C.'s decade of commuting to and fro, the timeless order of things was about to be junked and we'd all live under the same roof all the time, in exotic new surroundings. Maybe Mother had finally put her foot down and demanded liberation from her lonely, care-worn, crummy life. Maybe the incongruity of his being absentee father of six had finally shamed T.C. into action. Maybe he'd gotten a raise that would let him afford decent family living space in notoriously expensive Toronto. I never asked. I didn't especially care. With the innocent self-centeredness of youth, I could see it only as the granting of my most fervent wish, for my personal pleasure.

Simcoe, cradle of the dynasty, home to McCalls for generations, instantly receded into mere prologue to the cosmopolitan life that suddenly seemed only just and inevitable. I couldn't wait to taunt Larry and Gary and the others: We're moving to Toronto, and you're not; you poor hicks are consigned to small-town life forever. I'll write, of course, send postcards, even come back sometime to describe in person everything you're missing.

For a kid bursting to rush into the future, the weeks from September until the move in early November dragged. Our comfortable old house now seemed run-down, our school dinky, the town almost comically small-scale. How could I have stood it all those years?

The last Sunday evening at 101 Union Street, just before the household and life in Simcoe were dismantled forever, found T.C. and Grandfather Walt engrossed in their regular cribbage game at the card table in the living room and Mother packing up things in the kitchen. I wandered outside for a last ramble around the grounds and the neighborhood, to indulge my ever-present sense of history by collecting some final mental snapshots and sealing in memory as much as I could of the atmosphere.

It was a calm, clear night. Union Street was empty and quiet as usual, and that peculiar but familiar scent of decomposing chestnut skins hung in the air. Then, from the open living room window, came music—T.C.'s prized new original-cast recording of *Finian's Rainbow.* It was just as Ella Logan pitched into "How Are Things in Glocca Morra?" that everything tranquil and sweet and secure about the life and place I was about to leave rose up from somewhere within and seized me by the heart. For once I was powerless to shove an unwanted feeling aside. In that one long unguarded moment I was injected with a lifetime's supply of irrepressible loss and longing. I scuttled back inside.

• • •

The three-hour journey from Simcoe to Toronto on a crisp sunny Friday in early November 1947 was a triumphal progress across the bridge from nowhere to where the McCalls so obviously belonged. Simcoe already lay in the past. So long also to Jarvis, Hagersville, Caledonia—poor tired little burgs. Here came Hamilton, the Steel City, the halfway point and a mere preview of the cosmopolitanism about to ennoble us. Now we were rolling along the King's Highway, the royal road, every light stanchion bearing its proud George Rex shield.

Then we passed the stone lion monument—British lion, of course—heralding both the highway's end and our arrival at that proud bastion of Anglomania and Christian piety, Canada's greatest metropolis, Toronto the Good. And there, as if it had been paid to stand up and show off just for us, was the skyline, a big-city skyline, more awe-inspiring than Oz.

I'd seen it once before, a year and a half earlier, but that was only as a visitor. Now everything beneath it and within it, everything that was Toronto, everything it had was about to be mine. And it had everything, and I already knew it all by heart: the Canadian Bank of Commerce, the tallest building in the British empire; the Royal Ontario Museum, with real Egyptian mummies; Eaton's and Simpson's dueling department-store dynasties; movie houses by the dozen; Union Station, half the size of Simcoe itself; the N.H.L. Maple Leafs hockey team; a Triple-A baseball club of the same nickname; the Ontario Parliament buildings; an airport; a zoo; a harbor; a university; a financial district; a city hall. Short of an Empire State Building, what more could one possibly ask for in a hometown?

"Look, a streetcar!" "Hey, there's Maple Leaf Gardens!" Our excited jabber was too manic not to soon spend itself, and by the time T.C. had piloted us out of downtown and we were headed along Bloor Street toward the East End, near calm prevailed. This allowed me to note that even the street names were exotic: Drumsnab! Castlefrank! Bastedo! But now the buildings were sinking back down to normal scale. By the time we had crossed the mighty viaduct arching high above the Don Valley and reached Broadview Avenue and the beginning of Danforth Avenue, the babble had become a murmur. Where were we going? This wasn't my idea of Toronto anymore. Danforth Avenue was a narrow corridor of buildings, regularly punctuated by vast used-car lots and steadily descending in magnificence from four to three to two stories. BAKERY . . . SMOKE SHOP . . . WOOLWORTH'S . . . HOSIERY . . . BILLIARDS . . . MEAT . . . BAKERY . . . SMOKE SHOP. The skyline hadn't said anything about this. My initial visit had left the distinct impression that Toronto was one big urban miracle of broad boulevards and towers. Now, the farther east T.C. took us, the more the surroundings mocked my fancies of Toronto the Grand.

While T.C. continued unreeling his extemporaneous travelogue up front, I stole a glance at Hugh and detected a grin fast becoming a rictus. Coxwell Avenue. Glebeholme. Woodbine. Would it ever end? A four-story dump of a building: the Wembley Hotel. An Ontario Hydro substation and, looming up behind it, in huge block letters, on a giant steel latticework of a sign: ACME FARMERS DAIRY. T.C. slowed the car and turned off the street. Was he treating us to milk shakes?

"And here we are," he announced. We had arrived in the parking area of Danforth Court Apartments. Nobody spoke. Reserve judgment, I silently cautioned myself. My heart was beating fast, but with something other than anticipation.

We unloaded our baggage and followed T.C. to the nearest of a matched set of flat-topped three-story redbrick blockhouses. He led us up a narrow, echoing, bare-walled stairwell to a landing on the top floor too small for more than two people to stand at the same time and with a door on either side. He fiddled with his keys as the seven of us waited, trailing down the stairway. "Here we are," he boomed at last, and threw open the door to the McCall family home for the next five and a half years.

We were greeted by the overpowering aroma of latex paint and linseed oil and the sight of familiar furniture in unfamiliar poses. Everything else was brand-new. Everything was pristine. Everything was clean. And well before my eager, get-acquainted spin was over, some inner voice had begun to quaver that everything was wrong. This mean little set of rooms radiated all the homey welcome of a cardboard carton. A new and better life? Here?

I pretended to gaze out a window to hide the signs of my treasonous internal dialogue from the others. I prayed for the voice to shut up, but it wouldn't. I had been tricked. Trapped. From now on, "home" for the eight of us meant half the space on one floor of a small building in a gray urban nowhere—a space chopped up into a claustrophobic warren of tiny adjoining cells. The whole place, kitchen and single bathroom and closets included, would almost fit into the living room of 101 Union Street.

How much later pent-up agony might have been avoided had I let go with all the anger and sense of betrayal that was welling up in me then and there. But McCalls didn't make scenes—and certainly not within T.C.'s eyesight, unless they wanted to add his dudgeon to their woes; and not here and now, during this momentous family occasion. Besides, it was dark now and dinner would soon be on the stove, and over the radio—a brand-new Rogers-Majestic in a blond-wood cabinet, emblematic of our new start—here came CFRB's Jim Hunter with the evening news.

Hugh was already recording the day's events in his diary as I climbed up onto the top mattress of our new bunk bed that first night. Mike lay on his back in the separate single bed that was his by right as eldest sibling. Conversation, atypically, lagged. Maybe we had talked ourselves out; maybe each of us needed to order and settle his impressions of the day. We listened to the strange new night noises of the city: the whirr of the streetcars coasting along Danforth Avenue, the clanging of their bells, the popping of car exhausts and, in the foreground, the buzzing of the ACME FARMERS DAIRY sign, metronomically blinking otherworldly neon light through the window and across our room.

Soon enough I was beyond its reach, headed back as fast as my panicky imagination and Morpheus could take me, past the Toronto skyline and the lion monument, back down the King's Highway to Hamilton and Caledonia and Hagersville and Jarvis, back along

Highway #3 past George Culver's farm and down the hill and over the L.E.& N. tracks to Simcoe, back to 101 Union Street. Back home.

The real big city, as we had surmised, lay miles westward back down Danforth Avenue and over the Don Valley viaduct. The Toronto that had so entranced Hugh and me on our maiden visit the year before bore no resemblance to the easternmost reaches of Danforth Avenue. You could walk for miles in any direction—and in that first strange, floating, disoriented weekend Mike and Hugh and I did—without encountering a single big-city thrill. This wasn't the way it was supposed to be at all. A new sensation—panic—was already starting to slither up from my gut to my brain.

The next week would sharply accelerate its progress, beginning first thing Monday morning with the terrifying specter of a new school, made more terrifying by T.C.'s contemptuous refusal to come along and help shepherd us through the enrollment process. Finally, after much snuffling and with disgusted mutters of "gutless pansies," he relented.

I had, as usual, let my imagination run riot in envisioning school in Toronto. It would be a sort of campus, shaming Simcoe's hopelessly small-time idea of public school education with big-city sophistication. It would all be a benign variation on *Tom Brown's School Days:* Everybody would wear uniforms and those little English-style caps. There would be leaded windows in the classrooms overlooking manicured greenswards shaded by tall oak trees, in whose shade I would often repose while regaling my admiring new friends with tales of Simcoe life.

The Gledhill Public School would have made a perfect Victorian jail in a David Lean film. It was a chunky brown-stone fortress, heavy and dark on the outside, dim and grim inside. Its sheer drabness was sufficient to crush the spirit of Puck himself. Dung-brown, disease-green, mustard-yellow—there must have been an incurable depressive charged with buying the paint for the Toronto educational system. The whole place seemed carefully designed to impress upon its wards that youth and education were meant to be no fun at all.

Hugh and I were separated and packed off to different classrooms, where our advent went unremarked. We rejoined at recess period in mid-morning, set loose in what looked to be a perfect replica of the exercise yard at Alcatraz. A greeting committee was waiting, one of whom presently stepped forward to deliver a punch in the face that I had no choice but to take as Gledhill's own way of saying Welcome.

If I hadn't figured it out before, that welcoming gesture left no doubt: I wasn't in Simcoe anymore.

HIGH SCHOOL

In September 1948 I delivered myself to the mercies of the institution on Greenwood Avenue known as Danforth Technical High School. I entered the place as if I were wearing a Lord Fauntleroy suit and rolling a hoop.

I had chosen Danforth Tech because it offered an art course, and drawing was the most comfortable endeavor I knew. In this as in all matters educational, T.C. declined not only to interfere but even to consult. Outside guidance would have been valuable; I learned only as the door thudded shut behind me that "Danforth Technical School" was a euphemism for "trade school" and that halfway serious art instruction would start only two years later, in grade eleven. Until then I would be consigned to a kind of boot camp, a basement labyrinth redolent of wood shavings and machine oil and an all-male, blue-collar, bare-knuckle education in the lowlier industrial arts.

My classmates didn't actually pick nits out of each other's body hair, but they did impress me as being closer to the lower primates than any creatures wearing clothes I'd ever encountered. Their preference for physical mayhem over intellectual development disrupted my train of thought from day one. The teaching staff appeared to regard their wards as learning-proof; time had long since evaporated the fuel from their lamps of learning; chalk dust had dried out their hearts. I had never known that education could be so dull.

At home, a year out of Simcoe, the McCall family was now individually and collectively in psychic free fall. I dreaded leaving 2377 Danforth in the mornings to go to school, and dreaded leaving school in the afternoons to go home. The once-eager student watched himself turn into a dunce. As was virtually foreordained from day one, I failed grade nine. T.C.'s reaction, after an initial burst of door slamming and an even colder than usual shoulder around the apartment, was to distance himself even further from all connection with my academic career.

I fled the next year to Malvern Collegiate in hopes of reversing my losing streak in a more traditional academic curriculum and less oppressive surroundings, and failed grade nine again.

The only alternative to a third round in grade nine was a kind of academic amputation: enrolling in Malvern's "commercial" course, a cul-de-sac especially designed to convert confirmed underachievers like myself into the bank tellers and office clerks of tomorrow by deleting most academic subjects from the curriculum in favor of bookkeeping, typing, and other rudimentary office skills. It would at least nominally shove me forward into grade ten, at the cost of sacrificing all chance of a proper high school graduation certificate and any hope I might have had about going on to university. By then I hardly cared. There were more urgent things on my mind.

It is late one November night in 1949 in the living room at 2377 Danforth. T.C. is away on another business trip. Mother is drunk again. Certain atmospherics, as usual, cling in memory: the reek from a just-finished apartment repainting, "Blueberry Hill," a current Louis Armstrong hit, on the radio. Mike and Hugh and I are stewing in our bedroom when Mike decides to break the McCall taboo against direct encounters and get to the root of Mother's addiction, once and for all. Why, why, why this suicidal slide into alcoholism? What is so wrong in her life? Isn't there some way to help, to stop her from continuing to inflict this misery on herself and her family?

Mike leaves the bedroom, determined for all our sakes to pry out the truth. Hugh and I lie in our bunks, hearts thumping, desperately trying not to tune in on the muffled exchange on the other side of the wall. Ten minutes pass, twenty, then half an hour. He must have gotten her to open up, and if he has, maybe he'll be coming back with an idea, a plan, some hope.

He comes back a few minutes later in tears. Panic engulfs Hugh and me. What happened? What's wrong? At first Mike refuses to talk, burying his face in his pillow, but our whimpering beseechings finally wear him down. Swearing us to silence, he spills the secret that spins us into despair. Mother has cancer. She has taken to drinking out of fear and hopelessness. She is going to die. Not T.C., not anybody, is to know.

It's a comment on the dark emotional underworld in which the McCall family functioned that we were as good as our word. To bring it out into the open, to tell T.C. and beg him to seek medical or other help and at least try to fight it, never occurred to Mike or Hugh or me. In silence, betraying our dread secret by neither word nor gesture, we would have to watch our mother slowly die.

Covertly watching Mother's every move, measuring her struggle against the disease devouring her from within, became the center of my existence. There were ups and downs, good days and bad days, signs of hope—an uptick in mood—dashed by hints of doom—a cough, a headache. I alternated in torturing myself with images of death and bolstering myself with dreams of miraculous remission. Not even Mike and Hugh and I ever openly discussed the matter among ourselves. It would only make the nightmare more real.

Nine months later and Mother still hadn't died or, I began to realize, even appreciably sickened. Then came the August afternoon in 1950 when I found myself alone in an uncharacteristically deserted apartment. A dash to the bedside table in my parents' room where the family secrets were kept. A desperate rummaging, for what I didn't even know. But in a minute or less I found it: a doctor's letter, dated two weeks before. The hysterectomy had been a complete success; and in case Mother might be worried, there was no sign of cancer.

The nightmare faded as quickly as it had come on. I never knew whether it had all been a deliberate lie, a piece of emotional black-mail Mother had cold-bloodedly concocted on the spur of the moment to protect her addiction, or a genuine fear mercifully dispelled. For the first few weeks I was too relieved to care. Afterward, it didn't seem to matter. The drinking continued. The confrontations ceased.

TRONNA

> Morality hangs over the City of Toronto like smog over Los Ange-
> les. On Sunday no newspaper publishes there, the movie houses are
> closed and it is not possible, if one were so minded, to brighten the
> cheerless day by buying a drink. Perhaps as a result of this seventh-
> day suppression of profane desires, the norms of entertainment
> value are distorted, at least in the sporting fellowship, so that a fight
> which might attract 374 persons to Madison Square Garden was able
> to draw 5,200 in Toronto last week.

The above observation appeared in *Sports Illustrated* magazine in
1956. By that time Toronto's reputation as not so much a city as a
vacuum-sealed container of perfectly preserved late-Victorian Anglican rectitude was already beginning to melt. I'm doomed by my past
to remember Toronto—Toronto the Good in its own opinion,
Tronna in the local argot, Hogtown to the rest of Canada—from an
earlier time.

You can't fool me. Knock down all the glittery false fronts, sweep
away all the props and extras that allow the Toronto of today to
masquerade as a Swiss-run cold-weather version of Los Angeles, and
there it will be—that stone-gray civic bulwark against fun and fleshly
pleasures, Hogtown now and forever.

His Worship the Mayor, Hiram McCallum himself, once again
heads a mob of outraged Christian citizenry out to banish the painting titled *Sailors and Floozies* from an art show at the Canadian Na-

tional Exhibition, on the grounds of lewdness too raw for God-fearing Torontonians and their children to gaze upon. Workmen, again in the name of public morality, are dismantling the just-erected sign over a newly opened East End tavern with its suggestively filthy double entendre: the Coxwell Inn. The beady-eyed Pecksniffs at the Ontario Board of Censors are scrutinizing every foot of new film before it reaches the projectors of the local movie houses, bent on eradicating every overt or subliminal incitement to carnal pleasure.

Toronto the Good it was, if "good" was narrowly defined as a million middle-class white Protestants of Anglo-Saxon descent marching in lockstep along the path of moral righteousness. Something about the place suggested, even to an irreligious thirteen-year-old, that it had decided around the time of Queen Victoria's diamond jubilee just to stop and freeze everything, then and there. Had Victoria herself appeared downtown one typical pewter-gray Sunday in 1948, just to check up, she would have found a gratifyingly stone-dead Sabbath being observed, as 100 percent joy-free as she could have hoped. Toronto's moral tone was set and assiduously monitored for the slightest signs of slippage by the Lord's Day Alliance, a self-appointed star chamber of churchly hard-liners, whose dour vision of the Christian life had a way of getting itself transmuted into law. No Sunday sports. No Sunday drinking. No Sunday shopping. This accorded with the views and values of Toronto's barely postcolonial ruling class of Anglo-Saxon politicians, divines, lawyers, business leaders, and the odd Colonel Jingo. Their devout Anglophilia, Anglicanism, temperance, and solemnity set the model for the municipality and much of the nation—backward Papist French Quebec, of course, excepted.

As far as I could see, Toronto's architectural clock had stopped dead circa 1890. City Hall was an argument in stone against the very idea of progress, a soot-blackened Gothic eyesore hideous enough to frighten small children. Torontonians' idea of a high time on a Sunday afternoon—not that a Toronto Sunday afternoon overflowed with diversions—was to visit Casa Loma, the shell of a rich man's folly of a Scottish castle, complete with secret panels, erected

Toronto, 1948. Virtually every landmark in the city sooner or later got the same photographic treatment from T.C.: Hugh and I—no matter how hot the weather, always in jacket and tie—planted in the foreground, regarding it with grave circumspection. This is the Ontario Legislature building at Queens Park.

decades earlier in the middle of the city and long since abandoned by its bankrupted laird.

The entertainment climax of a Toronto year came with the annual late-summer extravaganza of the "Ex"—the Canadian National Exhibition, staged on its own permanent grounds, which were studded with Beaux Arts Halls of Electricity and Palaces of Agriculture. Here was a 1937 Canadian high school geography textbook come to life, where you could learn more about mining and foresting and fisheries than you ever thought you needed or wanted to know, before peeling off to stroll the yokels' paradise of a midway.

Even the downtown streetcars seemed to clang forth from a time warp; they were gaunt antiques called "trippers," and riding their hard wooden benches as they jolted and wobbled along made me half believe that by the time I finally reached my stop, I would be back in 1915.

The veritable heart of Toronto and all Ontario sedately pulsed close to downtown at Queens Park, the seat of the provincial government, adjacent to the Royal Ontario Museum and the campus of the University of Toronto. The Ontario Legislature building, its architectural style described by Frank Lloyd Wright as "Early Penitentiary," stood smack in the center. Dominating the greensward before it was a statue of Victoria Regina herself, squinting southward down University Avenue, the broad boulevard that bore you down to the lakefront and to mighty Union Station, the hub of train travel that still brought steam locomotives chuffing in and out from all over the dominion.

The Toronto of pre-expressway days dribbled out along the lakeshore into a harbor flanked by grain elevators and an ugly smudge of dark Satanic mills, which never seemed to produce anything but smoke, amid a motley of dead machinery and dead scows and dead-end canals. On hot August nights it emitted a collective stench of chemicals, bilge, and industrial putrescence that made you roll up the windows while driving through.

That the city wasn't designed for idle pleasure could be quickly confirmed by seeking it. Mike and Hugh and I, in our earliest Toronto days, made almost weekly Sunday attempts to wrest a few hours of distraction, if not recreation, from our newly adopted home. We'd walk the four miles west along Danforth Avenue and across the viaduct spanning the Don River to downtown without encountering a single store open for business. No doubt by some oversight on the civic fathers' part, the Royal Ontario Museum wasn't locked shut, affording a welcome hour of distraction, until the silence and stillness came to feel too much like what we'd been seeking to escape in the first place. Bloor Street. Bay Street. Church Street. King Street. College Street. Yonge Street. Nothing doing; nobody home. Elsewhere in Hogtown in those cheerless days, I'm prepared to admit, high times must have been had by somebody, somewhere. But not by anybody our intrepid threesome ever observed. From our halfhearted Sunday wanderings I remember mainly the emptiness: the deserted sidewalks, empty trolleys rolling by, dark store windows. You could have rolled Hiram McCallum down Bay Street and he would have had a clear run all the way to the lakeshore.

Toronto couldn't have offered much more in the way of pleasure to our parents. Canada's historic torrid romance with bland food and the citizenry's general reluctance to put on the dog combined to produce restaurant anhedonia. It was cheaper to indulge the native meat loaf fever at home than in Bassel's or Bowles's or some other hash house; and prices at the few restaurants that came close to celebrating fine food—the stately dining rooms of the Royal York and Prince Edward hotels, for instance—were too steep.

Toronto nightlife veered dangerously toward debauchery in early 1948 with the opening of Club Norman—a nightclub! How many innocent Toronto lambs were driven berserk by the Satanic blend of liquor and live music is not recorded. Meanwhile, confirmed dipsomaniacs slunk into one or another "beverage room," drinking dens as far from cozy cheer as a committee of killjoy teetotaling Ontario Bible-thumpers could devise: Stygian lairs reeking of stale cigarette smoke and stale beer, noisy as bowling alleys. Beverage rooms even provided separate entrances for Ladies with Escorts and Ladies without Escorts, the better to keep an eye on the Hesters in their midst.

The city's upper crust, following the English model in all things, made their own, no doubt decorous, form of whoopee amongst their own kind at private retreats such as the Granite Club or in their stately mansions in the enclave of Rosedale or its near rival Forest Hill. Each magnificent Tudor or Georgian or thatched Cotswold cottage therein was another elaborate architectural curtsy to the English Way. No Toronto grandee would have dreamed of building himself something Moorish or Mediterranean or Canadian—even if there had been an indigenous Canadian architectural style—or to furnish his manse in anything but as exact a replica of the interiors displayed in *Country Life* as money could buy.

"A zebra skin, brought back by Mr. Fleming from a hunting expedition in the Soudan, is used on the polished floor," intones a 1933 *Canadian Homes* review of one such Anglophiliac palazzo. That Mr. Fleming could have saved a lot of time and money by driving north two hours and bagging a moose instead was evidently not considered. There are no moose in England.

The earlier McCall aversion to mingling in Simcoe society was transferred intact to Toronto. Parents and offspring alike, our social reach seldom extended beyond the front door of our own apartment. Business entertainment on the Ontario government's cuff occasionally took T.C. and Mother out on the town, but having family friends would have required that we be a functioning family. There were no casual family get-togethers, dropping-by's, dinner invitations received or tendered. The eight of us could hardly have been less social if we'd all been under house arrest.

It didn't help that of the thirty-two families jammed into those apartments at Danforth Court, ours was not only the largest but by far the oldest; virtually none of the hundred or so neighboring kids was even close in age to Mike or Hugh or me. Danforth Court itself existed as a self-contained enclave, as foreign as a space colony plunked down in that settled old blue-collar neighborhood; the populations failed to interact.

The environment of the Danforth (as Torontonians insisted on calling the street, for reasons as obscure then as now) only helped to rub in the sense of isolation. The Danforth was a strip of mercantile monotony crawling shop by shop from Broadview Avenue to the city's easternmost edge. In our immediate section of it there was a decrepit Joy gasoline station, with the trademark miniature castle evidently long since sacked; Len Upthegrove's alleyway used-car lot, narrower than its proprietor's name; a furniture store where I could stand watching test patterns from a Buffalo station and Charlie Chaplin two-reelers, free, on the TV in the show window; Empire Motors, flogging flyweight English Standard economy cars to a car-starved postwar market; an off-brand church with its unchanging bulletin-board message WASTE NOT YOUR LIVES IN VAIN REGRET, clearly aimed directly at me; the Prince of Wales movie theater; a poolroom I never dared enter; a couple of greasy-spoon restaurants; a storefront window with nothing in it but a dusty poster showing a boy at prayer over the mantra GOD BLESS MOOSEHEART; and a "variety store," presided over by a garrulous scarecrow convinced that he alone was given to know exactly how the Rosicrucians, the pope, the Masons, and the barons of Bay Street had rigged the game of life against the Little Guy. If the McCall boys had a social life at the time, it was in our encounters with the proprietor and his lugubrious insights around the Coke cooler on long winter nights.

The Danforth also had, farther from home but well worth the twenty-minute walk, Harold Speaker's hobby shop. Model-building being a timeless consolation for the shut-in and the otherwise isolated, all five McCall boys took to it early and with zeal, and Speaker's was our supply depot. But even when we needed no sandpaper or airplane glue, a trip there could be the highlight of the day for Walt and me. We window-shopped the HO-gauge model trains and rolling stock on display and exchanged daydreams about the layout and equipment we'd choose if our apartment had the space and we had the money.

In this yearning, and the trek down the Danforth to Harold Speaker's, were the seeds of the one authentic miracle that ever touched my life or Walt's.

We had barely risen one hot August morning in 1949 before detecting the swift approach of boredom's enervating miasma, so out the door and onto the Danforth we went, sans money, sans plan. "Let's go down to Harold Speaker's and look at the trains," Walt finally suggested.

We were halfway there, just past Woodbine where Danforth takes a shallow westward downhill run. Street cleaners were already at work back behind us, sending a torrent of water flowing past us in the gutter. The debris swirling in the current caught my eye. Shreds of paper, wrappers, a two-dollar bill, another two-dollar bill, another.

"Walt!" I cried. "Look!" Look, nothing. Walt was already scrambling to scoop up as many of the rushing, spinning pink bills as his two hands could reach. Our sudden sopping fortune came to almost twenty dollars, enough for each of us to buy his HO-gauge rolling stock of choice. I chose a B&O reefer; Walt, I think, took a Santa Fe caboose. Harold was mystified by the moist state of our currency, but he let us be. The rich don't have to justify themselves.

The Danforth, an even farther walk from home than Harold Speaker's, also had Lyndhurst Motors, authorized Nash sales and service; and in October 1948 the show windows were soaped white. N-Day was near, when the windows would be wiped clean and the all-new Nash, the first since before the war, was revealed.

To almost everybody in 1948, any new-car unveiling rated favorably in terms of drama with encountering a freshly arrived meteorite in the living room. To Walt and me, budding car nuts, the excitement was doubled. And when it came to Nash cars, you could multiply that by a factor of a thousand.

Walt and I were Nash nuts; or rather, I was a Nash nut who had infected him. And while most such zealots seem never to be able to quite recall what triggered their obsession, I could remember the very day and instant. It was at the Ex on my first Toronto visit in 1946, in the hall provided for displaying new cars. I goggled at the Tucker Torpedo and the new Kaiser-Frazers, but Nash had decorated its stand with foot-long scale models of Nashes past and present: beautiful, professionally hand-built models of such glossy perfection that to contemplate them made me weak in the knees with admiration— and desire.

No sooner had I gotten back home to Simcoe than I tore out a page from my scribbler and dashed off a note to Nash, requesting return shipment of all or any models, signed Nash Fan.

Nash actually bothered to reply, politely declining my request but thanking me for my interest, etc., etc. That sealed it. Any disappointment I might have felt at losing out on those models was temporary, and softened at any rate by knowing full well that my chances were slim. But a giant car company nice enough even to acknowledge a letter from an eleven-year-old kid was my kind of car company. It was Nash for me, Nash now, Nash always and forever.

Then at last it was N-Day and off to Lyndhurst Motors to come face-to-face at last with the all-new '49 Nash. Walt and I arrived already panting from our mile-and-a-half sprint; what we saw took the rest of our breath away. There it sat on the showroom floor amid the banners and placards and bunting: the 1949 Nash Airflyte Ambassador sedan, a huge, bloated, eclair-shaped blob that not only didn't look like a Nash, it didn't look like a car. The gift of our adulation had been betrayed by the ugliest automobile ever conceived. In a world already too full of disappointments, even Nash had let us down. It was a long, silent walk back home.

Only fond memories attach to Margaret's Delicatessen on the Danforth, where one hungry after-school day Walt and I found, to our amazement and greedy delight, that you could buy—for a quarter—a generous paper sackful of yesterday's doughnuts. Buy them we did; and, after splurging another quarter on an industrial-size bottle of Canada Dry Tom Collins Mix, raced home to lock ourselves in the bathroom and gorge on rapidly superannuating pastries washed down with mouthfuls of tart carbonated lemon-and-lime. Let Mike and Hugh hammer all they wanted on the locked bathroom door. This moment, this feast, was all ours.

On Halloween night in 1950 Hugh and I rode the streetcar down to the Odeon at Bloor and Yonge to see a revival of Charlie Chaplin's *City Lights*, from 1931. I emerged transfixed. Shortly afterward I found a full-page still of Charlie huddled in a cabin, a famous scene from *The Gold Rush*, in one of T.C.'s litter of photography magazines and tore it out. I'd use it to build a diorama, my personal homage to the little genius.

T.C. knew better. On the reverse side of that very page, he quickly noted, happened to be a nude "art study," which he determined in his customary instinctive flash to be my real and hidden interest, adding that of budding sexual pervert to my already cluttered paternal charge sheet. Outraged attempts to argue otherwise, to save my good name and Charlie's, elicited only a knowing smirk.

That T.C. had a dirty mind himself I discovered abruptly late one night a few months later, to my lasting glee and his lasting mortification. Arriving home earlier than expected from the movies, Hugh and I barged through the front door and into a darkened living room. T.C. was hunched over his slide projector; on the roll-up portable screen in the instant before the projector clicked off I glimpsed milky skin and proud, jutting breasts. The hypocritical son of a bitch was showing Mother his naughty pictures!

Now I had something on him. Within days, after a furtive lightning raid on a metal box on the floor of his bedroom closet, T.C.'s secret cache of slide transparencies—nothing more pornographic than young women showing their tits—became a treasure trove, from which I plucked a few of the juiciest for my own private subcollection. I had, for once, no fear of parental retribution. What could that living font of righteousness do, ask for his dirty pictures back?

But those who live by unclean thoughts die by unclean thoughts, and my own burning moment of shame would arrive soon enough. Clawing at the clothes in our bedroom closet one morning in the usual pre-school rush, I inadvertently jerked a coat off its hanger—and dumped my illicit load of slides all over the floor. Mike pounced. His cackles chased me from the room and all the way to school. To his credit, my appalling moment of shame remained our secret.

The summer of 1952 brought wrenching change to my life and that of the family. Mike left home. He was with almost no prior warning packed up and gone from the bedroom and the life we had shared minute by minute and hour by hour over the past five years, gone for a sailor—or, more accurately, a Royal Canadian Navy midshipman in training to be a naval aviator.

Mike had been grooming himself for a career in hotel management, with summer jobs at resort hotels from Niagara Falls to Banff, and was learning the food part of the business in a course at Ryerson Institute in Toronto. But Mike was also twenty-one and restless, and it didn't take much—in fact, it took a sixty-second radio Navy-

recruiting commercial he heard while lying on his bed one sultry afternoon—to move him to sign up, leave home, and begin his Navy
career at Cornwallis, Nova Scotia.

He returned on leave the following December, resplendent in his
British-style midshipman's uniform. He was starry-eyed and dis-
tracted, and a month later married the woman who had made him so.
We saw all too little of Mike in the following years as he moved
around the world and began raising a family in Halifax. I desperately
missed him. Family life wasn't the same without Mike as the buffer
against our parents and the world. His absence created a vacuum in
my life, and I would invest more time and energy than I like to admit,
even today, in searching for substitutes to fill it. I found myself a
whole series of surrogate big brothers in the years to come. They
were helpful—valuable, even; but none of them could ever replace
big brother Mike.

Toronto did its utmost to starve the American idea out of my
soul, aided by the Americans themselves, alas, who appeared to regard the Queen City as a Mecca for stayaways. Toronto was a long
drive from Highway #3. Visiting required a conscious, deliberate
act—"Say, hon, how's about a weekend up Toronto way? Hear tell
the parliament buildings are something to see, and the butter tarts are
superb!" My U.S. license-plate count nosedived. The thrilling sense
of contact faded.

But I was determined to keep alive my sense of identification with
things American. One way was by lying. Certain that nobody would
bother to check, I let it be known to my Malvern classmates that I'd
just arrived in town from down Norfolk, Virginia, way. This failed
to stir curiosity beyond a polite nod, but the repositioning titillated
its creator no end, and I was chagrined that the detailed American au-
tobiography I had invented for myself never got the chance to be
used.

Regular New York business trips were among T.C.'s official perks,
mainly semi-ceremonial occasions where he graciously submitted to
being shown the town by space salesmen for big American magazines
eager to run Ontario tourism advertising. He knocked 'em back at

Toots Shor's bar, shook hands with Winchell himself at the Stork Club, took in a Giants game up at the Polo Grounds. I was vicariously a step behind him every glamorous step of the way.

Steady incoming loads of complimentary American magazines maintained the most dependable lifeline: fat issues of *Holiday, Time, Life, Fortune, The Saturday Evening Post,* and *Collier's* and *The New Yorker,* of course, even *The Saturday Review of Literature* and *The Reporter,* combining to spray the American ambience into my life like an atomizer. From Toronto you could tune in the Buffalo radio stations for afternoon serials and the evening network shows, smuggling the taste of the USA into your very bedroom, uncut and intact.

And big league baseball hung over my life like a firmament of sixteen distant but brightly twinkling all-American planets. Fortune would eventually reward me by hurling an American baseball meteorite almost into my lap. A professional American baseball player— a major-league baseball player, no less—was discovered to be living virtually around the corner from 2377 Danforth, on Mortimer Street. He was Chet Laabs, playing out the string with the Triple-A Maple Leafs, but a longtime big-leaguer and indeed a starting regular on the American League's pennant-winning 1944 St. Louis Browns. Chet Laabs himself, a neighbor! Howdy, neighbor! A mute Canadian-style howdy, actually, and from a safe fifty feet or so away across the street, where I was content to watch as Chet emerged from his house, walked to his car, got in, and drove off to smite horsehide with hickory at Maple Leaf Stadium.

An American kid would at least have asked for his autograph. I still had a ways to go.

THE GREAT ESCAPE

School was the rock and T.C.'s idea of family life the hard place, but wedged into the space between was a cramped and stinky little ten-by-twelve bedroom with a door that shut them both out for hours at a time; and so to a knob, two hinges, and some screws do Hugh and I probably owe our sanity.

That room was our only sanctum on earth. Only within its walls could we shed our protective carapaces, relax our stomachs and sphincters, and just fool around doing whatever felt most soothing. Escape felt most soothing. Tunneling out from three flights up was impractical, so we set ourselves to tunneling out metaphysically.

Not that choices abounded. I still know every inch of that fetid little stalag by heart: two beds, a bureau, a desk, a chair. Barely room enough for two people to stand up at the same time, much less run and jump. TV existed then only in furniture-store windows and the living rooms of the rich, a luxurious novelty. We did own a radio that if you whacked just so would squawk to life for a while. Even then we knew card games to be the last resort of imbeciles; by that time we'd played Monopoly, a dim-witted horse-racing board game called Crosby Derby, and our crude mechanical hockey contraption unto catatonia; and that official seal of the well-lived boyhood, the electric train, clicked and clattered only in dreams.

You could lie in bed or sit at the desk. And what could you do at a desk? Well, paper and pencils were cheap and plentiful, and a ran-

OuR Room — June 9/51

What Hugh's diary didn't record of daily life at 2377 Danforth, his painstaking drawings did. This is a 1951 cutaway view of our bedroom—fantasy factory. The desk is shown unoccupied; the drawing is otherwise microscopically accurate.

dom stock of watercolors and inks and pens and brushes had followed us from 101 Union Street, because Hugh and I had always liked to draw.

But now pens and pencils—and cardboard and glue and scissors and X-Acto knives—became psychic digging tools as we commenced to try fantasizing our way out, into realms as faraway and as different from oppressive reality as imagination could contrive. It was fun, of course, and absorbing, the same idle-hours hobby pursued to one degree or another by half the teenage kids in the world. But our brand was more than play. It was a survival mechanism, and all the more crucial because it was the only one at hand.

We alternated shifts at that tiny battered desk day after day, week after week, month after month, for five and a half years. Any sharpening of artistic and writing skill was a mere by-product. It wasn't ambition that impelled us, it was need.

It drove T.C. crazy that two sons of his were squandering their teenage years hiding out in an airless cell, all life reduced to whatever the hell they were doing at a thirty-by-twenty-inch desktop. "Why don't you two get girlfriends, go to dances, get out?" We couldn't explain why, not even to ourselves. I wasn't unaware that this monomania was creating a certain imbalance. Bolder, more mentally healthy, more normal guys my age probably were up to all kinds of hijinks out there in the Toronto beyond my bedroom window, in a world that might have been their oyster but was my ever elusive unsolved riddle.

But Hugh and I were powerless to bring our bathysphere to the surface. The crushing pressures of our lives pinned us to that desk, and squeezed and squeezed until our desperate imaginations spewed out solvents—images, words, ideas—that filled the emptiness, made us laugh, made us feel better for a while.

What a cauldron of creative industry it became, that microscopic colony tucked away in one room of a small apartment in the wastes of East End Toronto. The escape industry. I shudder today at the memory of it, and so does Hugh—that such sustained, feverish, desperate sublimation was so necessary, and that among its costs was that it so bent what deserved to be normal, healthy young lives. But from this accident of circumstance, this small-scale improvised working example of necessity as the mother of invention, I would extract first a diversion, then a hobby, then a calling, and ultimately a professional career. A rotten start: I don't know where I'd be today without it.

It was here that the lust to write spontaneously combusted when I was thirteen. One day I happened to find my fingers fanned over the keyboard of a typewriter—T.C.'s personal, sacred, off-limits portable Royal typewriter, sneaked into the bedroom from its hall-closet niche one idle afternoon for something to do.

Apotheosis. The mechanical transcription of words—my words— onto the page, in a form of printing, seemed a granting of magical powers. Seeing my words march from left to right across the page in Roman letters made what I was writing suddenly important, official, as if I'd managed to shimmy halfway through the portal that led to the adult world and gotten hold of one of the controls. I began taking care that what I set down was worthy, which forced a new concern for sounding like a writer, which left no choice but to become a writer.

In so doing, I doubt that I was entirely unaware of the grander context. T.C. had been a writer by profession for most of his adult life, after also pounding the keyboard for fun and diversion in his teenage years. Inhaling the aromas of newsprint and hot lead as I wandered through the pressroom of the *Simcoe Reformer*, his journalistic alma mater, remains one of my earliest and most vivid memories.

Following in T.C.'s footsteps. Emulation—or perhaps a sneaky form of internecine competition? I favor the latter, and so, I think, does history. For example, T.C. never felt impelled to fan my flaming zeal to write by encouragement or even more than random notice. He would no more think of writing, language, reading, literature as topics for discussion with me as Early Renaissance madrigals. Far from tendering the product of my typewriting efforts for his comment or approval, I tended to hide them from his view. Nothing a thirteen-year-old kid had written could possibly merit putting aside whatever he was doing to read. And, anyway, I'd be betraying what a surreptitious battering his private personal Royal had been getting on a daily basis.

Four of the six McCall siblings would eventually earn livelihoods behind the typewriter—their own—and a fifth, Mike, easily could have. I'd like to think T.C. would have been proud, but I doubt it. "No goddamn initiative," I hear him splutter. "Just trailing along behind their old man."

And his personal experience of a writer's working life, at least the print journalist's working life, seemed to have left him with something less than affection for the knights of the keyboard and their calling. Once, a few years later, in an especially dark moment of my commercial-art career, I hit upon the idea of switching into journalism—cub reporter, say—as deliverance. After dinner one night, I ventured down to his basement woodworking shop for advice and counsel. He gave them freely. All newspapermen were drunken, shifty, cynical hacks. The hours were horrible; nobody earned a decent wage. It was a mug's game. Banish the foolish thought. And like an obedient son and an idiot, I did.

But I wrote, as I drew, with purpose. Parodies of the last book I'd read; short stories; text and captions for handmade illustrated pamphlets and books. The creative duality of writing and drawing gradually fused until it was all more or less the same.

But "writer-illustrator" was not a career ambition served by any known educational system. The road forked at an early point—nascent artists, this way; would-be writers, that way. And at a susceptible adolescent moment while I was pondering my plight, *Time* happened to quote an ancient Chinese proverb: "Man who chase two rabbits catch none." Thanks, *Time.* It seemed a barb addressed directly to me. Come on, kid, quick, make up your mind. Make your choice or end up a misfit, a failure, a bum. I made choices almost monthly for the next few years, seesawing back and forth in an agony of indecision between being Charles Dickens and Norman Rockwell.

It took only about thirty more years of trial and error—mostly error—before I realized that it was okay to try being both.

My body of work from late 1947 to mid-1953—drawings, paintings, comic strips, stories, essays, pamphlets, booklets, maps, models, dioramas—would fill the proverbial Albert Hall. Much of it would also fill the notebooks of a platoon of psychiatrists.

The problem wasn't that I created fantasy worlds but the nature of the fantasies. They were not pretty. What did it say about my secret self that I chose to roam so endlessly through an imaginative landscape of such unrelieved, fanatically detailed squalor? That I was comforting myself, of course, by imagining a world even darker and more hopeless than I felt my own to be.

I drew a Hogarthian mob clawing at a chute in a basement and titled it, proudly, "The Garbage Eaters." Nobody could capture human or inanimate decrepitude like me. I was master of the mildewed, wrinkled, torn, and ill-fitting wardrobe. I couldn't draw a

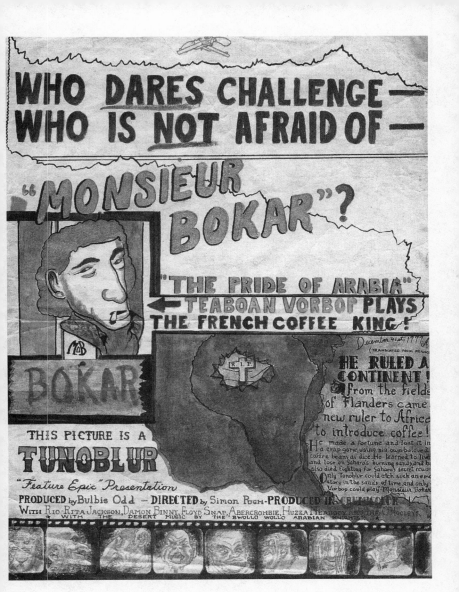

Circa 1950. A Tunoblur Studios movie poster and, on the following pages, a quartet of Puneranian vistas, Christmas at Cabbagetown Orphanage, the Commie-sponsored Ricardos hockey team, Li'l Grubber and cohorts. I thought all this compulsive wallowing in squalor was hilarious at the time. Today it seems pathetic—the desperate tactic of trying to buck up my spirits by imagining lives and worlds far bleaker than my own.

FAMED PUNERANIAN SUMMER RESORT TOWN, SMICKLEY-BY-THE-SEA, ON LAKE SNEDOE

A FAMED PUNERANIAN LANDMARK, 1924 TRACTOR, JUNK TRAGICALLY IN 1947 AT FISH

KING GUS' LIMOUSINE OUTSIDE OF HIS MANSION ON THE SUPERHIGHWAY OUT OF BOMSAK

A PUNERANIAN SOLDIER INVESTIGATES THE WRECKA A DOWNED ITALIAN FIGHTER PLANE FROM 1939 AT GR

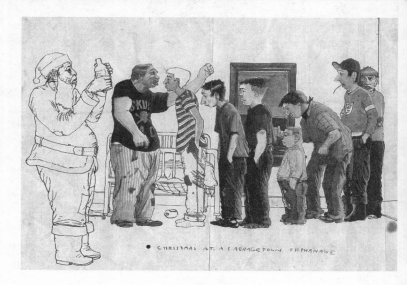

● CHRISTMAS AT A CABBAGETOWN ORPHANAGE

THE "TUMBLIN' ROVERS"

"GRUBBER" "LI'L BEANIE" "HICKER" "ROY" PORTER SLOAT LI'L HOGAN LI'L PEPPERMINT STICK "LI'L HOOKER"

"The Dangerous Eight"

The Good Ol' Rics!! ~Blobber~!!
Mar
1956

FLOURZ—
Fiv $5.

face that wasn't ugly, sallow, speckled with acne, and crowned with a mane of unkempt, greasy hair.

The urge to wallow in squalor spilled over into three dimensions: Out of cardboard and glue I built a scale-model run-down horsemeat store, lifelike down to the scale-model dab of real, rancid hamburger in the window. Even Hugh got sucked into the act. Out of a Laura Secord candy box he created Greed's Pool Hall, the sleaziest billiards parlor ever built, down to its ratty hole of a bathroom. (What does it say about me, and my suppressed rage at the time, that poor Hugh had no sooner completed it and momentarily left the room than I popped in a firecracker through the celluloid skylight and blew Greed's Pool Hall, bathroom and all, to smithereens?)

I moved from mere tableaux to chronicle, in pictures and words—life in mythical forlorn and impoverished neighborhoods, societies, whole complex families of mini-states—and stocked them exclusively with madmen and charlatans and dolts: I give you King Gus of Punerania, Count Igger de bo Slag—poor, dirty, ineffectual, and harmless—each as baffled by the goings-on around him as I was.

I invented the world's worst movie studio, Tunoblur, and gave it a stable of talentless oafs scraped off the streets for stars: Sid Malone, Rio Rita Jackson, the Gilhooley Boys, Teaboan Vorbop. I then concocted posters for the world's worst movies—e.g., *Oh, That Mustard Gas*—as their starring vehicles and, before the ink was dry, sat down at the typewriter to pan them mercilessly in the role of the acerbic critic Leeman Bonky, reporting in his regular film column "See What I Mean?"

Sports played too large a part of my imaginative life at the time to escape creative attention. I invented the Sumach Browns, the world's worst baseball team, drafted its roster from some mental dregs, wrote their bios, and painted their portraits: Jasmun Chickerby, the eighty-three-year-old ambidextrous hurler; Tang Onomuro, the Japanese shortstop; Tubby Yurk, the four-hundred-pound slugging outfielder; Bruce McSunnyworth, the loud-mouthed no-hit, no-field first sacker, me. I gave them teams to lose to—the Sackville Romans, the Chain City Gluemen, the New Huskard Barometerisers—and, complete with box scores, wrote up their epic failures for my own bedtime reading.

Hockey could not be ignored. I invented the Ricardos—the Rics, in the breezy style of my fanciful game reports—six identical chinless geeks and the world's rattiest, dirtiest, and worst hockey team, sponsored by the local Communist Party cell, bearing the hammer and sickle on the shirtfronts of their filthy moth-eaten yellow-and-red uniforms. I created a make-believe basement rink studded with brick pillars for them to play in, and ensured that crime (and Communism) did not pay by showing their opponents thumping them senseless en route to yet another humiliating loss.

And to cap the oeuvre I invented my alter ego: Li'l Grubber, a pumpkin-headed gnome in a huge tweed cap and ill-fitting ankle-length gabardine overcoat, whose sweet, sunny nature and sheer spunk couldn't be subdued. "The Adventures of Li'l Grubber"— and his faithful young sidekick, the orphan Li'l Peppermint Stick (a surrogate Hugh)—became not just my homemade comic strip, flowing from my pen at the rate of an installment or more per day, but my parallel existence.

I loved Li'l Grubber, the irrepressible scamp, inevitably triumphing in his ramshackle universe of poverty and oppression with nothing but his guile and wit. And no wonder, since he was me.

He started out as a street fighter, head of a gang called the Tumblin' Rovers, scrabbling for food and shelter in predictable McCall fantasy fashion in a black parody of urban blight inspired by Cabbagetown, the local Toronto slum. But Grubber was alive. I'd created him expressly to do the things I couldn't. Thus, in the full high noon of Li'l Grubber as recorded by his creator—now in color, the richer to make the experience—we see the methodical step-by-step ascent of a ragged dwarf from the netherworld.

What furtive, secret, liberating joy I sucked from that ascent! He gets a car, a rusted secondhand '41 Plymouth. He gives Peppermint Stick a brand-new deluxe Boston Bruins outfit. He models a flashy new wardrobe of business suits and leisure wear. The two of them are caught smiling out from amid palm trees under postcard skies on a deluxe Mexican holiday, a million miles from the slums. And . . . what's this? Why, you little devil! There he is, beaming before his brand-new Tudor-style cottage with its sweet little leaded windows, an early fifties bourgeois Toronto dream house. And . . . what's that? A brand-new Nash Airflyte in the drive!

Now that Li'l Grubber—and I—had reached something close to the heart of my secret dreams of security, surcease, contentment, there wasn't anywhere left to go. And anyway, the pleasure and the therapy had all been in the doing, in the daring to imagine these fantasies of normalcy and the thrill of watching them take form. So, goodbye, old friend, and good luck.

The Hugh & Bruce Fantasy Mill was open twenty-four hours a day, twelve months a year, and in summer so was the window. Along with faint wisps of air, it let in—how fitting this setting is, how poetically apt its every detail—the pungent reek of horseshit from the Acme Farmers Dairy stable right next door.

The lack of air-conditioning has never received proper study in its devastating effect on art and artists—for example, Hugh and me. Other than the local Bijou with its offer "It's C-o-o-l Inside," the phrase itself dripping with new-fallen snow, refrigerated indoor life was a sci-fi vision of the future. And with one electric fan to cool eight people distributed through five rooms—well, forget it. There was no relief from humid, stagnant, maddening summer city heat.

Ever keen to imagine new attractions on the low roads of life, I had hit upon the vision of a veritable citadel: a model of the world's crummiest baseball stadium. Over patient devoted weeks it rose, a ramshackle masterpiece of rickety wooden stands and a rough, bumpy infield and burnt-grass outfield ringed with fences advertising Black Sug Gasoline and other fanciful mercantile horrors.

Then, one hellish ninety-nine-degree August night as I sat putting the final touches on my palace of horsehide desuetude, some flaw, previously unnoticed, caught my eye. Perhaps a wrinkle in that paper outfield that I'd never glimpsed before, perhaps only some sloppy glue globs. Whatever it was, it was enough. Already murderous of mood from the sticky, unrelenting, inescapable heat, I snapped. I picked up the stadium and flung it across the room, where it exploded against a wall. It had no sooner landed than I was there to stomp it back to the last individual cardboard fragment and balsawood splinter.

How hot do you suppose it was in that room the night van Gogh cut off his ear?

Life on the other side of that bedroom door, meanwhile, seldom offered strong incentives to join it. Eight people attempting to find breathing room and preserve any sense of privacy in quarters as roomy as a piano crate will find ways, because they must. Everybody had his or her own defined zone, like wolves. We kids had our bedrooms, and Mother, the kitchen. The living room and everything in it, T.C. had long since claimed as his own, with Mother granted a visitor's pass. If he was in it, as a general rule, we weren't. We annoyed him; he saw us, and nine times out of ten he saw red. To be caught within his field of fire while scuttling out to the kitchen or making a dash for the front door was life-threatening. So there in splendid isolation in his living room, in a miasma of cigarette smoke, T.C. read, worked on his stamp collection, listened to his Guy Lombardo records or the radio, brooded, mildly tippled, and napped.

His sporadic absences—travel being part of the job description for Ontario's deputy minister of Travel and Publicity—never brought the relief we deserved. Alcohol had long since become fully established as Mother's zone of refuge, and she raced into it all the more avidly the minute T.C. was gone.

Mother drank as she did everything else—quietly, daintily, self-effacingly. The very lack of drunken fireworks made it seem more sinister and her more unreachable. She did it to get away from us and from her whole empty, dismal life, so there was no point in trying to follow her, no point in trying to talk to her. And even less point in rooting out her secret cache. She always had one bottle more somewhere. She just sat there, drifting further and further away in her self-induced fog, oblivious to our rage and, beneath it, our breaking hearts.

Mother's drinking had a soundtrack that always started playing once we had given up and gone to bed and she was alone. Oh God, not again. Song after song from T.C.'s collection of original-Broadway-cast recordings: "Some Enchanted Evening"; "Bewitched, Bothered, and Bewildered"; and, with a particular stab, "How Are Things in Glocca Morra?" Romantic music, glamorous music, music I hope I never have to hear again.

T.C.'S WAY OR
THE HIGHWAY

There was a period in early adolescence, an Era of Good Feeling, when correcting my behavior according to T.C.'s running commentary on its lapses still seemed the path to acceptance and all the rich pleasures beyond. Perhaps what I took as indifference was only his way of waiting for me to finally discover the obvious, get with the program, and allow him at last to release the fatherly affection he was holding back—for my benefit—until I did.

It didn't come naturally. He preferred athletes to intellectuals in his sons, "normal" interests to whatever I was up to day and night behind my bedroom door. Nevertheless, I'd try. I'd go out for team sports. I'd be so busy living the T.C.-sanctioned life that the bedroom would be not the cave where I hid out from him and other terrors but only the place where I rested between adventures. Or better yet, second thought suggested, maybe I could lead him to believe as much without actually going through with it. Blessed solitude, and the reading and writing and drawing that filled it, had by now become not what I liked to do but what I had to do; in some way that I sensed but could never define—to myself, much less to T.C.—equilibrium itself depended upon continuing intense private communication with the muse. I could no more give this up than I could abandon eating. With at least equal certainty I knew the gridiron, the basketball court, the towel snapping of the locker room, to be alien if not injurious to my spirit and my body. Wrong body, wrong gifts, wrong attitude: I was not and never would be a normal teenage boy.

Thus it was that on a late fall afternoon, on the way home from a football practice scrimmage I had never attended, I stopped to pick up handfuls of dirt and daub it all over my face and body; mussed up my hair; pulled out my shirttail; practiced my imitation of being winded. All for naught, for some reason. Not only did T.C. fail to take notice later at the dinner table, but Mike caught on well beforehand. "You faking little bugger," he sneered. "Who do you think you're fooling? You? Football? Ha!"

My eagerness to please reached its apogee after one particular evening at dinner the following summer. T.C.'s gaze fell on me. "That's some poolroom tan you've got there," he grunted. I'd never been in a poolroom, of course; he was obliquely alluding to my coloring, or lack of it, and would clearly prefer something ruddier—the glow of outdoorsy good health.

I arrived at the dinner table the very next evening, face and arms a brilliant orange—as vivid a picture of sunbaked vitality as half an hour before the bathroom mirror with Christine's box of Crayolas could conjure. Again, the compliments never came. Either T.C. saw through the ruse and decided not to call me on it or he'd forgotten it in the excitement of discovering some fresher failing among the quivering assembled.

Aw, the hell with it. If I couldn't win by trying to play on his terms, better to lose playing my own way. I scraped away the Crayola wax from my skin after dinner and closed the bedroom door behind me, imbued with new resolve.

My brothers and I placed vanity somewhere near necrophilia in the catalogue of vices at the time. This had nothing to do with any inherited Scots-Calvinist abhorrence of display or false pride; by abjuring a preoccupation with physical appearance we were simply making a virtue out of a fact of life. T.C., natty dresser, scrupulously well groomed and tonsured and fussy about his physical appearance to a point just short of dandyism, appropriated the family's entire supply for himself—and the bathroom that went with it.

Bathrooms are not only essential for proper grooming but essential at particular times of the day—specifically, in the morning, when most of the civilized world performs its ablutions and primps before the mirror. Ours being a single-bathroom household and T.C. by paternal right owning all rights of access, it was his prolonged ablutions and primping that hogged the brief window of grooming opportunity between 7:30 and 8:00 A.M., leaving the rest of us to run a brush over our scalps and scrub the unsightlier stains off our hands and faces in the kitchen sink before heading off for school. There was no time for such luxuries as brushing teeth, a hygienic lapse that would later be the makings of several dentists' fortunes. Even if we could have gotten our hands on it, we'd have no more dared use T.C.'s deodorant than his underwear.

I avoided mirrors in the mornings, knowing what I would see. I al-

Toronto, 1951. Sneer for the birdie! My helpless reaction to another of T.C.'s mandatory portrait sessions.

ways looked terrible, and probably smelled worse. Tom and Walt dwelled on an even lower rung; they were forced to scuttle about in such ragamuffin garb that it remains a mystery why their teachers or the Children's Aid Society never intervened. Neither the money for nor the interest in dressing us for success was ever there; it seemed achievement enough to our parents that all six of their kids managed to get themselves out of bed, dressed, more or less fed, and out the door on time every day.

By mid-winter, the one back-to-school outfit acquired around Labor Day was beginning to wilt from constant use, and I was reduced to plundering substitute ensembles from the pile of odds and ends and Mike's hand-me-downs on the closet floor. Discrimination was always racing the clock; better to be ragged than late for school. Anything that didn't smell positively rank and had fewer than two or three holes worn in it passed muster. I remember slipping on my usual pair of jeans one warmish spring morning and finding them even more clammy and greasy than usual; mildew had come to visit overnight. Rubber boots, being tough and versatile and cheap, were the footwear of choice.

These indifferent standards of hygiene and dress were so of a piece with McCall family life and so consistent with its values that complaining, much less aspiring to something better, would have smacked of treachery. And considering the way I viewed and defined myself vis-à-vis my peers at the time, they fit.

BOZ

I was never quite as alone as my physical estrangement from teenage and Toronto society in general might indicate. There were alternative sources of emotional nourishment. Perhaps foremost among them, from adolescence to early adulthood, was an irrepressible self-made Englishman whose inspiring influence was in no way mitigated by the fact that he happened to have been dead for eighty-odd years.

The Pickwick Papers, Great Expectations, A Tale of Two Cities—grade-nine English at Malvern Collegiate was a Charles Dickens festival. Dickens—soon Boz to intimates like myself—infatuated me from the moment Pip ran into Magwich in the graveyard in the first few pages of *Great Expectations.* Here was the sumptuous bath in extremes of feeling that I craved. Here were the drama, the humanity, the clear-cut good and evil, the purple sunsets streaked with gold that I was being cheated of in real life. Dickens despised bullies and cosseted losers. He was tenderhearted. Pumblechook, Chuzzlewit, Uriah Heep—his made-up names were funnier and more bizarre even than mine. Best of all, the moral compass that guided the great, gilded calliope of a Dickens novel on its roundabout epic journey reliably guided me again and again through an enchanted, overstuffed museum of nineteenth-century England to the inevitable, the triumphal, the unashamedly lachrymose happy ending, about which nobody seemed happier or more delighted than Boz himself.

Friendlessness, three canker sores in my mouth, another outburst of acne on my face, another zero in math? No matter when another date with Dombey & Sons or Nicholas Nickleby or Barnaby Rudge awaited me in my snug bedroom bunk after school on another dun February afternoon.

Naturally, I couldn't just leave it at a good read. When Edgar Johnson's two-volume Dickens biography fell into my hands in 1953, I devoured it as eagerly as a shopgirl devours a fan magazine. I disappeared into it, into Dickens's life and world, and emerged a close friend and confidant. To say that I came to identify myself with Charles Dickens would be an understatement. I came to half believe myself to be his living reincarnation. His saga paralleled mine. We were two identically unschooled young geniuses of humble origins with disappointing fathers, battling our way up from the bottom, sensitive, suffering, pouring our unhappiness into fantastic imaginary worlds.

Words on paper weren't enough for me. Working from a photograph in the Johnson biography, I proceeded to build as rigorously accurate a scale model as I could of Dickens's house at Rochester. I suspect the intent was only part homage and only part bookshelf curio and much more in the nature of an extra-long-shot, quasi-metaphysical experiment in trying to pull Boz forward into the third dimension—or, failing that, a desperate effort to conjure a variant of that Nabokovian stunt whereby the onlooker strolls into the painting and somehow wills himself through that tiny front door and up the stairs and into Dickens's study. We had so much to talk about, after all.

That house and my vain attempt to slip inside it was to be the apogee of my Dickens period. Unrequited enthusiasms, however ardent, eventually become boring. Having failed to overleap time and space and make eye-to-eye contact, I drifted away from the Dickens front door and the Dickens library shelf.

It was time. I was by then in my early twenties. I needed literature with fresh voices, more contemporary life lessons, dirty stuff.

HOCKEY

I was twelve, small for my age and almost anybody else's, and I probably never would have taken up stick and skates without the lively encouragement of my father. Flinging open the door of the bedroom where I sat pecking away on the portable Royal—his forbidden personal Royal portable—he regarded me for a long moment with a mixture of sorrow and contempt that I could feel on the back of my neck. Then came the inspiring words: "Sitting in here all day on your duff, wasting your life. For God's sake, get up and go out and do something."

Blunt it might be, but he did have a point. Not even I could stay indoors all winter. Not an endless steel-gray tunnel of a Toronto winter, not when indoors meant a tiny five-room behavioral sink of an apartment stewing with the compounded agonies of all eight members of Dysfunctional Family McCall.

But "doing something" beyond the ten-by-twelve-foot bedroom shared with Mike and Hugh posed challenges. We were new to Toronto, city of a thousand moods, all of them somber. I had no friends. It was stingingly cold outside. All the walks that could be taken had been taken, all the banks, churches, schools, and statues in this wonderland of late-nineteenth-century urban architectural gloom visited. I had discovered the Royal Ontario Museum, almost the only local institution not sealed shut every Sunday by the Lord's Day Alliance; but antiquity soon tends to pale on twelve-year-olds.

The fare at the Prince of Wales, the local movie house, changed only every couple of weeks. Ultimately, by process of elimination, I took the easy way out and followed the crowd of my peers. I took up hockey.

The brand of hockey available to me had only the element of frozen water in common with the official version of Canada's national pastime. The era of indoor arenas and organized kiddie leagues in every hamlet wasn't yet even a dream. The standard venue was a patch of outdoor ice universally and inexplicably known as a cushion. Thousands of cushions instantly materialized as soon as snow and the thermometer started falling in early November. Homemade cushions barely bigger than a bedsheet, and no more than a few steps from home, were for the goslings on bobskates. Sheets of ice double or triple this size, on a nearby front lawn or empty lot, allowed the older kids who could stay upright for more than seconds at a time to bat and chase a puck. The next step up was a leap: the big municipal public rinks, relative gladiatorial arenas aswarm with strangers steady on their skates, wielding new sticks, ready to play real hockey. It was a leap that age and pride dictated I make, tamping down the misgivings transmitted by size, experience, talent, and self-knowledge.

The municipal rink nearest to our apartment sat on a city playground, a bleak enclave hard by the C.N.R. railway tracks at Main and Gerrard streets, a ten-minute walk away. A fairly level rectangle of earth, about twice the size of a regulation hockey rink, had been hosed down until the water froze into a rumpled blanket of black ice, edged all around by a knee-high crust of filthy old snow as hard as concrete. Sticking out of it were orphan mittens, busted sticks, even the odd galosh, like debris from some Arctic plane crash. Memory insists that it was always January when I showed up at the cushion, always dusk, always freezing, and that I slowly laced up my skates and stumbled out into the fray with all the enthusiasm of a Tommy going over the top on the Somme in 1916.

Awaiting me were the silhouettes of dozens of neighborhood rink rats of all ages and sizes, in windbreakers and mackinaws and the occasional overcoat—anything but a proper hockey outfit, the sign of the hopeless tinhorn—and already formed into opposing twenty- or thirty-man gangs. You simply slipped into the melee, on the side of whichever gang happened at that particular moment to be in control of the puck.

The side never suspended play to acknowledge my arrival. I had been fumbling about on ice, without conspicuous success, since I first stood up unaided, and I could stand (or teeter, if on skates) as a living rebuke to the myth that something in the Canadian genes mints natural-born hockey players. There are probably Maoris with more innate talent for transportation atop two steel blades than I ever possessed.

Of course I loved hockey, the idea of hockey—native Canadians always have. It unleashes and sanctifies our equally repressed appetites for both primal violence and sensual grace. It enlivens dead winter. It gives Slav and Quebecois and Scot, Newfie and British Columbian, a common bond. It's exciting.

I just wasn't cut out to play it. I had inherited the small-boned physique of my mother's stringy lowland Scots forebears. Healthy enough, hardy even, but when was the last time a pencil-wristed, narrow-chested runt with all the intimidating physical presence of a hamster ever hoisted the Stanley Cup? At night, in my dreams, I was a crafty Max Bentley dipsy-doodling over the blue line to let go my feared wrist shot. By day I was an athletic phenom uncannily combining a fruit bat's metabolism with a tree sloth's reflexes, gifted with a sense of balance precarious enough that a cautionary siren should have sounded whenever I staggered onto the ice.

I was further handicapped by suffering from that dread and uniquely Canadian maladly known as weak ankles. The exact medical definition of this congenital handicap was never divulged, but the unanimous verdict of everyone who ever watched me skate—feet splayed outward, blades clawing the ice at a forty-five-degree angle as knees furiously pumped and body reeled—was always the same: weak ankles.

But you could have reinforced my ankles with iron bolts and skating would still have seemed to me a grotesquely unnatural physical act. Especially when the skates don't fit, and mine never did. "Mine" is misleading. Dad had made clear in frequent dinner-table tirades that his offspring's insatiable greed for food, clothing, and school supplies was leeching his already thin wallet of its last dollar. Skates? It would be attempted patricide to even ask. A pool of hand-me-downs and castoffs, stockpiled over the years, was the compromise solution.

C.C.M.'s fanciest skates wouldn't have begun to make up for my lack of control over the feet laced into them. But with big brother Mike's discards two sizes too big, a humiliating pair of girls' white figure skates a size too small, two left-footed boots, one in size nine and the other in size eleven—forget skill, I seldom achieved even comfort. In fact I became something of an expert on the variety and cruelty of tortures inflicted by skates that do not fit. I can feel it all decades later: feet chafed and blistered from rubbing to and fro inside loose boots; a network of previously unknown tendons and muscles, which had only tried to help, now knotted tight and screaming. Too many toes jammed into the hellhole of too small a boot, doubled under, mashed together into one red surge of pain with every forward stride. An hour or two of such imprisonment turned feet to pulp, extracted from the boot so gingerly, with so many "aaaaahs" and "oooooohs," that I know exactly how it must feel to have an appendix extracted without benefit of anesthesia.

But I was more fearful of T.C. than of bodily pain, less intimidated by the talent gulf between the rink rats and me than by the specter of fatherly rejection. So into the conflict I clumped and stumbled.

There were no referees and no rules in those twilight skirmishes at Main and Gerrard, and everybody kept his own subjective notion of the score. These weren't teams so much as two clashing packs of lone wolves. Everybody was bigger and stronger than me, yet even I could see that hockey talent was conferred on only a charmed few. There was a rough parallel, even here in this hockey equivalent of the primordial ooze, with the Darwinian principles that ruled in the

N.H.L.: To the quickest, toughest, hungriest of the mob inevitably went the puck, and the chance to carry it through shifting thickets of sticks and arms and legs, and then, if luck and balance and wind held, to haul off and fire a shot at the poor wretch cringing alone in front of his imaginary net.

I didn't even know how to pretend to be quick or tough or hungry. Fainthearted to begin with, fully preoccupied by the exhausting task of remaining erect, I found myself peripheral to the action swirling around me: startled when a stray puck whizzed between my legs, vulnerable as a Ming vase to a random body check from somebody who knew an easy mark when he saw one. Should instinct for once cut in and warn of a bruiser's approach on time, I'd save him the trouble and buckle to the ice in advance. If the puck should miraculously emerge from the melee and connect with the blade of my stick, I'd instantly—or as instantly as sluggish reflexes could manage—whirl and blindly whack it away rather than risk being crushed by the onrushing herd.

The one aspect of outdoor hockey that came easily to me was shivering. Unburdened by the pressures of being in the midst of the action, I was free to concentrate fully on being cold. Being cold is an almost completely negative experience, especially when the fingers are tingling in wet wool mittens and the toes have turned to marble in cotton socks and a Siberian wind whistles through corduroy pants as through a veil, turning half-formed gonads into numb little nuggets. The thermal revolution had yet to transform winter outerwear, and in any event it was McCall family policy to issue, every September at the start of another school year, a single all-season outfit rather than costly multiple sets to deal one at a time with climatic extremes. Two hours on the cushion often required five hours afterward to fully thaw, a reverse process of ears and digits and nuts infused with a burning sensation far beyond heat, in an aftermath almost as painful as the cold itself.

Thompson, on the other hand, must have generated body heat enough to warm an Eskimo village. Thompson was a chain-smoking, hyena-faced neighborhood lout who turned into a whirling Mercury on skates, able simultaneously to hog the puck and pepper team-mates and opponents alike with a nonstop barrage of taunts and ob-scenities while a Winchester perpetually smoldered in one corner of his smirk. He had an instinct for the game both wondrous and infu-riating to behold.

There always seemed to be a Thompson or two marauding through every pickup game on every cushion, like Visigoths rampag-ing through Rome. They dominated play with contemptuous ease. They made it seem so easy. What was unforgivable was that they took their natural gifts for granted, treated it all as a lark. I had always doubted the existence of God, but this cinched it. Hockey talent lav-ished on thugs like Thompson—while earnest, clean-cut, deserving kids like me nursed our wounds and watched.

Those frigid outings felt more like splitting rocks on a Georgia chain gang than high-spirited sporting fun: hard work, no reward. And yet I persevered. T.C.'s sneers made a powerful incentive; but there was also something larger and more positive at stake. For the prepubescent Canadian kid, shoving a rubber disc around a sheet of ice with a stick in the cold and dark was understood to be only partly sport. It was also part folk custom, part moral obligation, part pa-triotic act.

As with Soviet schoolkids being vetted for admission to the Young Communist Pioneers, offering oneself up for testing and evaluation of hockey talent was a duty of citizenship. Every Canadian kid knew himself to be part of the process. A kind of osmosis was at work on the cushions and rinks of the Dominion; from amid all those seething tides of would-be hockey players chopping and hacking away at the puck and one another through long winter afternoons, destiny's tots would sooner or later find one another; and someday, when a familiar name popped out from an N.H.L. team lineup, you might even be able to say, "Oh yeah. Used to play with him."

The process required no orders from above, no formal organiza-tion. It was a condition of Canadian life. To be a boy was to grow up knowing that hockey wasn't just the national game but a major chunk of Canada's national identity. And by flailing around on skates, your interests and those of your home and native land were one.

It became almost instantly obvious that I was letting both my country and my old man down. The country didn't notice. T.C. did. He had come fitted with Thompson-type sinews and synapses at birth, and exercised them effectively and pleasurably for life. He became a semi-pro baseball catcher, a badminton champion, an accomplished golfer. You could tell by his big supple hands, his agile dancer's feet, just by the way he threw a baseball, that he was an athlete. Alas for me, he could tell by my stiff hands, my heavy feet, just by the way I threw a ball, that I wasn't. The toll of absolute hockey incompetence on my fragile self-esteem was by then mounting. I'd rather do nothing than keep doing something this Sisyphean, parental wrath notwithstanding. The visits to Main and Gerrard tailed off. Back to the bedroom, back down my rabbit hole to indulge the furtive vices of pen and brush.

I had disappointed T.C. yet again. An even more curt formality in his relations with me, underlaid with an unmistakable distaste, was the penalty.

Hockey in the raw and brawling form it took on the big municipal cushions may have been over my head, but at that stage of life, after primary school and before sex, even I needed to work off energy. And hockey still fired my fantasies. Saturday nights were a family communion dedicated to Foster Hewitt's coast-to-coast play-by-play radio broadcast from Maple Leaf Gardens on *Hockey Night in Canada*. It was ritual every Sunday night for Hugh and Mike and me to lie in our beds in the dark as CKEY's Joe Crysdale emoted his telegraph-wire "re-creations" of Leafs games in distant Chicago or Boston or New York or Detroit. You could make a bottle of Kik Kola last an entire game by punching a nail hole in the cap and holding it over your mouth upside down so the contents, Chinese water torture-style, dribbled drop by drop onto your tongue.

Meanwhile, I had happily demoted myself from the big leagues over by the C.N.R. tracks to the driveway next to our apartment building. From flat rubber puck, hard to slide or even coax into motion on dry asphalt, to hairless used tennis ball. And from the overpowering competition of the Thompsons of the world to a gaggle

of malleable, harmless Danforth Court kids two or three years my
junior.

I was league commissioner, chief rulemaker, coach, spiritual
leader, commentator, and star goalie. I was also publisher, editor, and
reporter for the hand-penciled news sheet that covered the games,
racing upstairs to bat out perfervid accounts of the very contest I'd
just played in for a rapt readership of me. In time, after countless
consecutive lopsided victories had cemented my superstar status and,
like any underchallenged superstar, I became jaded, the pleasures of
writing up my exploits began to surpass the exploits themselves.
Writing about almost anything soon felt richer, more dramatic, more
satisfying than the thing itself. I became probably the only hockey
player who ever wrote himself right out of the game.

But while the fever lasted, it was a hockey feast. It was all so manageable, so perfectly scaled to my talents and resources and modified
ambitions. You might get winded, but you couldn't really get hurt
smacking tennis balls around a driveway in the company of tykes.
And it required surprisingly scant imaginative powers to convert
those dusty after-school free-for-alls into moments straight from the
gaudy annals of the N.H.L.

Something in me had always identified with goaltenders, those
lonely sentinels encumbered by their bulky, vaguely clownish pads,
called upon mainly to catch and kick. Even I could do that, or at least
do it better than stick-handling end to end down a crowded alleyway
of treacherous ice.

It would take more quarters than I could earn in a lifetime of
baby-sitting to buy real goaltending equipment. But in that league,
who needed it? We are now in the 2377 Danforth Avenue Hockey
Hall of Fame. In this glass case, Bruce McCall's goalie outfit. The leg
pads are two matching cardboard cartons stuffed with old *Globe and
Mails* and *Maclean's* magazines. Those are his dad's obsolete neckties,
used to lash the pads to his legs. Over here is the pillow off his bed.
Anybody? Right, chest protector. He used that first baseman's glove
as his puck (or, more accurately, ball-snaring) glove. He wore that
same Bruins jersey, with the holed elbows and spittle and dirt stains,
for his entire career. A great, great goalie, unbeatable in the clutch.

The source of all inspiration on and off the driveway asphalt was the spectacle, the mighty ongoing cavalcade, of the National Hockey League. Never mind the kids, their parents, their friends, and their teachers; the blindest, deafest old widow on the far side of Kapuskasing couldn't barricade her cabin stoutly enough to keep out news of N.H.L. scores and stars and team fortunes. N.H.L. hockey sparkled in the very air from October to April. I'm not sure *Hockey Night in Canada* really needed radio to seep into every household from Antigonish to Kamloops every Saturday night.

I managed to make just being a hockey fan difficult for myself. I had become the world's most ardent and probably Toronto's only New York Rangers fan.

It may now be impossible for anyone who never lived in the Toronto and the Ontario of that time to grasp the extent to which the Toronto Maple Leafs dominated the consciousness and held— no, demanded—the loyalty of the hockey faithful. There was as yet no television, much less cable television, and thus no choice of games or teams. *Hockey Night in Canada* was effectively Toronto Maple Leafs night in Canada for years, broadcast exclusively from Maple Leaf Gardens by a team-approved announcer and featuring the Leafs versus one or another of the league's five other teams.

Another factor favoring the Leafs was societal, and uniquely Canadian. Given that their historic and only domestic N.H.L. rival was Le Club Hockey des Habitants of Montreal—the Flying Frenchmen, the Habs, the hated Canadiens—the Maple Leafs shouldered the moral burden of upholding Canadian Anglophile culture, i.e., superiority, along with their duty to be a contending hockey club. No casual responsibility, the former. For years before it publicly erupted in Quebec's separatist urges, mutual English-French loathing acidified every Leafs-Canadiens confrontation. It was as much ethnic warfare as sporting contest. The Leafs weren't just Toronto's hometown team; for the English-speaking 80 percent of the population, they were Canada's team.

The franchise was owned and run with an iron hand by a local gravel tycoon and banty autocrat named Conn Smythe—Colonel

Conn Smythe as he preferred to be known, lest anyone forget his Canadian Army service at the side of the British in two world wars. Superpatriot Smythe had named his team (formerly the St. Pats) after Canada's national symbol, and he built Maple Leaf Gardens as their fitting shrine, a veritable La Scala of the sport, where the fans came attired in coats and ties, the Queen's Own Highlanders military band serenaded them with Strauss waltzes between periods, and neither drinking nor smoking nor the narrowly defined Canadian idea of rowdy behavior was tolerated.

The N.H.L. had always been the most feudal of major professional sports, and Smythe was its baron among barons. Word had it that he made sure there wasn't a promising young prospect in the whole vast province of Ontario who didn't find himself a Leafs chattel by the time his voice changed. The Smythe-Leafs regime seemed similar in its smothering conformity to life in a hockey version of Stroessner's Paraguay, and it all made me hate the Toronto Maple Leafs with a vengeance.

Why I had chosen to embrace the New York Rangers was in no way obscure. I was already spiritually halfway to being a New Yorker myself, pinnacle of a place that symbolized the glamour of America. I also liked the name—Rangers. I liked their flashy uniforms. I liked their knack for digging up eccentrics: Clint Albright, the first bespectacled player in the N.H.L.; Pentti Lund, the league's first European player, and a Finn at that; Gus Kyle, an ex-Mountie. But most seductive of all, I now realize, was the fact that the New York Rangers were perennial losers, just like me.

Deep study of *The Hockey News*, a weekly tabloid, made me a blabbing fount of Rangers trivia. I dressed the wooden pegs that served as my players in the family's mechanical hockey game in Ranger red, white, and blue. I believe to this day that the power of my fervent prayers vaulted the ragtag Cinderella Blueshirts into the Stanley Cup finals and seventh-game sudden-death overtime (and, naturally, defeat) in the giddy spring of 1950.

Since no living soul within a hundred miles shared my devotion, where could I go to sing my hymns of Ranger worship? Where else but to the church itself? The mailroom of the Ranger front office in distant New York City must have had to reserve a special pigeonhole just for my foolscap manifestos, part pep talks, part personal suggestions, part commiseration, illuminated with hand-drawn heroic vignettes from recent Ranger near wins. I addressed my effusions to what I knew must be a kindlier, humbler colonel than the hated Smythe—Colonel Kilpatrick, president of the Rangers. The colonel was of course far too busy trying to improve our team to ever reply; but that it all helped draw tighter the bond with my beloved Broadway Blueshirts was reward enough.

Being virtually the only Ranger fan in the province of Ontario wasn't only solitary. Sometimes it could get physically hazardous.

The local sporting goods stores stocked Maple Leafs jerseys in disgusting abundance, and a token few Canadiens jerseys for the pervert trade. And with the unerring instinct for the gesture that confounds as it deflates as it enrages, it was a Canadiens jersey that my parents laid out one Christmas under the tree, just for me. A surviving photograph taken that day on the fire escape shows a lad in a Montreal Canadiens shirt crouching with his stick in a halfhearted hockey playing pose. Years later the meek, unsmiling look on his face would be uncannily matched in those haunting North Vietnamese photos of captured American airmen.

Deliverance eventually came. Some merchandising mixup dumped a pile of Red Wings and Blackhawks and Bruins and Rangers jerseys in an East End Toronto sporting goods store. The proper vestments at last were mine—or at least a reasonable approximation. The colors and striping were right, but in place of the individual RANGERS lettering that ran diagonally from upper left to lower right down the front in authentic versions was a simple large felt R. No problem. Nothing a sheet of cardboard, some colored inks, a pair of scissors, and a tube of LePage's airplane glue couldn't fix, making me one with Bones Raleigh and Buddy O'Connor, et al.

It was with even more than my customary Ranger pride that I pulled on my authenticized jersey one Monday morning and headed for school. The effect on certain Leafs vassals among my Malvern classmates was electric, immediate, and vocal. "Rangers! You fuckin' little . . . c'mere!"

Long before lunchtime my lovingly hand-fashioned RANGERS legend read something more like R G R S, and I had learned a lesson. What availeth even LePage's airplane glue against Colonel Conn Smythe?

BASEBALL

"No wonder it hurts, you ninny, you've broken your nose!"

The Danforth Tech school nurse speaking, one May morning in 1953. Aha! That would explain my throbbing headache, the taste of blood in my mouth, the strange new sideways curve of my proboscis visible under the swelling.

All because of a lousy foul tip in a pickup baseball game the evening before. But as with all sports and me, nothing about playing baseball ever came as easily or naturally as it seemed to other guys. How would I know you shouldn't play catcher without a mask?

Hockey has and always will be there in my life, like a trusty family dog ever willing to uncurl from its bed over in the corner and be palpitating to go, cheerfully ready to lend itself again to my attentions. Sometimes it has waited patiently for years. Good dog, hockey! Baseball was always more complicated. For my first fourteen or so years on earth, it lay out there with Indian clubs and curling on the periphery of my sports interest, largely unplayed, its big-league sagas churning through season after season without so much as a nod from me. And then, wham! Almost from one day to the next, baseball fever—better, baseball malaria: long sieges of delirium now and then cooling off and even receding until you think the bug has gone and then, wham! Back again, more virulent than ever.

But my life with baseball was complicated more because it was fraught; and it was fraught because it tangled me up, but good, in T.C.'s footsteps. At age forty, the old man still had the gnarled fingers and beefy thighs of a catcher. He'd been good enough to play semi-pro ball on the sandlots around southern Ontario; he knew the game inside out as only serious ex-players do, and his interest never flagged.

By age fourteen I was running out of options if I was ever to snare any crumbs of paternal notice or affection, and perhaps at bottom I owed my sudden crush on the summer game to nothing more mysterious than that. Oedipus, play ball! Big deal. We would seem to have here only the age-old tradition of son and father united in a common zeal for sport, *Field of Dreams* with a 20 percent Canadian discount.

If so, I haven't fully aired the concept of "fraught." This was the same hapless Brucie, in body and reflexes and competitive spirit, to whom even parking-lot hockey had long since granted his unconditional release. My only natural baseball skill was my mouth: "Attaboy, hum baby, at's a way, babe!" Chicken-winged runts with lead weights in their asses and a fear of thrown objects seldom get to bat cleanup. The man I'd chosen to please with the gift of my emulation had a) high standards, therefore b) low interest, therefore c) no time for coaching or baseball palship.

This rebuff I took as merely temporary. I'd earn T.C.'s respect the honorable way, by making myself into one heads-up, hustling, hot-hitting catcher fit one day to sit exchanging tricks of the trade with the master himself. All the more challenging that I charged forth not only in the wrong body but also with transposed arms; our nascent pint-size Ernie Lombardi was what no catcher in baseball history had ever been: a southpaw, a lefty. Burden enough in practical terms, but T.C.'s considered view of lefties was already on record: congenital idiots.

But God knows I tried. I stole T.C.'s prized old decker, as catchers' mitts were then called, and wore it upside down and backward on my right hand every evening after supper, down in the alley that made a perfect warm-up bullpen. I'd wheedle Mike or Hugh or Walt or Tom—baseball haters all—to fire me their best until they wandered off, bored. I soon ventured off to the local sandlots in search of pickup games. Nobody had the heart to physically bar me, and my baseball fever flourished. Wow, the ball I almost caught! The ball I almost hit! I'd organize my own teams from among the neighborhood sprouts and hone my skills and fatten my ego by out-hitting and out-fielding the lot.

I was throwing and catching and batting and running in my sleep. Now that I had discovered the *Sporting News* (editor, J. G. Taylor Spink—even baseball's solons had baseball names!), I knew everything. Not only about the big-league game, but down to the lower orders in the back pages. Go, Highpoint-Thomasville Hi-Toms! Too bad about those Memphis Chicks!

The Toronto Maple Leafs' Triple-A club was at the time a farm team of the Philadelphia Phillies. The Phillies, in what could only have been a P.R. goodwill gesture, announced an amateur tryout camp in a Toronto park for lads my age. There I was on the appointed hot June morning, along with about a thousand other aspiring stars itching to strut their stuff. What would T.C. say when the Phillies signed a fifteen-year-old left-handed catching prodigy?

I never knew. I never touched a ball. I was lawn furniture in a melee of raw juvenile baseball talent as far over my head as the fungoes as I stood watching kids smaller than me race to snare one-handed and, for all I knew, eyes shut.

I didn't make the cut on the Canadian Legion team, either. That's an overstatement. The coach, probably from watching me warm up on the sidelines, never put me through my paces, and indeed never made eye contact.

Still, summer after summer—barred from even pickup games with my peers, who had evidently gotten together beforehand to declare me officially invisible when sides were chosen up—I persisted. What if my catcher dreams had run after a foul and somersaulted into the visiting-team dugout? What if nobody wanted to play on any nine I was part of? I still had my passion, my imagination, and my good left arm.

The blotch left by the thousands of tennis balls I hurled at the strike zone chalked on Acme Farmers Dairy's brick stable wall between 1950 and 1953 is surely still there today. I can still hear the chorus of multitudes rising in my ears as the strikeout totals mounted far past anything Walter Johnson ever dreamed.

I wasn't always unhittable. For a month or more in the summer of 1951 I was Klein Nachburger, the Hamburg Wheelhorse, whom I had invented in order to rescue from the rubble of war-torn Germany to become the New York Giants' stellar junkball lefty. Klein could start or relieve and had terrier guts. But maybe I was working him too often; his control would suddenly go haywire. When he/I faltered and had a few bad outings, I'd become the G.M. and send him/me down to Minneapolis in the AAA American Association to work on his/my stuff. Soon enough—often by 3 P.M. that very same day, in fact—good old Klein, hitch corrected, would be back again, mowing 'em down at the Polo Grounds.

I like to believe I would have discovered baseball and wallowed in it throughout adolescence even without the paternal element. Playing, following, just thinking about baseball discharged energies that, left unspent, might have one day sent me up on the roof of 2377 Danforth with a high-powered rifle.

If hockey was a kind of spontaneous, continuous ice-bound skirmish, baseball, in its intricacies of strategy and statistical formulas, approached the cerebral. There was no upper limit on how much you could know. You could immerse yourself in baseball, fold it in around you, shut out the world. And baseball's ambience soothed: summer days, green pastures, vast open spaces. Its sixteen big-league teams were sixteen families, from the rich, snobbish New York Yankees to the down-at-the-heels St. Louis Browns (my personal darlings), that you could live with, stew about, care for through the long, long season—from a safely vicarious remove.

And—now we approach the heart of it—baseball was American, played in fabulous faraway places like New York and Chicago and St. Louis by sun-bronzed, square-jawed Texans, Californians, North Carolinians, spewing tobacco juice, scratching their nuts: American demigods. Baseball fandom gave me more than a pastime; it made me an honorary American.

Hurling those tennis balls at a brick wall every day; pacing my reading to make the week's *Sporting News* last from one Monday to the next; taking the hour-long streetcar ride to and from Maple Leaf Stadium down by the lake to Maple Leafs games; tuning in to barely audible upstate New York radio stations to catch staticky wire re-creations of New York Giants and Brooklyn Dodgers afternoon games; drawing baseball scenes, including a hundred successive drawings in the upper-right-hand corner of textbook pages to create kinetic, movielike flip-o-grams; writing baseball epics ("Southpaws Aren't So Bad," whined my masterpiece, featuring a thinly disguised me)—all this still wasn't quite enough to achieve satiety.

There was also a baseball board game to fill long summer nights, a diamond and a spinner and some cards, me versus me via made-up teams with invented lineups, slogging through double- and triple- and quadra-headers—and their painstakingly recorded box scores—until Mr. Sandman finally said, Screw this, it's 1:30 A.M., and shut me down.

And there was bathroom baseball. A pencil, a notebook, and a pair of dice, and possession of the loo for half an hour or so transported me to somewhere as close to baseball Nirvana as I ever knew. I was the god who created a league, its teams, its players, its games, its odds, its fates. It was a crude dice game: 12 was a home run, 1 a groundout, and so forth. The players were mostly a handpicked elite of No-Stars culled from my personal major-league pantheon: slick-fielding Pale Hose; third-sacker Floyd Baker; lefty Senators hurler Ray Scarborough; Owen Friend, a second baseman borrowed from the Browns. Underachievers all. My kind of ballplayers.

Studded in among them for dramatic tension were bad guys of my own creation, composites of ballplayers and schoolmates (and father figures) who had earned my enmity. Now they were trapped. Now they were victims of Bruce's justice, baseball-style. The odds, after all, were up to me. And so the rigged moral drama played itself out. The dice tumbled, and if necessary tumbled again, and again, and again, until Floyd Baker (who had poled exactly one four-bagger in his entire big-league career) suddenly found the home run touch and Ray Scarborough was 25–1 and Buddy Hazen—my most malign creation, the most despicable human being ever to don major-league flannels (I could see his ratlike face)—was hitting a humiliating .193.

The bathroom had to be the venue. This was intensely, almost grimly private, this righting of baseball's and life's scales. It demanded concentration and could brook no distractions, no interruptions. I played hard and I played fast—as fast as I could, being eighteen players and two managers and scorekeeper. The thump and cry would come soon enough: "What the hell are you doing in there? Come on, people have to use the bathroom!"

But it was all set down in my notebook, every juicy, soul-satisfying whack of Floyd's bat, every Buddy Hazen whiff, to be savored later and to fuel anticipation of the next night's bathroom tilt.

"Got you a Phillies cap" came the postcard thunderbolt from Florida, in that telltale back-slanting, nib-crushing hand. Unburdened as usual by any pangs of guilt at leaving Mother behind, T.C. had ambled down in March 1950 with a Simcoe pal to golf and browse the grapefruit league for a week or so.

My own Phillies cap! It mattered not a whit that I couldn't have cared less about the Philadelphia Phillies. Beggars can't be choosers. The cheap souvenir-stand Detroit Tigers cap that T.C. had brought back from a visit to Briggs Stadium a couple of years before probably didn't have another season left. It had been serially transformed, following my hopscotching team loyalties, from a Tigers to a Cubs to a Reds to a White Sox to a Senators cap by means of homemade logos airplane-glued in place until ripped away to make room for the next, and was getting a bit crusty. It was sweat-caked and, worse, perfume-soaked—the cloying legacy of a prank by some giggling girls of Danforth Court.

In those days, before Major League Properties, Inc., authentic or even inauthentic big-league baseball caps were as scarce in Canada as papal miters. And why quibble about which team, anyway? What truly thrilled was that a caring dad had come through for his kid, without even being asked! Picked out and bought and carried all the way home from Florida just for me, that Phillies cap would be advertising Eddie Sawyer's amazing Whiz Kids team less than the renewed bond between T.C. and me. I knew it would eventually happen. What a dad. What a guy.

What a crock. When T.C. returned home and unpacked, there was no Phillies cap, only my instant realization that, of course, a fleeting good intention and the sending of a postcard had discharged his duty as far as he was concerned. He offered no explanation and, God knows, no apologies. I never inquired directly; I knew the rules. Bugging him, a man of his worries and concerns, about some crummy damn two-dollar baseball cap? Couldn't I ever, just once, think of anybody but myself?

That just about did it for baseball as the vehicle for dad-and-lad bonding. That was about the start, in fact, of a tight U-turn. Hereafter, I'd use baseball to bean the son of a bitch.

What destructive glee. Growing up in the Babe Ruth era had made T.C. a lifelong Yankees fan and American League diehard. (In an earlier internecine baseball version of the Oedipal dilemma, this had led him to stick it to his own old man, a deep-dyed National Leaguer going back to the 1890s.) Despising the Yankees came naturally to me. Their monotonously all-conquering ways were as offensive to me—living example and reflexive champion of underdogs everywhere—as the Maple Leaf dynasty was in hockey.

I almost feel sorry for the man in retrospect, maddened by my relentless snipes and digs. It was a labor of love to deride his Yankee loyalties. I composed a screed accusing the Yankee club of racism for being among the last to recruit black players. I did up a chart demonstrating that the St. Louis Cardinals had more often finished first, second, or third over a twenty-five-year span than the so-called Bronx Bombers and left it on T.C.'s bed in hopes of ruining his slumber. I typed out a devastating document proving that the Yankees had simply bought their recent pennants with late-season cash acquisitions like Johnny Mize, Johnny Hopp, Ewell Blackwell, and such, violating common decency if not baseball law, and bound it in hard covers with the Yankee pinstripes and NY escutcheon shown on the front being slowly overrun by a slimy black tide of shame.

Thereafter, I pursued my baseball interest and he pursued his, and the twain never met again as long as he lived.

GAINFUL EMPLOY

It occurred to me as I walked away from Malvern Collegiate and into the summer of 1952 that nobody had offered me summer work. Initiating my own job search would have called for powers of self-reliance as alien to my character as taking up the tango. Well, I could coast through a Danforth summer on a quarter a day or so; there would be the *Sporting News* every week, some sort of ball game on the radio every afternoon, the Acme Farmers Dairy brick wall for my personal bullpen, time for sunbathing and reading up on the flat graveled roof of our apartment building among the frying blobs of tar. But even I had to acknowledge, stimulated by ears burning from T.C.'s none too softly muttered imprecations, that a healthy seventeen-year-old ought to be making more of his summer than that. And distasteful as it would be to leave my ten-by-twelve-foot womb and engage with the world outside, even I sensed the need for a change of venue.

The paternal prod inspired me to start bombarding every tourist resort in Ontario for which I could find an address with eleventh-hour job pleas. I was, Sir or Madam, hustle personified. I would do anything, anywhere, for any wage. Say yes and I'm on my way.

Limberlost Lodge, one of innumerable summer hostelries in the Muskoka Lakes north of Toronto, bit by return mail. I could start immediately as factotum in charge of renting and tending to the small lakeside canoe flotilla, while instructing neophyte guests in canoeing technique. I decided in the instant that the fact that I'd never seen a canoe in the water, much less paddled one, shouldn't bother me if it didn't bother Limberlost Lodge. As for my profound distrust of all bodies of water outside the bathtub, I'd keep that to myself. Summer work, summer fun in fresh surroundings, that was the thing. That, and giving T.C. the gift of my vacant bunk.

On a glorious June Sunday, after a three-hour bus trip that seemed to be a progress from Babylon to Labrador, I reported for duty at Limberlost Lodge, a modest foothold in nature's surrounding domain. The kindly matron who had hired me showed me about. Fellow teenagers constituted most of the staff. The ambience was rustic to a fault. The tour concluded at my living quarters, a kind of woodshed, how quaint, one more facet of this adventure in new experience.

At sunset I found myself standing alone on the shore of Limberlost Lake, surrounded by canoes, water, the forest primeval, silence, and misery, gripped by the psychic bends from having transited too rapidly to a different state of being. What any normal seventeen-year-old would have seized as heady freedom left me with the sickening sense that everything familiar had fallen away and left me floating in a void. Too much space, too much time, no boundaries. I could feel myself sinking down; or was it panic, rising up? Come on, I'd get used to it! No I wouldn't. Two months tethered to a few square yards of beachfront in the middle of nowhere with no radio, no box scores—I felt kidnapped. It'd be fun! No it wouldn't. If I never had to clamber into one of those flimsy, tippy little canoes it would be none too soon. That placid lake out there was a sinister hole, waiting for the first opportunity to drown me. The forest primeval was dark and full of secrets, probably man-eating bears as well. I couldn't dance; girls scared me; my clothes were odd; I'd be the same hapless outsider among my teenage Limberlost Lodge colleagues as I was in high school.

Homesickness now came rolling in like ground mist to soften and distort reality, and I rode the tide. I pined for Danforth Court, the aroma of the Acme Farmers Dairy stables, for the warm embrace of what a hundred miles' distance, eight hours' absence, and my panic had magically transformed, as through a gauzy lens, into a snug and loving family. They were all probably even now huddled around the kitchen table, wailing why oh why had they ever let me go.

No repatriated prisoner of war was ever as suffused with sweet anticipation as I was on the bus ride home the next day. They'd all be so surprised to see me walk through that door. I'd been away since Sunday! True, my abrupt resignation as canoe boy had caught the nice lady in charge entirely by surprise, which would explain why I'd been ejected from Limberlost Lodge like a drunk from a bar. But I'd managed the feat of slinking away from that green hellhole of sylvan tranquillity with head held high, and I forgave her. How could she or I have known that I was far too sensitive for such menial chores in such alien surroundings, or how much my family needed me, and I needed them?

The first minute back in the family's bosom suggested that I might have somewhat miscalculated the effect of my return. The sight of me instantly froze T.C. into an iceberg that made any room in the apartment too small for the both of us. Hugh was uncustomarily distant. Even undemonstrative Mother could barely hide her contempt for the gutless twerp who'd aborted his first solo venture into the outside world almost before it started. The meaning of the word *pariah* landed with full force over the next few days. So this was all the thanks I got for loving my family. I retreated to the far corner of my bunk in a corner of the bedroom and rolled myself up into a ball of self-pity to wait it out in the anguished isolation of the tragically misunderstood, ostensibly until Labor Day.

Rustication was short-lived. If I couldn't or wouldn't seize the reins of my destiny, T.C. would. A week after my homecoming I was instructed, via his fifteen-second phone call, to report the following morning to the mailroom of the Ontario Department of Travel and Publicity at Queens Park, ready to do whatever I was told for twenty-five dollars a week. As a cover for this distasteful and potentially embarrassing act of nepotism into which I had forced him, T.C. announced that I would be working under an assumed name.

Thus did Bruce Gordon find himself one of numerous troglodytes milling about in a subterranean vault redolent of paper products and mold, where you had to look up to see a patch of daylight through tiny barred windows. Bruce Gordon's task was to fetch stacks of tourism brochures—Old Fort Henry, Sleeping Sentinel of the Centuries, Haliburton, Hello!, The Trenton Locks, Gateway to Adventure's Threshold—from their storage shelves and lug them to the mailroom for shipping. It was moron's work in a dank netherworld.

I felt like Gene Kelly in *Singin' in the Rain*. The streetcar delivered me downtown daily from the dreary Danforth into a world where the men wore suits and the women had high heels. My life had purpose: I was now one in the parade of wage-earning Torontonians headed for another day in stores and offices to oil the machinery that turned the wheels of commerce. The lines of command down to my mailroom lair from the department nerve center above were slack enough that the workday could be shaped to fit the workers—between brief flurries of effort, all the coffee breaks, bull sessions, naps on mailbags piled in corners that we wanted.

At lunchtime, a bag of grapes in hand, I strolled Yonge and Bay and College streets, glittering avenues of cosmopolitanism. Almost every lunchtime I detoured, for the thrill of it, through the block-long ground floor of Eaton's College Street, to savor that perfumy department-store smell, the air of well-being and civility, the sight of spending power at work, as well-heeled customers pawed over cashmere, leather, and silk, the merchandise of the gods.

My self-appointed guide to the protocols of life in the mailroom and the department was a guy I'll call Ted, a balding low-level functionary some years my senior, who in his soiled white shirt and clip-on tie had already assumed much the same dingy aspect as his environment. Ted not only adopted me and showed me the ropes but also shared his very special brand of wisdom.

"See that dame? Jew slut."

"Don't talk to that one. Polack bitch."

Ted, it seemed, had compiled an exhaustive personal dossier on every attractive female person in the Department of Travel and Publicity, based on ethnic background, then correlated this intelligence with the Ted take on recent world events. Poland and the Jews had attacked Germany in September 1939, according to Ted's historical analysis, which then spiraled forward in time to carom off one hair-raising disclosure after another before crash-landing in front of the secret cave where lurked the Elders of Zion, the perpetrators of it all. Not even Toronto in 1952, thousands of miles and seven years away from World War Two, was safe from the fiendish conspiracy. But it was the women—the young, friendly secretaries and clerks among whom he moved every day—who most exercised Ted. Each, behind her mask of wholesomeness, was a cunning Jezebel, racially poisoned, the enemy, evil incarnate.

It was funny in a way, but only for a few days, before it became the rancid frothings of a crackpot. No wonder I was his only friend, that nobody else in all of Queens Park would touch the guy with tongs. Poor Ted. If only he had ever gotten laid. Even I could see it. His bottled-up sexual agonies had putrefied into rage boiling so fiercely that only the most monstrous fantasies could sustain it. We were pals no more.

The luxuriously drowsy routine of the mailroom slid me through the days and weeks of the summer as in a gondola on calm water, until I came to prefer the life of Bruce Gordon to that of Bruce McCall, hands-down, and to wish the summer of '52 would never end. But end it did, and badly. I had managed to avoid even the sight of T.C. the whole time I was working under his very nose. By unspoken mutual assent, he never asked at the dinner table about life down in the bowels of his department, and I never volunteered comment. But just a few days before August ended and I was due to troop back to school again, some minor bungle—a phone call from home, as I recall—inadvertently tipped the mailroom crew to my real identity.

A mole, a fink, a sneaky double agent had wormed his way into their midst, no doubt squealing about their half-hour coffee breaks and irreverent comments to his old man and the other higher-ups. No no no, I protested. I was under orders! I never said a word! I'm one of you! My pleas went unheeded. I spent my remaining mailroom days in Coventry. It stained an idyllic summer; but at least it wasn't Limberlost Lodge.

IDYLL

Three years of scholastic futility had soured me on Malvern Collegiate Institute, even if Glenn Gould himself could be counted among the alumni. Three years of moping about on its social fringes, the perpetual loner, didn't help. Even more than the cretinous thugs of Danforth Tech, I had come to despise my fellow Malvernites—in their case for the sin of being normal. Malvern drew most of its student body from the relatively affluent area of the Beaches, from comfortable, stable, healthy families. I was jealous of the fat lunch bags their mothers packed for them, of their clothes, their spending money, their football games, the normalcy they seemed so complacently to take for granted.

For a while I attempted to register my own unique identity by becoming the class Communist, exploiting the McCarthy-era political orthodoxy that had reached all the way up into Canada and into the souls of Toronto's high school students. None of my incendiary book reviews or English essays or history papers, foaming with praise of the Great Leader Stalin and denunciations of the Wall Street Imperialists, could provoke so much as a yawn; not even my wallpaper-design project in art class—a pattern of Soviet hammers and sickles, cradling atomic bombs—raised an eyebrow.

Meanwhile, my compulsive passion for drawing had continued to blaze unabated, and insofar as I could foresee a future beyond high school, it was the life of an artist—a magazine illustrator like Norman Rockwell and my other heroes of *The Saturday Evening Post* and *Collier's*—that most often formed my daydreams. So I told myself that it was for the sake of my art that I was leaving Malvern and returning to Danforth Tech, and my fifth high school year, in September 1952.

Fate must have changed chief administrators over the past few years. From the moment I stepped once again over that angst-haunted threshold, things were different. Danforth Tech, in my absence, seemed to have become a liberated city, goon-free. I wasn't a leper anymore. My new classmates in the grade-eleven art class presented the astonishing, unprecedented pleasure of kindred souls; within weeks, Dave and April and Maurice and Don and Diane and Paul had become almost a surrogate family.

The hermetic seal that had isolated me from my adolescent environment for so long was popped at last. I threw myself into this soft, warm new pillow of high school life with what passed, with me, for abandon.

The Toronto Board of Education at some distant time must have invited Victoria herself to design the grade-eleven Danforth Tech art curriculum and then honored her memory by never changing it. What lessons in heraldry, stained glass, leathercrafts, and bas-relief sculpture had to do with training the commercial artists of the fifties, I never quite fathomed. I didn't much care. I was having too much fun, swept up in friendly competition with my classmates. My grades reversed their downward spiral. I even had after-school diversions outside my bedroom, skylarking about Toronto's East End with my crony and surrogate big brother Dave.

And on the evening of March 23, 1953, after only two or three months of careful consideration and planning, I ventured forth on my first date. I had honored the occasion by washing my face and armpits and donning my smartest outfit, a wine-colored corduroy jacket and powder-blue summer trousers, the ones with a normal crease plus a second, lateral, crease across the knees from having hung on a wire hanger for the better part of two years. On Terry, my date, I had no carnal designs. I just wanted to feel what it was like to be in the presence of a girl.

It was a sedate outing. Sedate to the outskirts of pointlessness. I walked the half mile or so to Terry's house, and we wandered about the neighborhood for an hour in the knuckle-reddening chill of a March evening. It no more occurred to me to buy her a cup of coffee than to whisk her off to El Mocambo. The most meaningful part of the evening was my long walk home, luxuriating in my heady new sense of fullness. I had gone on a date! I might as well have been wearing top hat and tails.

Toronto's creaking iron gate was beginning to open for me, revealing excitements and pleasures within that now, after five long dreary years, made it seem a kind of Paris.

But once again, what fate had given with one hand it quickly snatched away with the other. The evening of March 23, 1953, was to be memorable for another significant and infinitely less pleasurable event.

I returned home to find Mother ironing in the kitchen, with the radio tuned to an N.H.L. playoff game. She was sober.

"Guess what?" she said. "T.C. just called. He's taking a new job with Chrysler and we're moving to Windsor in June."

Of course. My new life had been too good for retribution to be long in striking. I would immediately wage an insistent campaign to stay behind in Toronto for the final year of high school and board somewhere, but it fell on deaf parental ears. Anyway, larger interests than mine were at stake—although, as usual, shielded from me. After fourteen years as a civil servant, T.C. had finally had a bellyful of being overworked, underpaid, and an unwilling pawn in various political shenanigans. His loyalty was exhausted, and so was he.

Bittersweet might have been coined to describe those final three months of Danforth Tech and Toronto. I was already enveloped in a nostalgic fog for the life I hadn't yet put behind me, and saw and lived the precious remaining days in a kind of elegiac trance, at pains to experience and record forever the last tiny details of the happiest life I'd known.

My friend Dave treated me on my last night in Toronto to a chocolate milk shake and a slab of strawberry shortcake at the

Gainsborough coffee shop on Danforth. Afterward we sat in his parents' living room in the dark, listening to my LP record of the famous 1938 Benny Goodman concert at Carnegie Hall. I walked home around midnight along the Danforth. The splendid, sweet, magical Danforth.

Part III

IN EXILE

WELCOME TO CANADA'S
SUN PARLOR!

In mid-afternoon of June 23, 1953, a gray day almost as sullen as I was, mother's friend Macil Keeffe drove her and Hugh and me from 2377 Danforth to Union Station for the train trip that would deliver us from Toronto to our new home and new life in Windsor, 240 miles southwest. The rest of the brood, dispersed for the duration among the Simcoe relatives, would be fetched and brought to Windsor the next weekend. Hugh and I had rummaged up proper jackets and ties for the trip, I remember, obedient to the code, long since lapsed, that required travelers to show respect before the might and mystery of traversing vast distances aboard a self-propelled conveyance—in this case, a steam-powered C.N.R. train.

Mother must have secretly shared something of our sense of the occasion as a ride to oblivion, the Last Mile, because she splurged on parlor-car seats, and there—amid the cigarette smoke and flea-bitten plush, Cokes for us, a beer for her—the three of us lolled and joked across southwestern Ontario. It was gallows humor, of course. We pulled in to Windsor at dusk. T.C. was there waiting with his factory-fresh Plymouth Cranbrook; so was our new hometown, and off we went for our introductory tour.

I saw Windsor as Napoleon Bonaparte must have seen St. Helena, with sinking heart amid unbearable memories of all he had left behind. I was in no mood to marvel, exult, or celebrate. Windsor could have been the French Riviera and I'd have hated it on principle for presuming to supplant my recently lost paradise. It was no Riviera but a city of two hundred thousand or so, in Essex County—"Canada's Sun Parlor" in chamber of commerce-ese, for reasons I never did divine. What I saw through my haze of self-pity as T.C. conducted our guided tour was an entire city of Danforth Avenues. Few buildings rose above three stories. Along identical-looking streets as straight as string huddled identical-looking little houses on tiny plots, a living Monopoly board of Baltics and Mediterraneans. "Downtown" was overstating things compared with Toronto—and perversely, I sat there comparing everything with Toronto. That motley of squat office buildings and shops dribbling out at the edge of the Detroit River exuded all the glamour, all the pulsing energy, of Gopher Prairie.

Windsor even lacked a pedigree. Hiram Walker had founded his distillery there, and built a park nearby and a mansion in the middle of it. By accident of geography—it lay right across the river—Windsor was Canada's car-making equivalent of Detroit, its gaudiest monuments the factories and foundries dotted throughout the municipal area. Half the city's working population manned the assembly lines "to Chrysler's," in local parlance, or "to Ford's." Otherwise, there was little to distinguish this from any of those other centers of production that exist in a modern industrial society. Prohibition-era rum-running antics aside, it had no history. Nothing memorable, even by modest Canadian standards of memorability, had ever happened there.

And poor Windsor was a caricature of the Canadian dilemma. It lay under mighty Detroit, and was forever in its shadow. It couldn't compete with the drive and energy and stature of the fifth largest city in the United States, and didn't even try. A night out, deluxe shopping, art, and theater—all the good things in life—waited at the far end of the Windsor–Detroit tunnel or the Ambassador Bridge.

If there ever was such a thing as a Canadian Dream, it didn't stand a chance of fulfillment here. Stranded on the southernmost tip of Canadian soil, so surrounded by the USA that Detroit was actually its neighbor to the north, Windsor found itself geographically and culturally severed from the rest of Canada. It was not quite Canadian and not quite American. It was . . . Windsor.

It was now almost dark, and we headed off to meet our new family home. Something to celebrate at last—a real house at last, the first T.C. had ever owned. The move to Windsor had at least brought us escape from the stifling confines of an overcrowded flat surrounded by an asphalt moat in the middle of a gritty urban nowhere.

The house at 1793 Byng Road was not quite what I had imagined when T.C. described our new dream home in suburbia. It was a brick bungalow on a patch of grass barely larger than its shadow, identical to every other bungalow around it in a low-budget development thrown up by the federal Central Mortgage and Housing Authority after the war, to give a few returning veterans and their families somewhere affordable to live.

It wasn't deliverance from 2377 Danforth, it was more like 2377

Windsor, 1953. The entire family musters for a rare group shot in the back-yard at 1793 Byng Road on Labor Day weekend. Walt, Hugh, Mike, I, and Tom stand behind Chris, who stands between Peg and T.C. A couple of days later my feckless high school career would be declared *finis* and my equally feck-less commercial art career would begin.

Danforth shipped to a new location. It might be adequate to house a family of three but would have to accommodate seven. Again, the single bathroom; an even more cramped kitchen and dining nook; bedrooms barely large enough for beds. The place was a flimsy reverberating sound box. Everybody anywhere inside, even from behind closed doors, could hear everybody else's footsteps and coughs and arguments. Every private gurgle and fart resonated from behind the ground-floor bathroom, down the hallway, and into a living room, soon to be redolent with the scent of bacon fat and reheated coffee and other olfactory delights wafting in from the adjacent kitchen.

Hugh and I were assigned one of the two upstairs rooms and Tom and Walt the other, both cells jammed under the sharply slanting eaves so that the walls on either side sloped inward, tentlike, and you could stand erect only in the middle, in a three-foot-wide alley between the beds. Even I could touch the ceilings. The living room was smaller than the living room on Danforth. Astonishingly, inconceivably, we had traded an apartment for a house and downsized our living space.

Whatever faint enthusiasm I had succeeded in manufacturing about the move was being undone, fast. What in God's name could have been in T.C.'s mind? How could the public relations manager of Chrysler of Canada Ltd. consign himself, not to mention his teeming family, to these few square feet of living space, in an antiseptic blank of a neighborhood, in a Minsk of a city—and expect us, as he obviously did, to be as wowed, as grateful, as if we'd just been transposed to Tara?

Coexisting in such quarters would have put a strain on the Brady Bunch; populate it with a secretive alcoholic, a moody tyrant, and five troubled offspring and you had the house of the seven time bombs. Hugh and I knew as much before we'd spent our first night under its roof, and the look in Tom's and Walt's—and even ten-year-old Chris's—eyes soon after they arrived disclosed that they did, too.

It was time for another pep talk with myself. Hold on, I counseled. Pull back and see the picture overall. This was more than just a move, it was a whole new start. Maybe Mother would take it to heart and stop her drinking. Maybe our loose-knit family would close ranks; maybe T.C., with more money and a car and a house and everything, would become a real dad—take us to Tigers games, Red Wings games, on excursions to the beach at Point Pelee. Maybe I'd fall in with kindred spirits, meet girls, star in art class, belong. Yes, it was far too early for whining. So our new hometown and our new home weren't perfect; still, Windsor was a new chapter, a new adventure. Why not make the most of it? Who could tell? A few months from now, Mother sober and out of the shadows, T.C. not ogre but pal, family life no longer fraught but rollicking, the fresh start in new surroundings giving my charm and talent their chance to shine at last, my former existence—Toronto itself—would be seen as mere prologue to an infinitely richer life.

Ten days later I was on the noon bus back to Toronto. No sooner had the last moving carton been unpacked than McCall family life resumed in Windsor where it had left off on Danforth Avenue a few days before. T.C. went golfing. He had already reneged on his first commitment as new-style dad: Hugh and I were left to go by ourselves to Briggs Stadium and the Tigers game he had vowed only a few days before that we'd take in together; like the dad of old, he was enraged at being reminded. Mother went back to the bottle and seldom left the house. She could hardly be blamed. Our new neighborhood baked and dozed under the hot June sun in unrelieved silence and torpor, of a deadliness I had never experienced before. Day or night, not a human soul ever seemed to be abroad on any street within a mile of Byng Road. Like Hugh and Tom and Walt and Chris, I was alone and bored and prey to homesickness for the life I'd left behind.

I had prepared the ground beforehand in a desperate flurry of clandestine phone calls to Toronto, cadging a second summer round in the Department of Travel and Publicity's basement warren in Queens Park and free lodgings in the apartment of some vacationing family friends. I knew my runaway flight back to Toronto could only bring a temporary reprieve from Windsor. School awaited again in September, and that part of me still enmeshed in our family drama—a large part, since there was too much at stake, too many suspenseful plotlines still unresolved—belonged back there in the midst of it. According to a report from mother, T.C. had not blown the expected box of fuses at my unauthorized departure. Quite the opposite; he rather admired it as my first ever display of gumption.

Giddy with my newfound sense of freedom and independence, sprung from the hour-to-hour psychodrama of our family life and Windsor, I made the most of my amazing save of the summer of '53. As September loomed and the return to Windsor drew imminent, the ache of again leaving Toronto was even worse than it had been in June. The desire to defy T.C. and find some way, any way, to remain for another year at Danforth Tech rekindled itself. But not quite hotly enough, alas, to stand up to him when the dreaded phone call and even more dreaded summons came—as, sooner rather than later, it would. My summer had been a joyride, but it had also been an aberration. Life was not what you wanted to do but what you had to do; T.C. had taught me that much.

At the last possible hour of Labor Day weekend I was on the bus to Windsor again. My summer of freedom was behind me. I didn't know it yet, but so was my adolescence.

CAR MAN

The continuation of my high school career in Windsor lasted forty-five minutes, long enough for the principal of Lowe Vocational High School to reveal that there was no commercial art course in his school or the city of Windsor or all of Essex County and, that being the case, that my academic credentials qualified me to repeat grade eleven in one more round of bookkeeping, calculator-pounding, and other of the dismal arts of clerkship—take it or leave it. I opted to leave it, and was home in time for lunch.

Time for stock-taking. I was eighteen years old, for God's sake. Failing grade nine twice and then taking three more years to overcome grades ten and eleven had all but consumed my adolescence. Art was my vocation, and the educational system in its omniscience had me pegged as a future bank teller.

We see here a boy adrift at sea on a raft, drifting further and further away from his destiny. But fate's currents can shift in sudden and dramatic ways. Home for lunch in time to hear my lament, T.C. rose to the crisis with his usual bracing blend of exasperation and command. "Well, now that you've screwed up your education, I guess you have to go work. A guy I know told me there's an art studio downtown looking for help. Go see them—and for Christ's sake, brush your hair."

Twenty-four hours later I had stepped from the foundering scow of formal education into the career I had dreamed of. I could now call myself a commercial artist. They'd even pay me—thirty-five dollars a week, plus all the art supplies I wanted, free! Sweeter still, they'd pay me to draw and paint cars! Windsor Advertising Artists Ltd. was a three-man (now three men and an apprentice) commercial art studio clamped like a limpet onto its one and only account, big and lucrative: all advertising and catalog illustration for Dodge and DeSoto cars and Dodge trucks in Canada.

The protocol of the business was the Canadian dilemma in the proverbial nutshell. The advertising agency that commissioned and supervised Windsor Advertising Artists' work was American, across the river in Detroit. It was their layouts we had to execute, their scrutiny every illustration had to pass. Whatever mix of politics, money, and cronyism accounted for a tiny Windsor studio's grip on the business interposing itself in the dialogue between American advertising genius and the Canadian consumer, I never knew. But it was clear that the Americans involved didn't much care for it or our work or us.

Under such circumstances the agency didn't come to us, we went to them. More accurately, I went to them, the studio dogsbody dispatched back and forth through the Windsor–Detroit tunnel, often two or three times a day, to deliver artwork for approval and pick up new layouts and generally dance attendance on the art director in charge. The studio was a supplier, and tradesmen use the rear entrance. I'd take the freight elevator to the fourth floor of Ross Roy, Inc., on East Jefferson and await the art director's pleasure. "Gruff" hardly describes his manner when finally he deigned to receive me. "This is shit. I gave you guys the paint chip and it's still the wrong shade of pink. Can't Rudy paint a goddamn circle? Look at those headlights! Make all the fixes I've noted and have it back here tomorrow."

Rudy the artist would fume, of course, when I returned to deliver these critiques. "That asshole. I'm not changing anything." I nodded gravely in loyal agreement with the man who signed my paychecks, but mentally, inside, I was shaking my head. Didn't Rudy get it? He ought to listen; the Americans were smarter, more sophisticated, knew better. They deserved to call the shots.

• • •

I remember the place like a former hostage remembers his basement corner. For the next six years my working world and much of my life would be a walled-in space about six by ten feet, occupied by a large drawing board, a taboret, and one extra chair. To my left, large windows gave out on a low-lying jagged skyline—the hind ends of the three- and four-story brick buildings on Ouellette Avenue, Windsor's main artery—and in the foreground, on Pelissier Street directly below, the subterranean grotto of the Niagara Grill, Art Kane's Men's Clothiers, an insurance office, a parking lot. Opposite the open door on my right was a countertop where all the spraying and gluing and wrapping typical of an art studio were performed, an area fragrant with the aromas of rubber cement, gum-eraser crumbs, and the lethal benzine fumes that medical science swears should have burned my lungs to bacon long ago. The thump-thump-thump of the air compressor in a back room feeding the airbrushes, the heavy grinding of air conditioners turned on in May and left running until October, the mingled babble of multiple radios—Norman Rockwell's Vermont studio wasn't anything like this.

My Windsor Advertising Artists colleagues were Rudy, Nick, and Wilf. Rudy and Nick were the artists, and nothing at all like the pipe-smoking eminences depicted in ads for the Famous Artists School. Rudy was a dark Armenian, dour, taciturn, a master Car Man and co-owner of the studio, whose love of art and creativity began and ended with the money he was paid and whose love of his fellow man was invisible. Nick, Rudy's protégé and the number-two artist, was in his mid-twenties and blazed with raw talent that was already shaping him into an illustration ace. He also blazed with ambition, temper, and a lust to live down his impoverished origins. This took various forms: spending more than he made (on used Buicks and other luxuries), learning Italian, dressing for success—in a homburg and velvet-collared banker's chesterfield coat—and taking a La Salle Institute correspondence accounting course, among endless serial efforts at self-improvement, all soon abandoned.

Wilf, co-owner with Rudy, was the "contact man," a nebulous job description that seemed to require his dashing in at 11:00 A.M. and right out again for lunch till three, then spending most evenings interviewing dry martinis in the bar of the nearby Norton-Palmer Hotel. Wilf talked out of the side of his mouth, dressed like a bandleader, and glided as effortlessly as Fred Astaire around the matter of doing any work. Wilf was my favorite. He had style. He also had boxes of barely used shoes, elegant Lobb and Church wingtips, that he donated to me. They were the first good shoes I'd ever worn, and as a bonus, if I scrunched up my toes just so and walked sort of on the outsides of my feet, they almost fit.

It required only a few weeks of working studio life to separate me from boyish fantasies of the craft I'd thought myself destined to pursue. Creativity had as much to do with commercial art—or car art—as it did with Martinizing shirts. There was one technique and one technique only for rendering cars for advertising, and it was as formalized and unresponsive to improvisation as a Japanese tea ceremony. The goal was waxworks realism—not a tire tread askew; the means—and the very reason most advertisers preferred their cars drawn and painted, not photographed—was to visually lie and cheat.

Every new painting started with a black-and-white photograph of a car taken from the exact angle desired—usually three-quarter front and slightly above—sliced with a knife at critical points into sections. The sections were then moved apart until the car had optically gained a foot more of length in the hood, in the doors, and in the tail. The tires were shoved so far up into the wheel cutouts as to strongly suggest a missing suspension system. Pasted down on a piece of cardboard, spaces intact, this painstaking reconstruction was then painstakingly traced onto vellum paper. And, presto, that runty Dodge Crusader sedan now looked as if it weighed six tons, sat an inch off the ground, and tapered off into infinity.

Rendering this fantastic beast in rainbow hues—this was the three-tone pastel fifties, after all—demanded patience, exactitude, advanced eye-hand coordination, and absolutely no imagination, and it yielded all the creative adventure of turning table legs on a lathe.

Windsor Advertising Artists, 1954. Hugh points while I hold a French-language Dodge ad. As with most moments in that office, it marked no particular occasion.

Airbrush the body for that otherworldly mirror smoothness and shine, adding the same reflections and the same twinkling highlights in the same places. Airbrush the interior fabrics. Airbrush the tires. Paint in the chrome, cobalt-blue above, yellow-ocher below. Grab a fine-point brush and detail the Dodge escutcheon on the hood, the fine-mesh grille, the windshield wipers, the five perfect zigzag treads on the tires.

Meanwhile, think happy. Paint with an idiot smile in your mind, if not on your lips. Uncomplicate nature, simplify complexity, make that Dodge look its Sunday best, because it's headed for the never-never land of advertising, land of no bug-splat and of highways you could eat off, land where puppies frolic and humanoid couples dress in tuxedos and ball gowns and freckle-faced girls in pigtails staff their lemonade stands.

Now, hand over the finished painting and start on the next one.

Diligence and faithful observance of the rules would in time yield the sturdy competence that assured the more than decent income of a certified professional Car Man. Rudy was a Car Man. Nick was a Car Man. I was a mere apprentice-in-training, but with practice, practice, practice, I could one day be a Car Man, too.

It was on an ordinary weekday afternoon in my second month in the studio as I sat at my drawing board gazing out at the leaden November sky that the worm of unbidden truth finally worked its way to the surface.

I barely had a life as it was, and life in a tiny atelier on a side street in Windsor was only further sealing me off. Familiarity had already served to evaporate the initial mystery and allure of car art. The commercial-art milieu in which I ostensibly sought a niche was not glamorous. It was factory life, with long and irregular hours a fixture in the rush to meet whimsical, impossible, and ever-changing agency deadlines. The atmosphere was raffish. The big-time Detroit commercial artists as I'd observed them—the Car Men, the figure men, the background men—were not the studious craftsmen of my imagination, not the role models I craved. They were happy-go-lucky social outsiders if not outcasts, nocturnal creatures, drinkers, philanderers, oddballs who had chosen lives that mocked fifties ideas of stability and respectability.

Then, too, I already knew I was never going to be any good at being a Car Man. There was no feeling allowed, no mischief, no wit, nothing of oneself. A finished car ad wasn't a personal accomplishment but a fusion of specialists' skills. In some other studio a background man was painting the happy landscape your car would be shown thundering through, and in another, a figure man was rendering its delirious occupants. Finished car and background and figures would all be cut out and glued in place to create the final picture. You learned the Car Man's trade by copying the work of others, until your work was sound enough to be itself worthy of copying. My initial practice exercises inevitably dissolved into cars with square wheels or cars covered in flannel or a Studebaker with a Rolls-Royce grille and Cadillac tail fins. Rudy found this unamusing. He also found that my ellipses were coming out potato-shaped, that in my hands an airbrush became a runaway spray gun, that my finest painted lines were other artists' practice brushstrokes.

Reverie concluded. I didn't want to be a Car Man. But the dread of admitting as much led me to steadfastly say otherwise—and to nobody more than myself—for the next six years. Two thousand days is long enough to teach a horse to count, but it wasn't long enough for me to gain minimal Car Man competence.

Meanwhile, Bill Windsor, a refugee from hand-lettering Canadian Club whisky labels at the Hiram Walker distillery out along Riverside Drive, had decided to broaden his oeuvre and accepted Windsor Advertising Artists' low pay and long hours for the chance to become a Car Man. He had surpassed my level in weeks and was a full-fledged Car Man in a year. I chortled at our new apprentice, Louie, dumb as a box of hammers, but within a year Louie had also left me behind.

It was all a drawn-out lesson in the damnation that awaits when you don't care enough. I never managed to break the magic one-hundred-dollar-a-week barrier; indeed, at sixty-five dollars a week, in terms of drawing-board productivity, I was overpaid. Rudy should have fired me within the first six months for the incorrigible dud I was, but it was a measure of my irrelevance that he never got around to it. My chicken-feed salary was more than covered by my messenger and housekeeping duties. At my sixty-five dollars a week, neither Rudy nor anyone else at Windsor Advertising Artists much cared whether or not I made artistic progress; any achievements at the drawing board constituted a kind of bonus, a minor windfall. Thus was an exquisite career equilibrium achieved and perpetuated: I was too scared to quit and didn't matter enough to be fired.

It got to be the highlight of my studio day to visit the Windsor outpost of Grant Advertising, successor agency to Ross Roy, just across University Avenue. At least it was brightly lit and co-ed, and verbal jousting with the receptionist—"Thank God it's Friday!"; "Cold out there!"—provided practice in the art of social conversation, otherwise rare enough that I might soon be in danger of being mistaken for a boy raised by the wolves. My caste didn't qualify me for complimentary cups of coffee or a chair, but milling about the reception area for ten or fifteen minutes dribbled just enough fuel into my tank to fortify me for another few hours in my studio cell.

Christmas Day, 1955. Breakfast, the perfunctory family exchange of gifts. By 10:30 A.M. I'm downtown, in my familiar seat at the studio drawing board. The studio is deserted. There is no need to be there, except that I can't think of anywhere else to go or any other way to fill the long hours until Christmas dinner. I sit there waiting for habit to engage, to be absorbed into the familiar routine of rendering a car. It doesn't quite take this time. Even my faithful companion, the radio, declines to lull me with the familiar programs. Only Christmas music, nonstop. After half an hour of arranging my paint jars and washing my brushes and cleaning my airbrush, I leave.

Skulking in my little cubicle at Windsor Advertising Artists month after month, year after year, may have been a waste—was a waste, complete, total, absolute. But it was also probably inevitable. I needed a safe place to lie low until I sorted things out and the master plan, if any, was at last revealed.

Windsor, 1955. T.C., Mother, me, and Hugh, at a local nightclub celebrating my twentieth birthday. It was the first and last time in my grown-up life that I got the chance to dine out with my parents.

• • •

One indisputable benefit did derive from that job at the studio. It got me out of the house.

Come join the McCall family dinner table circa 1955. It is the family's sole communal activity and meeting place and T.C.'s one daily exposure to his miscreant brood. He presides at the head of the Formica table in the cramped kitchen "dining area." He stabs at his food like Ahab at Moby Dick, feeding on his anger as much as his meal. The very experience of breaking bread with us has already set off some powerful mixture of rage and despair—expressed either in surly muteness, to the click of five desperately masticating McCall mandibles, or in sporadic grillings of his captive offspring, designed to smash through our lies and evasions and expose the truth.

"Who took five dollars from my coat pocket this morning?

"Why didn't you help your mother with the dishes last night?

"Peg, can't you get Tommy to stop that goddamn stuttering? He's just trying to get attention."

Unaccountably, T.C.'s gimlet eye for human weakness passes over Mother at the table's other end. She is drunk, gently reeling in place from the cheap wine she has been secretly nipping at since early afternoon, frowning with the effort of acting sober, picking at her food in slow motion and with exaggeratedly dainty gestures, not about to betray herself by trying to talk.

The minutes are hours, the food eaten but untasted. Tom and Walt and Chris, heads down, chew and cower, praying for it to be over soon so they can escape without receiving direct hits. Hugh, ever adaptable, ever cheerful Hugh, is performing his role as human solvent. Depending on my adrenaline level at the moment, I sit there either blabbering nonstop to try to mask or deflect the tension or simmering in a helpless rage whose chilling effect on the assembled duplicates T.C.'s.

Dinner is finally over, but it isn't over yet. T.C. has imposed a ludicrous little thumbscrew of punctilio at his dinner table. It is absurd, it is hypocritical in this tumbledown farce of a household, but we must ask to be excused. The others mumble their obloquies and vamoose. I seethe, refusing to acknowledge the tyrant's power. The impasse can turn into a test of wills lasting half an hour, forty-five minutes, until I've outwaited him and he gets up and leaves and the edict is moot.

One evening much later, emboldened by God knows what sudden gust of pugnacity, I simply got up and left the table with him still sitting there. I did it the next evening and after every dinner thereafter, and he never said a word. It was the only clear-cut victory over Tom C. McCall that I would ever achieve.

RADIO DAYS

Cuban cigar rollers have their readers; commercial artists in the fifties had their radios—as today they also have their cassette players and CDs. The solitude, the instinctive and often almost mechanical process of drawing and painting, can often be trusted to the hands while large portions of the mind lie idle and free to wander, open not only to take in but to concentrate actively on outside input.

The radio in my cubicle was almost always on. What it fed into my ears and mind over thousands of listening hours made radio not only my primary link to the outside world but, such as it was, a surrogate form of education. This was the fifties. Those thousands of listening hours streamed intellectual pap and gruel into my ears. Popular music in that pre-Elvis era still languished in Tin Pan Alley mush and corn. The only daytime audience was housewives, and large daily blocks of programming were given over to cultural Neanderthals like the housewives' darling Arthur Godfrey, to whose Monday-through-Friday morning show—the living psychodrama of a nasty egomaniac in folksy trappings—I confess to having developed a perverse addiction.

But tiny atolls of quality did speckle radio's vast sea of mediocrity in the fifties. There was Edward R. Murrow, intoning his Savile Row sentences in a nightly CBS News commentary; the comedians Bob and Ray; the magisterial Edward P. Morgan on ABC; locally, the U.A.W.'s house scourge, Guy Nunn, keeping the flame of liberalism alive—balanced by the breathtakingly snide and inflammatory McCarthyite insinuations of Mutual's Fulton Lewis, Jr.

And there was, thank God, the radio service of the Canadian Broadcasting Corporation. CBC Radio brought the BBC news from London via shortwave every noon hour, and in-depth world and national news every night at ten. Moreover, the CBC regularly broadcast hour-long documentaries in the best tradition of serious noncommercial radio, bringing enlightenment to coal miners in Glace Bay and farmers in Saskatchewan and struggling commercial artists on Pelissier Street in Windsor. There were erudite and witty CBC and BBC quiz shows; the *Goon Show* and *Hancock!* comedy shows, English humor at its rich and eccentric best; thoughtful film criticism; poetry readings; altogether, a bracing antidote to the Arthur Godfreys of the world.

The Windsor radio outlet of the Canadian Broadcasting Corporation was station CBE, a lonely outpost justified only by the corporation's charter to provide radio service to all of Canada—even to parts of it, like Windsor, inundated by American radio and not noticeably hungry for the patented CBC diet of information, uplift, and heavy doses of classical music.

It was over CBE in 1956 that I began noticing a new presence, a part-time announcer who was manifestly in love with the sound of his own mellifluous voice, but who defied funereal CBC announcer convention by cracking wise at every opportunity. I began to discern something close to an alter ego. This guy saw through the same crap, prized the same heroes I did. He found the same things idiotic or ridiculous or funny. He was a celebrity, a radio personality, a self-proclaimed cultural arbiter, and I was a nobody. But the affinity was too obvious to ignore, and by now, three years into a life devoid of friends, my desperate sense of loneliness and isolation justified desperate measures. Mustering all my wit and poise, over several office lunch hours I composed a mock-scholarly critique of his on-air performance, typed it up on good paper, and mailed it off.

Within a month, Alex was the closest friend I had ever had. The teasing hints I'd picked up over the radio were not misleading. Our views meshed perfectly—our views on everything from Windsor as

Canada's anal canal to the genius of Ernie Kovacs and W. C. Fields and the knavery of rock and roll to our individual and mutual talents as cultural critics nonpareil.

We met evenings and weekends at every opportunity, yet even so there was never time enough for me to blurt out everything I was bursting to say or for Alex to pronounce on all the things—usually connected with the slights inflicted upon him by petty men blind to his brilliance, blocking his rightful rise—that he needed to get off his chest. Here in one person were the college bull sessions I'd missed, the big brother I'd lost, the soul mate I'd craved, the validation I needed, the worldly success who would show me how it was done, the model of sophistication and worldliness whose example I could study at close range and which might one day rub off on me, the means of escape from my clammy state of exile from the world: a friend.

Alex was, admittedly, a lot to take. He had the ego of a grand opera tenor, the hauteur of a Lord Chesterfield and, though endowed with the build of a jockey, carried himself as if he were wearing a trilby and cape and wielding a malacca cane. As was once said of Walter Winchell, Alex could strut sitting down. He was a ham, a snob, a popinjay, a trendy, and narcissistically self-obsessed; he never passed a mirror without pausing for an admiring glance, and was forever pressing me to take his picture, draw his noble profile.

But Alex had the right. He was on the radio. I willingly indulged his affectations and pomposities. His air of jaunty self-confidence perfectly complemented my own hangdog diffidence. He was not one more interchangeable human part. He was larger than life, and to be around him magnified my own view—of myself, of life's possibilities. And we made a comfortable fit: Alex liked having an acolyte as much as I liked having a mentor.

To my astonishment, Alex's lavish act charmed only about one in every thirty people exposed to it. He raised the neck hairs on the other twenty-nine—including T.C., who detected in him a kind of latter-day Dorian Gray and sensed something evil beneath those gaudy trappings. Such reactions, of course, only reinforced my belief in his uniqueness and superiority. From Oscar Wilde to Orson

Welles, the genius was ever misunderstood and resented by the drones. And Alex was a genius. He'd allowed as much himself.

The underlying objective truth about Alex was either pathetic or hilarious, depending on one's bias. This debonair man of the world went home every night not to his bachelor pad but to a room in his parents' humble house, where a doting mother did his laundry, ironed his shirts, made his bed, and fed him his favorite meals. His salary as a part-time announcer amounted to peanuts; his fancy wardrobe, his car, his spending money—his entire lifestyle—depended on free room and board. More injurious to his vanity was the fact that Alex's parents were blue-collar Hungarian immigrants who had never assimilated and still spoke only the Magyar tongue at home. This he interpreted in the time-honored way of ambitious immigrant offspring as embarrassing and déclassé, a social millstone, and he kept his origins and his parents as sealed off from the rest of his life as if he'd bricked them up behind a wall.

Only someone as ingenuous as I was in those years could have seen Alex as a paragon of glamour and accomplishment. In fact, he occupied something close to the lowest of rungs in his chosen field—he was the juniormost announcer on a three-man staff at a radio station that defined small-time broadcasting and that couldn't even exist were it not subsidized by the Canadian taxpayer. Nor did Alex's claims as a certified intellectual and cultural pooh-bah bear close scrutiny. In truth, his educational background was hardly more distinguished than my own—he was a fellow high school dropout no less, albeit a deficiency in his case later partially redressed by part-time night courses at the local Assumption University. That he talked himself into a radio job and palmed himself off ever afterward as a combination of Oxford don and cultural expert was a marvel of self-invention. And as impostors since time immemorial have discovered to their relief and joy, the world was by and large entirely willing to take him at his word.

We'd drive 120 miles over to London, Ontario, and back in an evening just to see a W. C. Fields movie. Alex and Hugh and I piled into his beat-up old Mercury for aimless winter Sunday rambles through the dreary landscape of Essex County, rolling salons and

Hugh took this picture—reluctantly—of the author, at age twenty-one, posing as an author, in imitation of how successful real authors always seemed to pose on book jackets.

spontaneous lectures, featuring Dr. Alex. Ayn Rand's *The Fountainhead* was a fascist tract. Steve Allen was hip. Billy Graham was a menace; religion, a joke; Chaplin, a god. Our friendship thrived on a bottomless fund of shared enthusiasms and joint dislikes—perhaps more of the latter, because we were young and arrogant and considered ourselves hard-minded and merciless in our spiritual and intellectual purity. But beneath all that, Alex and I saw the world through similar lenses: as powerless outsiders aching to be where the action was, clueless for all our bluster about how to crack the magic circle, while reassuring each other daily that we both belonged there. Alex had become my intellectual conscience just at the time in life when I had decided that rigorous intellectual honesty was one's highest duty to oneself.

And then along came Jane, and quickly afterward an intellectual and moral dilemma not inaccurately described as soul-searing.

Jane had materialized like a rainbow in June 1958 suddenly to brighten, warm, and sweeten my life with the gift of romance. She was tall and long-haired and comely—comelier than a first girlfriend had any business being. Her family had moved in right across the street from 1793 Byng Road, and after stealthy weeks of scouting and observation and courage-screwing-up, I untangled the lifelong bonds of diffidence and struck. Jane made it all so relaxed, so natural. We progressed with thrilling speed and ease from companions to lovers, perfectly matched in our inexperience and our impatience to taste the pleasures of the flesh. We were soon inseparable, this kind and wholesome and desirable girl and I. Her entry into my life had vaulted me from the valley to the peak.

Alex disapproved of Jane. Her unpretentious nature contained too little intellectual starch to please him, and his early hints soon escalated into a virtual order to drop her. Flouting the advice of my personal Svengali was asking for trouble; what if he were to withdraw his favor and abandon his side of our friendship on grounds of my intellectual impurity and moral cowardice? On the other hand, I had thrown myself heart and soul into my romance with Jane. The prize of the total, uncritical affection and loyalty of an attractive young woman, the indescribable pleasure of sex, not to mention the miraculous fact of her presence in my life, were redeeming at warp speed all those hollow, sterile years of distant longing.

I waffled and wavered, torn and queasy with ambivalence that neither Alex nor Jane, from their individual opposing sides, could understand or would long tolerate. The Big Boy Drive-In out on the farther reaches of Tecumseh Road became the site of marathon nightly encounter sessions as Jane and Alex pleaded their separate cases in the pressure-chamber intimacy of the front seat of my car. The dilemma had invaded my being and left me awash. I vacillated, asquirm in the knowledge that this was one decision neither T.C. nor big brother Mike nor anybody else but me could make.

I decided to give up Jane. Alex was pleased. Jane was devastated. After two weeks I was in a more miserable state than I had ever found myself during those empty girl-less years. I soon relented. Giving up Jane was the one thing I couldn't do, for Alex or anybody.

Alex was displeased. But by now I had begun to see the crisis through Jane's eyes: Alex, possessive, selfish, manipulative, was jealous and enraged at having to share me with her, and out to wreck the relationship at all costs. He'd just have to suppress his darker impulses and accept it. Eventually, grudgingly he did, though at the cost of a certain tempering of the old easy camaraderie and a sharp diminution in the time we spent together. But the bond between Alex and me would soon thereafter shrivel and die—not because of Jane, but because of his own moral dishonesty.

Alex was the only genuine satyr I had ever known or ever would know. Sex was for him like cigarettes to a three-pack-a-day man—a compulsion. He was a sexual predator, coupling indiscriminately with housewives, friends' wives, young girls, anywhere and anytime. Initially, to me, who had barely spoken with much less touched a female anywhere near my own age since puberty, this trait was a source of wonderment and envy and yet another proof of Alex's superior place in the world. That his pursuit led him time and again over various moral boundary lines failed to disturb him, moral philosopher supreme; why should it bother me?

It didn't, until one day when Jane reported that Alex had recently gotten her out on his little outboard boat and attempted another conquest. I couldn't decide which was more loathsome, his effort at cuckolding his best friend or his hypocrisy in castigating Jane to me while coveting her body for himself. I tore down to the CBE studios in a blind rage to confront him at his seat behind the microphone. His sangfroid was absolute and his apology distinctly offhand.

It was less than a month later that I moved to Toronto. Alex, the good with the bad, was soon all but forgotten.

CARS

What's the point of being a boy if you don't grasp the fact that cars are the package excitement comes in? I certainly did. By age ten I was the kind of boy who knew every Dodge and Hudson and Packard of every model year by heart, tore the car ads from magazines, rushed to George Milligan's showroom to see the new Packard the day it arrived in town.

It was self-evident from earliest youth that mankind inhabited a closed automotive universe revolving around a gigantic single planet called Detroit, and that the sole automotive life form in it—directly evolved from the Big Bang of Henry Ford's Model T back at the dawn of time—was American-made, and the bigger the better. And no matter how much bigger or how much better, it would be bunted into oblivion twelve months later by the irresistible force of innovation, i.e., a styling face-lift.

But one day in 1952, scouring the remainder bins of a Toronto bookstore in search of cheap diversion, brother Hugh fished out a compendium of prewar articles glorifying British exploits in speed. The Schneider Trophy Supermarine float-planes; Malcolm Campbell's Bluebird land-speed-record car; and . . . what was this? Lord Carnarvon could have been no more boggled the day they pried open Tutankhamen's bedroom door. It was an entire epoch of automotive prehistory. All through the twenties and thirties, it transpired, Europe had reveled in an automotive golden age. And nobody had told me.

They called it motor racing over there. It was Olympian combat. Titans—Mercedes-Benz, Auto-Union, Alfa-Romeo—clashed in epic road races, in cars piloted by dashing demigods named Caracciola and Nuvolari and Seaman. Meanwhile, Europeans habitually elevated automobiles into rolling sculpture. Ateliers in Paris and Berlin and Turin minted exquisite one-off creations on chassis whose names sounded like fine wines: Talbot-Lago, Delahaye, Isotta-Fraschini, Lagonda, Hispano-Suiza. Together with Bentley, Bugatti, Frazer-Nash, Maserati, BMW, Jaguar, Citroën, ad infinitum, the noble marques of England and the Continent formed a menagerie more colorful and varied than the birds of the Amazon. Europeans didn't blunder about in rolling sofas and road yachts; they leapt into sports cars, GT cars, coupes, lithe and lively machines built for pleasure and play. The American automobile overnight receded into irrelevance, a plow horse among stallions. At age seventeen—still a pedestrian—I became an acolyte, a propagandist, a crusader for the European and against the American automotive culture.

Best of all, the sports car dramatically symbolized freedom and self-expression and daring nonconformity. It was flamboyantly individualistic, even selfish: only two seats, for God's sake. It was impractical. You looked silly driving one in regulation suit and tie. It was all about speed, and it exuded a frisson of danger. It was flagrantly anti-bourgeois. The sports car cocked a snook at everything—John Foster Dulles, the Rotary Club, *Your Hit Parade,* golf, *The Saturday Evening Post,* suburbia—that middle-class America in the fifties held sacred.

And if, in the process, this emerging sports car mania might just happen to stir up a bit of mischief in the McCall family, well, what the hell, I had to openly break with T.C. sometime, and I couldn't imagine a worthier issue.

T.C. hugged convention like a koala bear hugs a tree. He knew in his bones that "European" was a synonym for decadent, corrupt, profligate. A stodgy Dodge was good enough for him—for any normal person. His own flesh and blood's affinity for European cars verged on perversion.

It rapidly escalated in his eyes to something like attempted patri-

cide in 1953, when he took his job at Chrysler. When you hired
T. C. McCall you got his heart and soul, plus his Doberman loyalty
at no extra cost. Never especially car-minded before, he became
overnight a walking, talking, full-time one-man lobby for the American Association of Automobile Manufacturers. And a splenetic one:
no matter that the foreign car invasion was still no more than a lone
rowboat far out to sea, that 99.5 percent of the market belonged to
the domestic industry. Any North American caught even thinking
about cars with offshore nameplates deserved to be caned. The sight
of a foreign puddlejumper parked within eyeshot of his house was a
personal affront. And any son of his caught up in this idiotic fad was
a professional embarrassment and an ingrate. No, make that a viper
nursing at his breast.

Sorry, T.C., but I was too far gone. If my deviant automotive beliefs brought family exile and martyrdom, so be it. Sports cars by now
more than dominated my life; they were the prism through which I
saw life. It was all so clear. If only everything were as enlightened and
creative and bold—as fresh—as the sports car; what a wonderful
world it would be.

A year or so later, the liberation signified by a driver's license was
a tangible and even more urgent automotive goal. Driving anything
had mushroomed from an ambition to an imperative. I'd even suspend my purity of soul and man the wheel of T.C.'s Detroit blun-
derbuss if necessary. It was necessary. Novice drivers under twenty
are seldom bombarded by keys to other people's cars. Once attained,
of course, the official sanction of a license to drive turned into a
greedy need for more and more driving, far more than the odd quick
spin in the old man's sedan could ever satisfy. There was no alternative. I had to have a car.

Like everyone else, I dreamed of nestling into the all-conquering
new Jaguar XK-120, or lording it over all mankind in an Aston
Martin, or lording it over even Aston Martins in a Bentley Conti-
nental. What I settled for was three hundred and fifty dollars' worth
of Ford Anglia, a tinny little thirty-horsepower relic of prewar English economy-car design barely gripping the lowest known rung of

automotive status, barely good for 63 MPH in a strong tailwind, homely as a meat loaf, stark as a monk's cell.

Hugh was half-owner; only by pooling our puny resources could we aspire even to an Anglia. We tended it as if it were a Rolls. Feeling at least halfway certified for admission to the sports car fraternity, we bought Kangol driving caps and mesh-backed driving gloves and long woolen English scarves. We enrolled in the local sports-car club, joining our fellow zealots one evening per month at the local Grange Hall to watch films of the Monte Carlo and Redex Round Australia rallies of three or four years before. We drove in Sunday rallies. I became editor of *The Crankshaft Journal,* the club newsletter, and turned it into a screed packed with anti-Detroit polemics and almost no news. If T.C. had ever seen an issue I'd have been disinherited on the spot.

Six months into the giddy experience of car ownership, Hugh and I worked up the nerve to drive the Anglia all the way from Windsor to Toronto, 240 miles across table-flat southwestern Ontario. We rolled to a stop six hours later in Toronto, as flushed with triumph as Lindbergh landing at Le Bourget. But a genteel year behind the wheel of the Anglia was enough. Hormones and the lure of the sports car ever more insistently churned, and driving this thing was like dating a nun. Back to the used-car bazaar in search of something more robust.

If it had been a dog at the A.S.P.C.A., that used 1953 Morgan Plus Four would have had to be put down. Morgans had always been an idiosyncratic footnote in the annals of the sports car, crafted in the low hundreds annually by an old family-run English firm where the clock of technological progress had stopped dead around 1923. The archetypal Morgan was old-fashioned going on antediluvian, from its part-wood chassis to its mid-thirties bodywork. It was hard-riding and spartan. But its rarity and character, its very primitivism, gave it cachet wherever aficionados gathered. The Mog: sui generis.

Our Mog proved to be a thousand-dollar investment in disillusion and heartache. Only after it was legally too late did Hugh and I discover that its previous backyard-mechanic owner had planed the head

of the Standard four-cylinder engine in a misguided effort to boost
its power. Maybe he'd used a wood plane. The job was bungled; the
engine was sick. The four-speed manual transmission snatched and
jammed in every gear. The electrical system's frequent short-outs
vouched for the notorious nickname of its maker, Lucas: Prince of
Darkness. The frame flexed so violently over bumps and potholes
that the hood and doors popped open.

But at least it wasn't an M.G. The mass-market sports car world
of the time formed a competing, all-English trinity of M.G., Austin-
Healey, and Triumph that engendered a partisanship as fierce as that
among Muslim, Jew, and Hindu. I viewed the new M.G.-A as a char-
acterless sop to know-nothing American dilettantes, Austin-Healey
as an overpriced lounge lizard's sports car, and the stumpy Triumph
TR-3 as doughty underdog, sans pedigree but by far the best
performance-for-dollar buy extant. Hugh's and my English-born
friend Mike Barber disagreed. He had just taken delivery of a brand-
new M.G.-A.

With its Triumph-built engine, the Morgan was at least lineally
part Triumph. Honor demanded a showdown. Purring new M.G.-A
and lumpy-idling Morgan Plus Four met side by side on an unopened twenty-mile stretch of the new Highway 401 outside Windsor one blustery December Sunday afternoon. It was a rolling start
in a flat-out, straight-line run from standstill to valve float. And may
the car with the higher maximum speed win.

The torquier Morgan shot ahead, but by 70 MPH Mike's M.G. had
drawn abreast. I mashed foot to floor and held it there. One car
length, two car lengths; the M.G. receded. My engine's rising scream
now leveled off to a steady shriek and the speedometer reading leveled off at 90 MPH. Had it been in working order, the Morgan's
tachometer needle would by now be nudging into the red zone. Suddenly a vicious, ripping noise and howling cockpit turbulence: the
weather-beaten canvas roof had just sheared itself in two, straight
down the middle, and co-driver Hugh grappled with the flapping
remnants. Then, seconds later, a shudder, a clatter, and suddenly only
the sound of the wind and the co-owners' whimpers as the speedome-

ter needle arced backward from 80 to 60 to 40 toward 0 and the powerless Morgan rolled to a stop.

The damage assessment was the Morgan's autopsy. "She's thrown a rod," explained Bert, the kindly Yorkshireman proprietor of British Motorcycles & Cars. Resuscitating it would cost quadruple what the corpse was worth. We withdrew to the corner desk in Bert's Hogarthian pit of a garage to mull our options.

Bert happened to be an authorized Triumph dealer, and an hour later Hugh and I emerged the co-owners of a spanking new 1956 Triumph TR-3 in British racing green. Avuncular Bert's willingness to extend generous terms, and our ability to rationalize when it came to money and cars, had lofted us from the slums to the near pinnacle. The penury threatened by the monthly payments would be worth it. The new-car smell alone rendered Hugh and me almost drunk. We drove home in triumph in our new Triumph, insisting that even T.C. take it out for a spin. He came back shaking his head in condescending amusement, but what the hell did he know? A day with a new Triumph TR-3 was better than a night with Ava Gardner. How could two guys be so lucky?

Twenty-four hours later, with the TR-3 a crumpled ball of wreckage steaming in a cornfield near London, Ontario, I felt lucky to be alive. I'd been creeping along roads glazed by black ice and powdered with windblown snow, en route to celebrate New Year's Eve in Toronto with my friend Dave, when a car towing a trailer lumbered off a side road and directly into my path. The Triumph hit a patch of glare ice just as I reflexively stomped the brake pedal and started a long, lazy spin, and an oncoming Oldsmobile did the rest. The Olds had hit smack on the passenger side and smashed through almost to the transmission tunnel. If Hugh had been with me, he'd probably have been killed. This was of scant solace. The Triumph was a total write-off. I felt as if a newborn baby had died.

But sports-car life must continue. The insurance check bought TR-3 number two. Why it didn't also end up in the scrapyard, and I in the morgue, is a question perhaps best left alone. I'd regularly steal away in it to thunder over the back roads of Essex County, sickening myself with fear, careening along far too fast for my skills. Speed is narcotic to the young, and I became an addict. What an obnoxious jerk I must have been to my fellow drivers, what a pathetic show-off, what a public nuisance. But then, a sports-car driver was supposed to be. And the stiff cost of the TR-3 was being at least emotionally amortized. I was now a certified top-down-in-December, foot-to-the-floor, give-and-ask-no-quarter, bravura sports-car driver.

A year into my seniority, indeed, the joys of Triumph driving were starting to wane. Fast car, strong car—for its price and class—but after all, still only a common Triumph. Drivers of my sophistication hankered for a more challenging steed.

The risk of financial suicide was once again brushed aside. Hugh and I, for only a few dollars more per month, could graduate to the inner circle of sports-car connoisseurship. We could own a ruby-red 1956 Porsche 356 coupe, barely used—and by an anal-compulsive engineer at that. And one hasty session of breathtaking rationalizations later, we did. Porsches were a bold enough departure from conventional sports-car design of the day to seem almost Martian: rear-engined, air-cooled, soft-sprung, sinuously round and flowing of shape. Their designer and namesake, Dr. Ing. Ferdinand Porsche, former engineering chief of Mercedes-Benz, creator of the Volkswagen (and the Tiger Tank), was a genius. The Porsche did carry one minor liability. It was German, and T.C. disliked the Germans. No, he despised them, and all their works, babies, and puppies included, with every fiber of his being.

The Porsche relationship proved to be, even for Hugh and me, a strange one. In our hearts we knew it was too good a car, too fine an object, to be wasted on the likes of us. Porsche owners were famed for their perfectionism; we were slobs. We had it repainted German racing silver, and the job was botched. I ran it in the grueling Canadian Winter Rally and smashed it into a fencepost in the middle of a blizzard in the middle of the night. No sooner had it been patched together again than I missed a shift during a local time trial, cracked the bell housing and, being out of work and lacking anywhere near the price of repair, finally surrendered.

The enforced demotion to a VW Beetle drew the curtains on act one of my sports-car saga. I would climb the sports-car ladder from the bottom up a second time, but maturity would make it a mellower journey. By then I had long before cast aside my driving gloves, my hoard of car magazines, my lust to go fast for the sheer thrilling sake of going fast. I sometimes shudder at the energy and passion I poured into the cause of the sports car, day after day, for years. I shudder more to think where all that energy and passion might otherwise have gone.

DOWN BUT NOT OUT

I looked down from my studio window on Emperor Haile Selassie of Ethiopia in the course of his state visit, and Queen Elizabeth II and Prince Philip on theirs. I once stood this far from Paul Whiteman, the ineptly yclept King of Jazz, in a drugstore, and late one clear winter night while walking home from a movie I watched a flying saucer hover for half an hour before an airliner approached and it zoomed away at about half the speed of light.

Remarkably little else of interest crossed my life's horizon in the Windsor years. All the more incentive to exercise the inner resources. There was barely a time in that fallow era when I was not partnered with the mind of one or another author in the adventure of one or another book. Diversion and entertainment, naturally; but—at least as alluring—education. My shallow dive through high school's intellectual depths had left both a sense of mental depletion and the urgent desire to correct it. Reading became self-improvement. History, biography, and a peppering of the classics promised to plug the most glaring holes.

The more I read, of course, the more it fed the compulsion to write. Lacking the faintest idea of who I was, I lacked even the rudiments of a style of my own, with the result that I usually took on the style of whoever I happened to be reading at the time. This no doubt baffled and amazed the recipients of the long, dense, lovingly composed letters that served as my chief writing outlet. One week a few pages from Hemingway; the next, Thurber; the next, Churchill or Robert Lewis Taylor or Mackinlay Kantor.

With the other hand, so to speak, I persevered in drawing: in another tiny bedroom, with the same crowded desktop as in the Toronto days the focal point, with all too similar motivation for tunneling deep into my own psychic recesses. Drawing solely for my own relief and pleasure now smacked of onanism. Still far too diffident to even dream of trying to market my personal visions professionally, I satisfied myself by sending them to friends. Developing skill and polish—I was now more than a ten-year veteran at it—made my handiwork a bit harder for the addressees to throw away, but I still had to pick my targets with care. Not for everyone, these gnarled, dark, mercilessly detailed vignettes of low or desperate lives.

I was, as usual, primarily writing those letters and drawing those pictures not for the pleasure of my friends but to try to soothe and unkink myself. In this I was pursuing a form of self-therapy at the same time, in the same place, and in essentially the same way as Hugh in the room beside me and Walt just across the hall.

Odd ducks the three of us, by almost any definition of the norm. But I think, in retrospect, that what most sharply differentiated Hugh and Walt and me from our contemporaries—and most of the world—was that we preferred to be senders more than receivers, that we manufactured far more entertainment than we bought or passively consumed. And in the making of it we not only fought to keep our demons at bay but gradually, almost haphazardly, drew forth and nurtured something that would far outlive the need to produce or perish and reward the three of us, in different ways, more than almost anything else in our lives.

The endless standoff with T.C. left the natural desire for paternal attention and approbation hanging. Mother could not be lured out from her self-created limbo more than an inch or two at a time. Enter T.C.'s own second-in-command in the Chrysler public relations department, his old air force crony Don Tucker, and his jolly and maternal English-born wife, Madelaine.

The Tuckers had much to recommend them: no kids of their own, hospitality unbounded, a preference for Django Reinhardt over Guy Lombardo, and an infinite willingness to listen as Hugh and I, overlapping each other in our eagerness to vent our rage, blabbed ourselves hoarse on Friday nights with our anti-T.C. diatribes at their dinner table and later, until the wee hours, in the den of their suburban Windsor house. Worldly, wisecracking Don had another heady attraction: true-life anecdotes from his wartime experience as a navigator in the R.C.A.F. bomber group. It still puzzles me what diversion a middle-aged couple might have found in two lost souls in their early twenties, but we became better friends with the Tuckers than we had ever been with our parents.

T.C. couldn't overtly block the relationship, but this chumminess of ours with the Tuckers was not to his liking. We had halfway stolen away two of his and Mother's close friends. Whether it was connected or not I never knew; but their friendship thereafter did wither, and within a year or so, Don had left Chrysler and the Tuckers had left town.

We had few Windsor friends of our own age—one, to be precise. He was Mike Barber, son of a postwar English immigrant and co-enthusiast with Hugh of the sport of cycling. I had neither the interest in cycling nor the bike to ride even if I did, but we became a threesome after I'd horned in. Mike was upbeat, energetic, and full of ideas, all of them exactly opposite to mine. I'm not sure we even much liked each other, but neither was exactly inundated by alternatives, and the political and philosophical debates-turned-squabbles that seemed to erupt within five minutes of our laying eyes on one another were more interesting than another evening in T.C.'s taut living room, watching Lawrence Welk.

Sports cars, driving them, and myriad related diversions burgeoned in Windsor. The sports car's value as a girlfriend substitute—don't let's be coy, as a subliminal sexual outlet—has not yet been dealt with in the clinical literature as fully as it deserves. Hugh and I had always used the movies as cheap escape, an excuse to get out of the house for an evening, without exercising any particular discrimination. We found the magic of great movies one night when a neighborhood bijou inexplicably replaced its standard cheesy Hollywood bill of fare with *Citizen Kane*. It was but a short step to foreign films, shown to fervent clutches of fifties cultural deviants in one or another suburban Detroit art theater, and a not much longer step from there to the awakening of a whole new and exciting realm of possibilities.

High school–dropout–turned–pilgrim, I had made it across a river and stumbled onto the great plain leading to the foothills of something that at its higher elevations was called culture. To T.C.'s ever-lengthening list of my shortcomings, he could now add "effete snob."

COLLAPSE

Sputnik's sudden appearance in the heavens in the fall of 1957 may have rendered a dispiriting jolt to the free world, but at 1793 Byng Road things were cautiously looking up.

T.C.'s congenital petulance seemed to be in temporary remission, and Mother hadn't arrived drunk at dinner in weeks. That hypertense household was experiencing, for the first time in memory, something tantalizingly close to normalcy. It was still too early and fragile to trust, but after a month or more of almost hourly checks of the situation, I had begun to allow myself a measure of relief.

One particular after-dinner Sunday evening in mid-November was normalcy itself. I sat upstairs at my drawing board, finishing the latest assignment from the Famous Artists Schools correspondence course. Hugh read, Walt fussed with his umpteenth fire-truck model of the week, Chris pored over her homework, and the parents, downstairs in the living room, were tuned in as usual to their regular Sunday night TV fest of Jack Benny, *The Ed Sullivan Show,* and *What's My Line?*

Suddenly silence, followed by sounds of an unusual commotion. I raced downstairs to find Mother doubled up in her chair and T.C. on the phone, calling an ambulance. She was in terrible pain, and walking around or lying down gave no relief. Within minutes T.C., Hugh, Walt, Chris, and I were milling helplessly around the stricken, moaning victim. The ambulance was taking forever. Finally it arrived, and Mother was taken away on a stretcher, with T.C. following in his car.

It had all happened so fast. Those of us left to wait at home, hearts racing, spent the next several hours bouncing from room to room and chair to chair in varying states of clammy panic, waiting for word from the hospital. We tried to dispel or submerge our fears by reassuring one another with medical hypotheses—digestive upset, probably; maybe severe gas; ruptured appendix—that desperately skirted what each of us secretly dreaded. At about 3:00 A.M. T.C. returned home and we gathered for the news. He sat looking down at the floor and spoke even more tersely than usual, as if the more words he used, the less he could maintain self-control. A ruptured aorta . . . extremely serious . . . the best doctors . . . resting comfortably . . . more information tomorrow, now let's all get some rest.

She was "stabilized" the next day, and an eminent expert was being flown in. Soon twenty-four hours had passed since the attack, and she was still alive. I allowed my hopes to sneak upward a smidgeon. There was nothing for any of us to do but wait and, meanwhile, go through the motions of everyday life. But concentration on anything but that tiny figure clinging to life in her hospital bed, by who knew how fragile a thread, was not only impossible—it was almost obscene.

Chris, age fourteen, held herself together somehow, and her example shamed the rest of us into at least a semblance of sangfroid. Alone in bed in the dark, however, I gave in to the terror and despair inside me and forced myself, scene by excruciating scene, to imagine the worst.

Tuesday morning, Hugh and I were allowed a hospital visit—another favorable omen. There she was, seemingly more annoyed than gravely ill, wisecracking about hospital food and her stupid gown. That was all it took. We had been so overwrought. We weren't accustomed to medical scares. It would be a battle, but Mother would pull through.

Back to the studio and a regular workday. A measure of calm, even optimism, had returned. T.C. was taking no chances and stayed at the hospital virtually full-time.

It was six in the morning on Wednesday when he returned and gathered us together in the living room where Mother had been struck sixty hours and several lifetimes ago. His mood was almost relaxed; his energy, drained during the past couple of days, seemed restored.

Your mother, he said, died during the night. The damage had been too great; there was nothing the doctors could do. She had gone peacefully, without pain. Here T.C. paused, and as if this were a signal that the point had finally been reached, that it was all right now, that it wouldn't be held against us, all of us began to cry. He was near the end of his self-control, but with one massive deep breath he recovered to finish what he had to say. The funeral would be in Simcoe in a couple of days.

Helen Margaret Gilbertson "Peg" McCall was forty-nine years old.

In the unbearably long and hollow days that immediately followed I attempted to comfort Chris, but the best I could manage was to try and drug her a few minutes at a time with *Reader's Digest* platitudes and whatever thirdhand wisdom I might have randomly acquired from reading and the movies. Who was I to console Chris or anybody? "Mother" and "death," arguably the two most emotionally charged ideas extant, had collided, and the repercussion collapsed the antipain defense system I had believed invulnerable, and I was lost.

We all were lost, but none of us more than T.C. The sudden snatching away of his wife, lover, friend, partner, confidante, the mother of his children, his high school sweetheart of thirty years' standing, turned T.C. overnight into a figure of pity. He now faced what I believe he had never realized before: It was Peg—her sacrifices, her tolerance of his selfishness and whims, her absorbing the dirty work, the knowledge that she would always be there to comfort and console him—who had underwritten his own existence all those years, allowed him the freedom to rampage through life doing whatever the hell he wanted while she dealt with the consequences. The props had been truly knocked out from under him. He never managed to reassemble them. After a brief, halfhearted effort, he never even bothered to try.

For the first time in his life he now needed us, but we could do little to comfort him. The gulf he had created over all those years of intimacy denied was too vast. I'm ashamed in retrospect at how little I even tried. More often than not in the strange months immediately following Mother's death, his fumbling suggestions for taking in a movie or dining out, his sudden interest in my life and career, were met with the same cold indifference I had learned from him. He had never let me in. Why should I now pretend to be his pal?

No doubt partly because Hugh, Walt, Chris, and I were each still groping so desperately for emotional footholds ourselves, none of us was impelled to greatly exert ourselves on his behalf. His hurt and anger at the rebuff took the form of withdrawal, and life at Byng Road, never exactly boisterous, assumed the impersonality of a boardinghouse.

In time, he no longer bothered with face-to-face encounters. We would mount the stairs to our rooms after an evening at work to find individual crisp copies of neatly typed memos placed on our beds: terse, stinging reviews of whatever real or imagined transgression had most recently offended him.

Within a year he had found his way to Simcoe and Eleanor Beale, an old friend from youth and a recent divorcee. They shared memories and loneliness, and a couple of months later he announced that they would be married. It seemed right and proper. We all liked Eleanor, as modest and witty as Mother herself. Marriage, all agreed, would be good for both of them. But deep down I was enraged, and so too, I found, were most of my siblings. The Stepmother Syndrome gained momentum, fast. Nobody could replace Mother. It was far too soon even to try.

Perhaps this reaction and the coolness it engendered served to beat T.C. down. Perhaps he himself couldn't move on from memories of his thirty-odd years with Peg. In any event, the trips to Simcoe suddenly stopped. It was quietly let to be known that the marriage was off.

From then on, T.C. simply gave up. Chris had been packed off to board at the Bishop Strachan school in Toronto. Hugh and I had finally declared our independence and moved to our own apartment, a decision made easier by the increasingly dire state of life with T.C. We barely bothered making conversation anymore. In the silence of night, night after night in that flimsy little house, I could hear his grieving sobs, and the sound of such inconsolable misery was unnerving. Starting afresh in some less haunted place promised not only independence but escape.

T.C. went apathetically through the motions of a life alone. Golf and his other hobbies lost their appeal. He got fatter and careless about his housekeeping and the appearance in which he had always taken such pride. His only recreation was nostalgia for his life with Peg, which he made a project, tape-recording hour upon hour of reminiscences, a narrative of his and their life against a background of sentimentally evocative music.

In August 1959 he decided to take a vacation trip to a resort in Quebec and to take Chris with him. The first stop was Toronto and an evening with his good friends the Waddells. He and Chris returned late that night to their hotel and their shared single room and went to bed. An hour or so later Chris was awakened by a cry. T.C. sat up in his bed, clutched his chest, and died.

Thomas Cameron "T.C." McCall was forty-nine years old.

In the immediate aftermath of his sudden passing, the newspaper obituaries offered a soothing epitaph—T.C.'s career résumé, his war service, his six progeny, the untimely end of a solid, honorable, productive life. And for a while, such a simple and straightforward summary seemed the only proper one. He was gone; respect alone called for all the anger, the bitterness, the conflict, to be put behind at last. Rest in peace, as they say.

But the enigma of T.C. would not rest—not for long, not in my mind. As the shock and pain of his death receded, mourning gave way to the need for a more balanced judgment of the man under whose rule I had lived my whole life. I dared to think forbidden thoughts. I conjured an alternative epitaph.

His thirty years' war with his own life, his compulsion from the onset of adulthood to invest the best of himself elsewhere, knowing it could only mean the ruin of any hope for a normal family life, and that it would be left to his wife and kids to bear so much of the cost—what had it profited him in the end? What had been the point? He had lost Peg early, in no small part through his own selfishness and neglect. Never had he faced the facts of her alcoholism and depression, much less attempted to intervene for the sake of her and her children. And all that busyness of his, the self-granted ten-year hiatus from home and fatherhood, the work and worry in the name of a career, had won him a series of booby prizes—jobs that frustrated far more than they ever fulfilled him. And his famous industry and dedication and loyalty had always been bought cheap: In the end, he had lifted himself only slightly from where he'd begun, to a feeble grip on the lower rungs of the middle class. He had his golf club membership and his expensive cameras; but he could never afford a new car, a proper vacation for Peg and himself—much less for the whole family—or more than a minimum of life's comforts and conveniences for his wife or his family. The net of that thirty years of toil, his estate, amounted to the half-paid mortgage on a less-than-modest house, a small life insurance policy, some worn-out furniture, a set of Wilson golf clubs, a stamp collection, a few good suits, a typewriter, and his cameras. If he'd just hunkered down in Simcoe and become editor of the *Reformer*, he'd have ended up materially far better off than that. And the unrelenting emotional stress and physical self-abuse of the distorted life he had invented for himself were instrumental in cutting him down in what should have been his prime.

When we came back to the house in Windsor after the funeral in Simcoe, his stamp paraphernalia still lay spread out on the living room coffee table; his martini shaker sat on the kitchen counter; his bed was unmade; his mail lay there unopened. It took less than a day to banish all vestiges of his last desolate days and the last painful reminders of his intimate physical existence. It would take years to dispel the sense of bobbing helplessly in his wake.

INTO THE ABYSS

In the fall of 1959 I was not only an orphan but an orphan about to join the breadlines.

This came as more of a shock than it should have. The assistant manager of Baghdad's third-largest sign shop was probably more attuned to commercial art and advertising trends than anybody at Windsor Advertising Artists. Neither I nor anyone else shackled to the timeless ox-wheel of life at the corner of Pelissier and University had noticed until too late that our craft was about to go the way of the antimacassar and the stovepipe hat. Advertising didn't need illustrators to lower and lengthen and prettify cars anymore: The stylists were now doing it at the source, so all the admen needed to do was photograph the longer, lower, sleeker new Bulgemobile for 1960.

The news that Dodge and DeSoto were going photographic came out of the blue in June 1959, just as the studio was gearing up again for the annual mad scramble of catalogue season. There would be no mad scramble this summer, or ever again. Overnight W.A.A., its craftwork, and its tiny guild of artisans had become obsolete. On the bright side, it meant the first summer in six years with weekends off and no rushing back to the office weeknights before sunset. But the looming shadow of unemployment robbed my new freedom of its pleasure. By July, the scraps of color-photo-retouching work tossed the studio's way weren't even enough to fill Rudy's time sheet. The rest of us were left to mill and wonder and wait. The passengers on the *Titanic* must have experienced similar feelings of shock and help-lessness on that night to remember. For those of us in that doomed suite of rooms at Pelissier and University in Windsor, as for them, the thought of the whole thing sinking—and sinking fast—had simply never occurred.

By Labor Day, after T.C.'s funeral and as Hugh and I moved back to 1793 Byng Road, I could feel the water starting to lap around my ankles. Dismal as it might be, this was the only job I'd ever had, my familiar little cubicle the only refuge from the harsh, real outside world. T.C.'s pathological fear of joblessness and lectures on the topic were rebroadcast nightly from the grave, in stereo. The cost of six years squandered on half learning a dead-end trade was suddenly, mercilessly coming due.

Rudy thrashed about in a belated effort to reconstitute the studio and stay afloat, but there was no demand for our kind of service in Windsor or Detroit or anywhere else. There was one long shot: A big Toronto studio had expressed mild interest in taking Windsor Advertising Artists on a sort of trade, in exchange for what remained of Rudy's hold on Dodge–DeSoto art business and whatever profit might still be milked from it.

Large, taciturn men duly appeared in the studio one evening, to huddle with Rudy and then to examine our portfolios one by one, in person, the way a prospective buyer examines a horse's teeth. My samples were sifted in silence. Shock or awe? The latter, I decided. I had to. This deal was the lifeline, all that could keep me from plunging into the bottomless void of unemployment and disgrace.

Negotiations lumbered through October and into November. Rudy threw us periodic tidbits, vague reports nonetheless pounced upon like chicken entrails for omens. A coward dies a thousand deaths; I must have been up to about 5,063 when Rudy finally gathered the four-man staff in the waiting room at dusk one Friday in mid-December. This was it. I realized that I had never counted how many brown and yellow squares there were in that linoleum floor. I kept my eyes down and the count running as Rudy delivered the news. I now found myself somehow under water as well, so the droning voice came from far away, ebbing and receding, difficult to follow with the loud hum in my ears. Studio closing end of month . . . going to Toronto . . . can't take anybody . . . couple of weeks' pay . . . help clean up this place.

Two hundred and twenty brown squares; 226, yellow. Better do a recount—that seems off. And if I heard it right, as of December 31, 1959, I was going to be out of work, on my own, and probably, within six months, a hobo.

Hugh and I arose uncustomarily late the next morning to move silently through the motions of the first day of the rest of our blasted lives. What did out-of-work people do with their time? Tidy up the house, evidently, read the paper, nap, all the while trying to find their bearings amid the sudden sense of infinite empty space stretching away in all directions, including under the feet.

Lodging at 1793 Byng was rent-free; the estate was paying the mortgage until probate. Hugh and I had three hundred dollars in cash between us and the poorhouse. Tomorrow or the next day or the day after that—it was never supposed to have come to this for the proud McCalls. Thank God T.C. never lived to see the day—we would have to endure the humiliation of queuing up in line at the unemployment office for our weekly dole.

The shame of being jobless was a burden more onerous than any practical consequences. It would take weeks to crawl out from under it, to work up the nerve to start scanning the want ads, much less start making the rounds. I retired to bed for most of the next few weeks, rising only to wallow in late-night-talk therapy with Jane or Alex while sitting in a car sipping hot chocolate at the Big Boy Drive-In, a neutral site. Limbo had no directional signs. I was no savvier than a high school kid about where and how to trade my slender skills for a paycheck; for all I'd learned about the commercial-art business in those years at Windsor Advertising Artists, I might as well have spent them spelunking. I didn't even know anybody to ask for advice.

The New Year arrived, and the start of a new decade. I was lying prone on the living room sofa, watching the *Million Dollar Movie* and killing another dateless January afternoon, when some membrane deep in the back of my mind was suddenly breached and the truth rushed in. Goddammit, I knew I had no earthly right, but I felt good. I felt better than I had on my best day in the past six years. For the first time in my life I felt free. T.C. was gone. His ghost had lifted, and with it his power over me. His house of zones packed in perpetual tension was dissolved; 1793 Byng Road was now just a place. And his pathology was no longer the law. Jesus, the man had been wrong. No job at all was in fact healthier than the joyless treadmill of that studio leeching away my spirit and my time and teaching me nothing I wanted or needed to know. This state of being wasn't disgrace, it was freedom. And I had enough money for cigarettes and Pepsis and gas for the car. What more did I really need?

Thus commenced six of the most agreeable months in my twenty-five years. Breaking forms releases energy, McLuhan or somebody once said, and those six months could stand as proof. Hugh and I threw ourselves into remaking the household. We blitzed the place. For the price of a few cans of paint, a few yards of fabric, much elbow grease, and some minor demolition, the shabbiness and ennui of years were dispelled in a couple of weeks. That once run-down bungalow glowed. I wrote and illustrated an article—a sneering satire on car nuts called "The Aficianados" (complete with misspelling)—and this time submitted it for publication. Bingo! A sale! A mere twenty-five dollars, from the barely readable *Canada Track & Traffic* at that, but self-esteem like mine was too hungry to be choosy. I read my piece over and over in a daze of admiration and wonder at my first published work, and positioned that ratty *Track & Traffic* on the coffee table just so, as if it were a hundred-dollar book on French châteaux.

Up in his improvised bedroom atelier, meanwhile, Hugh was filling at least some of his empty time with productive work. He'd made a connection with a young New York editor who needed a batch of illustrations for the book he was writing on automotive design. Hugh got no money up-front, but if a publisher was found, he'd be paid for his efforts.

A real living, working New York editor! As a published writer, I was now not only drawn but entitled to the company of literary professionals, and in short order I had shouldered Hugh aside and taken up a correspondence with his New York contact. It was less a correspondence, in fact, than my plea for long-distance editorial advice and tutoring. What a good sport he was, patiently reading and commenting on the shapeless reams of prose inflicted on him week after week. What, if any, craft lessons I might have absorbed from the exchange are lost to memory. That didn't really matter. To intersect with a professional when I was so immediately out of the starting gate as a writer—that was what mattered. And if not wildly encouraging, neither had he been overtly discouraging. I had been pulled across some invisible line. I was no longer a would-be, an amateur, a dilettante. I was now a serious writer.

Spring brought hope, or perhaps idleness now spanning nearly six months brought guilt; but in March I began my earnest search for work. Oh, darn. There didn't seem to be any. Two or three forays to Toronto and the major commercial art studios elicited varying degrees of polite apathy. Well, I'd tried. Meanwhile I conjured up fresh, nonautomotive samples in an improvised bedroom atelier, and drove in blissful aimlessness around Essex County on soft April afternoons. Baseball was back, and the Stanley Cup playoffs were in full swing. Call me a family black sheep, a dropout, a bum, but my cup runneth over. I didn't care if I ever had a job again.

Part IV

OBSCURITY'S

EMBRACE

TORONTO REDUX

My luck couldn't hold forever. In June 1960 appeared the dread specter of employment, beckoning me to the drawing board again at a Toronto commercial art studio willing to trust—at a munificent $125 a week, no less—that despite my satchel full of mediocre automobile renderings, there lurked in me a productive professional hand.

The chains that had bound me for seven years to Windsor were struck at last. And Toronto this second time around would be different, because I was different—a wage-earning adult free to follow my own destiny, doubly energized by the move from the center of nothing to the center of Canada. My own apartment, my own life, in the big city: Ah, so that was the master plan. Everything before had been just a kind of hazing. Life begins at twenty-five.

Windsor Advertising Artists hadn't prepared me for the commercial-art big leagues. My arrival at work in the studio on Yonge Street that first Monday morning was unheralded to the point of going unnoticed. Rudy, Nick, and Wilf had at least said good morning. "McCall, is it?" The office manager, Les, convincingly disguising his euphoria at my advent, conducted me through a hangar-size open space, more humming fluorescent-lit mill room than tranquil studio, and pointed to the one empty spot in a long row of drawing boards. No cozy room of my own, not even a cubicle. The nearest window was thirty feet away. This would require some adjustment.

I had no sooner adjusted the height of my chair than Les handed me the day's assignment—an oil can, full color, need it fast. No tot lost in a train station ever felt so alone. An all too familiar taste of panic simultaneously arrived. I hadn't even found my bearings yet. Where was the john? Who were all these guys jabbering and clowning around even as they worked? And, anyway, how do you paint an oil can? I was a Car Man. Wasn't there an Oil Can Man around somewhere? What if I screw up, first try?

The first hitch had arisen in my bold new life. It would be only the first in a rapid hiccup of hitches, creating the strong suspicion that Toronto hadn't finished with me quite yet.

I was blasting down Oriole Parkway in my tiny Austin-Healey Sprite one Saturday afternoon a couple of weeks later, brooding upon my fourth try at the oil can, when my train of thought was violently interrupted by two tons of Ford. We collided almost head-on. I should have been erased from the face of the earth, but God had clearly spared me to finish that oil can. Albeit limping Frankenstein-style and wearing a turban of medical gauze, I was sufficiently repaired a few days later to stump back to the drawing board for try number five.

Try number five was never to be, at least not in my hands. Mustering as decent an imitation of sincere regret as circumstances allowed, Les called me in minutes after my arrival to deliver what could only come as a vast relief to both parties. Sorry, Bruce, but the studio—sudden slack times, last in first out, you know how it is— anyway, well, in the time-honored phrase, they were going to have to let me go. And without rancor, I went.

My plan for reconquering the Queen City had gotten a bit off schedule early on. But unemployment was starting to show a pernicious knack for agreeing with me, and vice versa. Those years in Windsor—years without summers, without more than three weeks of vacation to punctuate the ennui from 1953 to 1959—had made idleness, once the strangeness and guilt wore off, more luxurious than wealth. I had time now to recover from my injuries, to repaint the living room of my lightless aerie on the second floor of a run-down little house on Millwood Road from suicide indigo to cheery peach, to sleep in and goof off as much as I wanted. It was a fuller life, this latest enforced lull, than I'd ever known in the working world. It gave me time, as summer yielded to a golden Ontario autumn, to take in every game of an exciting Yankees–Pirates World Series on TV every afternoon in those pre-nocturnal baseball days; to bone up on the upstart John F. Kennedy's campaign for the U.S. presidency; to read; and to lay plans for my next career.

I had decided to take to heart the broad hints lately delivered by commercial art. No hard feelings: If commercial art didn't need me, so what? I could finally admit that I had never liked it, either. On the other hand, career alternatives for a failed twenty-five-year-old Car Man with a partial high school education were not exactly dizzying in their variety. All I'd ever done besides draw for the past decade was write; ergo, by simple subtraction, writing was it.

The flyweight rented portable all but jitterbugged off the coffee-table-cum-dining-table-cum-desk. Glossing over the incidental fact that I had never worked a day in publishing, I announced to every known publication in the dominion of Canada my availability to consider offers for a journalistic position, commencing more or less immediately.

My direct-mail salvo stirred a brisk response. Publications rushed to decline my offer. October had long since withered into November when the money started running out. The phone was disconnected by now, and my Volvo sat idle for want of gas funds. Loud rustling noises from the kitchen late at night began to suggest that I had competition for the hot dogs and rolls on which I subsisted. It would be months, and the discovery of a good many pre-gnawed frankfurters and rolls later, before I happened upon the corpse of the mouse— drowned headfirst in a carton of molasses, poor wretch—that had waged that stealthy fight for food.

But against the minor, clearly temporary, and in any event merely physical irritations of joblessness and poverty were the infinitely more important pluses: I was young and free and not in Windsor, and poised on the brink of a new and exciting chapter in my life, blank though it might still be. And I had a typewriter and paper. Cadging letters now flowed forth. From Mike, from Hugh, from Aunt Eva in Simcoe, I extracted the occasional tens and twenties that were all I needed to make it through another couple of weeks or so if I was careful. So I'd be careful. It wasn't as if I'd had to suddenly climb down from some sybaritic summit, after all; a lifelong leanness in the area of creature comforts now stood me in good stead.

Not to mention a lifelong anti-despair strategy. The wider world receded once again. Life became the living room corner where I sat hunched over the typewriter from breakfast till late in the evening, swaddled in the old reliable refuge of telling myself weird and amazing stories to keep the bogeyman at bay. It worked, as it always had and always would. Isolation and privation and three bucks in the pocket might not be a sociologist's idea of an elixir, but they jump-started the imagination and sent it racing fast enough to outrun reality. The semi-delirious fantasies piled up around my ankles in reams.

I unhesitatingly recommend serendipity as a career starter. The last hot dog was about to be devoured the day a letter arrived, the first in weeks. It was from the editor of a trade magazine in Toronto. He couldn't offer me a job, but he was willing to talk to me if that would help.

I was sitting in his office within twenty-four hours. "Are you by chance related to Tom McCall?" I hadn't been there three minutes before it was established—small world, whattaya know, talk about coincidence—that the editor and T.C. had crossed paths and shared many a beer during the war. Say no more, young man! Any son of good old Tom McCall deserved all possible help. Maclean-Hunter, where we sat, was a Canadian publishing giant churning out dozens of monthly trade titles in addition to the consumer magazines *Maclean's* and *Chatelaine.* The editor would send me upstairs to talk to the director of editorial personnel.

"Are you by chance related to Tom McCall?" Fortune and Royd

Beamish, ex–Canadian Army press officer, wartime colleague of T.C.'s, were both smiling upon me. Two hours ago I'd been fighting a mouse for my next meal; now I was ensconced on a couch with a cup of coffee in my hand in a spacious office with Utrillo prints on the walls, overlooking University Avenue, the world about to be at my feet.

"Tell you what, Bruce. You just sit tight awhile. The first opening in our copy trainee program is yours. Tom McCall's boy. My God. Small world. Be in touch!"

There remained, of course, the minor detail of bridging that indefinite period between Royd Beamish's calling and my expiring of starvation. But once you get its attention, fortune doesn't fool around. Rescue came the next day. The want ad leapt out at me. The A. V. Roe Company, a former aviation power now reduced to stamping out vending machines and aluminum canoes, needed hack artists to churn out pamphlets and catalogues. A day later there I sat, one hack artist among scores, in a former drafting room in suburban Downsview retouching black-and-white photographs of the new A. V. Roe line of pots and pans.

It was a unionized shop, as the steward's visit quickly made apparent. That, and the torpid clock-watching sullenness of the place. Pettiness was job one. Sal the steward prowled the room in search of unfair practices or rules infractions. Unionization evidently meant that you didn't do a lick more work than you had to, that you memorized the rules and regulations and played them like a zither to avoid all possible exertion and responsibility, that you stretched your coffee break to the full fifteen minutes, and dropped everything at twelve noon and five o'clock on the dot. And Sal was there to ensure that you complied, like it or not.

By Thursday night of that first week at A. V. Roe, painting oil cans seemed an idyll and painting cars a dream of paradise. In four short days I'd slid all the way back down into ambition's basement, back down into anonymity among witless churls in the commercial art equivalent of a blacking factory. How long could I even . . . And the phone rang. "Royd Beamish here, Bruce. You can start Monday, if that's convenient?"

It was convenient. Landing a job you wanted pales by comparison with the pleasure of quitting a job you hate. The next day was triply glorious. I not only retired forever from commercial art and from A. V. Roe, but I gave a final finger by walking away with the take from that week's office lottery. Ten to one, Sal filed a grievance.

JOURNALIST

Life in Toronto in winter is cold and wet and slushy, and when the threads holding the soles to your only pair of shoes rot away and finally let go altogether, those soles not only flap with every footfall but become scoops, shoveling back cold water and treating the underside of your foot to an icy splash with every step.

This is not only uncomfortable for the wearer, but potentially degrading socially. It is incumbent upon a newly hired sixty-dollar-a-week trade magazine trainee, anxious for the acceptance and respect of his new colleagues, to maintain certain minimum standards of dress—i.e., not to look like a bum. My solution to the problem was ingenious, cheap, and effective. Each night before retiring I would uncap my thirty-nine-cent bottle of rubber cement, slather the flapping soles, and clamp them fast against the shoes with bindings fashioned from my two neckties, to dry and seal. If I stepped lively around puddles and otherwise exercised a modicum of precaution through the following day, the fix lasted almost exactly twenty-four hours.

It would be months before I could afford a new pair of shoes, much less a new sports jacket or suit to replace the worn and spotted examples in my modest wardrobe. But such concerns weighed lightly. My feet might be submerged in water now and then and I might be ill-clad by comparison with the hundreds of others who filed every morning into the Maclean-Hunter building on University

Avenue, but my new life as a writer was submerging me in only positive thoughts and feelings.

I was stationed at a desk in an open area on an upper floor of Maclean-Hunter, and I was on top of the world. The editorial milieu fit like a favorite cardigan almost from the minute I entered that room one December morning in 1960. This wasn't Windsor Advertising Artists or A. V. Roe, this wasn't the ox-slow pace, and these weren't the ox-dumb people. The Editorial Services Department of Maclean-Hunter hummed with purpose. My new office mates—Terry, fellow cub; Clyde, assistant manager; Jack, supervisor; Madelaine, secretary—spoke in complete sentences. They were friendly and helpful to one another and to me, and they laughed a lot.

And my job was to write. There wasn't a lowlier form of writing at Maclean-Hunter, or perhaps in all Toronto, than the kind plied by an Editorial Services trainee. The department was a catch basin for the periodic overflow of routine fare—new-product columns, industry personnel changes, and the like—from *Canadian Paint & Varnish*, *Canadian Pit and Quarry*, *The Canadian Baker*, and the twenty or so other M-H trade magazines hived on the office floors below. The intellectual challenge was manageable. It chiefly involved reducing piles of windy press releases into so many brief, brisk informational nuggets ostensibly useful to readers of *Canadian Paint & Varnish* et al., whoever they were.

I might as well have been minting "Talk of the Town" items for *The New Yorker*. The very idea that I was being paid to tickle the keys of a typewriter thrilled me. I was shot through with pride, and with determination to be the fastest, the most accurate, the best goddamn Editorial Services writer in Maclean-Hunter history. It was Editorial Services' good fortune to be providing typewriter and paper to a just-burst dam of writing energy, and my inconceivable good fortune to be actually encouraged to vent a pent-up lifelong urge. I couldn't write enough. Proper, formal English grammar and I were only passing strangers, but avid years of reading had honed my eyes and my ear. I thought I knew exactly how a decent English sentence was supposed to look and sound. I itched to blaze a verbal trail of pellucid, muscular prose that drew forth everything I knew and believed, every principle and every trick picked up and stored away over the years and now, suddenly, gloriously, the tools of my trade.

Nothing in life had ever come as easily to me as writing. Coming to Maclean-Hunter was coming home. To feel in my natural element after those fumbling, stumbling, half-assed years of futility in commercial art changed how life itself felt. I was no longer grimly hanging on, dragged wherever destiny chose to take me; I was in command. I was good at something, and because I was, I could hold up my head and look the world in the face.

It would be ten writing-filled years before I even picked up a paintbrush again, and even then, only in the nature of a hobby.

THE CANADIAN DRIVER

My friend in those yeasty early days back in Toronto—I seldom managed more than one at any time—was Eric, erstwhile Malvernite, compulsive smooth talker, hypnotizing weaver of intricate schemes, indefatigably cheerful companion, and fellow car nut. Our idea of a good time was to take our Volvos out on the roads near his trailer-size tract house on the outskirts of suburban Mississauga and chase each other at reckless speeds until one or the other's nerve failed. Our idea of an even better time was to sit around afterward to jaw about it, and about cars and racing and anything else connected with the world of cars.

Car magazines came in for discussion that inevitably escalated to dissection. Of course those monthly issues of *Autocar* and *Motor* from England, and *Road & Track* and *Sports Cars Illustrated* from the U.S., fed us the news and reviews and race reports that in our isolation we seized upon like P.O.W.s clawing at a Red Cross parcel. Humber offers automatic transmission on the Super Snipe! VW may produce a bigger Beetle! Corvette gets fuel injection!

But something in both of us—perhaps nothing more than our mutual infatuation with them—also responded to magazines as a creative and intellectual form. Debates about the relative merits of *Road & Track* and *Sports Cars Illustrated*, their editorial styles and star writers, were as frequent and as spirited as our opinions about the relative merits of Stirling Moss versus Phil Hill as Grand Prix driving talents, or the Alfa-Romeo Giuletta versus the Jaguar XK-150 as cars.

We'd never actually driven an Alfa or a Jag or actually seen Moss or Hill race, and maybe we never would. But out of the heat of our magazine blather it began to occur to us—dimly at first, then suddenly so clearly and obviously that little else mattered—that the way to publishing a car magazine of our own lay wide open.

Canada's car-minded millions, we decided, were being ill served by their sole magazine. The amateurish monthly *Canada Track & Traffic* had been around a year or so; bad, we agreed—laughable in comparison to its English and American models. And if anybody was capable of rescuing Canada's national car magazine honor, it was Eric and me.

You had to look beyond our formal credentials, true: Eric's professional status was somewhere between clerk and the juniormost of junior officers in a huge Toronto trust company. I was pulling down sixty dollars a week as a Maclean-Hunter editorial dogsbody.

But Eric's business acumen and my editorial genius, as we tirelessly reassured each other, only appeared to be lying dormant. They were simply awaiting a challenge worthy of them. And this was it. We could not only do better than *Track & Traffic.* We could do much better, and get rich, while wallowing in our dreamland world of cars.

Eric would raise the money and act as publisher while I handled the contents under the title of editor. It had to be only a part-time effort at first, but soon enough we'd plow *Track & Traffic* under and monopolize Canadian car journalism, and the rest would be magazine history.

Henry R. Luce and Briton Hadden had nothing on us. So in a kind of spontaneous combustion was Pegasus Publishing Ltd. formed and *The Canadian Driver* conceived, and so began our all-consuming second careers, pursued over weekends and lunch hours, in after-work bull sessions and the endless telephone bull sessions that followed them. We never revealed our imminent coup to the outside world, for fear that some publishing giant might steal the idea out from under us. And anyway, we were too far gone emotionally to have our illusions dashed by any outsider's common sense.

If we had had a shoestring, it would have been a shoestring operation. As it was, I wheedled the various talents of friends and acquaintances to design and fill the inaugural May issue, finding within myself talents for salesmanship and browbeating that had never surfaced before and haven't since. Eric, with a near mystical confidence that swept aside my every new doubt and worry like crumbs, busied himself with targeting potential angels.

Our business plan owed nothing to real-world magazine economics and everything to our bottomless ability, driven by need, to convince ourselves that whatever we wanted to believe was true. Advertising and newsstand proceeds from the first sensational issue of *The Canadian Driver* would finance issue two, and so on, until, by issue three—four at the very outside—ad and newsstand revenues would so exceed costs that *The Canadian Driver* would roar into the black and Eric and I could start ordering our new Aston Martin DB-3s.

Meanwhile, the editorial package was taking shape. It resembled a half-filled laundry bag. From the outset, I steered clear of hard news—news of any kind, in fact. *Road & Track* and my other car-magazine models were proving easier to analyze over the kitchen table than to emulate in print. The debut issue of *The Canadian Driver* was all too rapidly evolving into whatever an untrained twenty-six-year-old car freak could coax from his own brain while sitting alone at a typewriter without a news item, a file, or a fact in sight. Eric had begged the use of a Corvair from a dealer friend for two hours one Saturday afternoon; that would be the road test. Our road-testing equipment consisted of a borrowed stopwatch, which didn't discourage my writing a two-page article on *The Canadian Driver* road-test philosophy.

I found myself as surprised as the next man that the editorial mix for the first issue of Canada's hot new car magazine was already shaping up into a wan compendium of history, think-pieces, time-killers, space-fillers.

I could dilate for hours, in detail, on what a superior car magazine should editorially entail; the stumbling block was that I hadn't a clue as to how one went about achieving it. I had invented my job, not earned it, and not out of experience but out of daydreams. The editor-in-chief of Canada's bold, authoritative new car magazine faced the challenge of knowing nobody in the industry or the sports car and racing bodies that *The Canadian Driver* was ostensibly in business to serve; and in any event was much too diffident personally to approach them, not to mention too callow to know how.

This might have normally provoked a crisis. But by now, swept up as we were in the drama and the dream of publishing our very own car magazine, it hardly seemed to matter what its actual contents would or wouldn't be; the mere existence of *The Canadian Driver,* of such noble intent and sophisticated sensibility—Eric and Bruce, for God's sake, guys who lived and breathed sports cars, guys who had studied the best American and English car magazines the way medical students study spleens—would capture the loyalty of car-conscious Canadians from Cape Breton Island to Victoria, B.C., on sight and on faith.

Eric's money-raising efforts quickly revealed that the rich were indeed different from car-crazed would-be car magazine publishers like him and me: They couldn't care less. The originally lavish editorial budget began a weekly series of downward revisions. Well, we could do without a color cover after all; nah, the magazine didn't really need so many editorial pages at the outset; come to think of it, a full-time staff could wait. Our dreams of glory were still intact; so what if the smashing debut originally expected would have to be somewhat modified? Look at *Life* and *Time* and even *The New Yorker.* None of them was an overnight success, either. How shrewd of Eric and me to uncover that historic truth; even our setbacks were advances.

By March, only a few weeks before *The Canadian Driver's* scheduled debut—shrewdly geared to the annual postwinter boom in car interest and buying, thus sure to make a car magazine pure advertiser catnip—Eric finally hit paydirt. It was a molehill. The racing playboys, the venture capitalists, the bankers all lacked vision and nerve. He had found the necessary daring in a couple of similarly car-crazed Toronto brothers who were sufficiently generous, or at least gullible, to loan Pegasus Publishing enough of their modest recent family inheritance to fund most of issue number one, if we could tolerate further contractions of the original cost forecast. Of course we could! By now, promises had been made to friends about payment. A printer had been contracted. Frankly, it was now a bit too late to turn back.

Eric's fund-raising and my editorial burdens had left the vital task of advertising sales untended. No sweat. We had Nat, a genial Irishman, car mechanic, and part-time racing driver, who brought one matchless credential to the challenge of selling ads for *The Canadian Driver:* He was out of a job, and he'd work on commission.

Off went Nat, clutching a dummy issue of *The Canadian Driver* that bore no resemblance to the emaciated-looking little black-and-white version soon to go on press, to sell space. Back he came, with disturbing speed. To our dismay—not to mention poor Nat's—the expected advertisers instantly chose en masse to decline the honor of appearing in historic issue number one. Six weeks from D-Day, those multitudes of Canadian car enthusiasts pining for a quality magazine to call their own had proven of interest to no advertiser except for one Esso gas station/repair shop/Borgward dealer in the East End of Toronto, ready to splurge on a quarter-page black-and-white ad, at a price so far beyond discount as to be virtually gratis.

The dream was foundering fast. None of our editorial contributors had been paid; our puny grubstake would barely cover printing costs, and only if the magazine's pages were further reduced. We were evicted for nonpayment of rent from the dank little room we had rented as Pegasus Publishing world headquarters; the electric typewriter, also rented, was overdue to go back. And the two brothers were starting to ask questions.

Eric's response to the festering crisis was, literally, to whistle in the dark. Now, instead of mesmerizing me with new plans, new forecasts, new enthusiasm, he would hear my pleas—and whistle, as single-mindedly as he had formerly described bright horizons. Outright legal action was by now threatening Pegasus Publishing Ltd. from numerous creditors, who had discovered that *The Canadian Driver* might not in fact be quite as solidly moored financially as they had been given to believe. Eric had soon whistled himself all the way into denial; and when that could no longer be sustained, when it was obvious that *The Canadian Driver* was dead on arrival at the handful of newsstands witless enough to stock it, he simply vanished.

There would be no second issue of *The Canadian Driver.* Its sole distinction was to be the least-noted event in the history of Canadian magazines.

WORLD'S WORST MAGAZINE
NEEDS EDITOR

Canada Track & Traffic had escaped my best efforts to extinguish it—but come, come, no hard feelings. Indeed, within days of *The Canadian Driver's* next-to-invisible demise, *Canada Track & Traffic* became the vehicle for my meteoric rise from trade magazine editorial drudge to editor-in-chief.

Out of the blue one day, as I sat hunched in my Maclean-Hunter cubicle composing yet another fifty-word paean to modern slurry technology, the phone rang. It was Jerry, co-owner of *Track & Traffic*, offering me the number two editorial job. Given my entrenched opinion of that magazine as the print equivalent of a leper colony, I accepted with what might appear to be unseemly haste the opportunity to don the bell and have my bodily extremities decompose. But for this once, I'd decided to act on instinct, and the very next day proved my instincts flawless. The incumbent editor of *Track & Traffic* quit. I was his successor, head editorial leper.

So what if there were no other visible rivals for leadership of that one-man department, paying a cool hundred bucks a week? Somebody was actually willing to pay me more money than I'd ever hoped to earn to drive other people's cars and write about them. Leprosy was a small price to pay.

I did have to turn my back on status symbols like the mighty Maclean-Hunter building on University Avenue. *CT&T* headquarters was a walk-up aerie in a gloomy old brick factory building at

King and Bathurst streets in Toronto's weary West End, next door to what was billed as Canada's oldest tavern, the Wheat Sheaf.

The magazine had been born in financial desperation, brainstorm of a small-time job printer trying to amortize his linotype's downtime. It never did manage to outlive the spirit of those origins. By my advent, it was in the hands of Jerry and his Montreal backer Norm, a couple of amateur racing drivers keeping alive hopes for the magazine's eventual success on the car nuts' congenital delusion that the world is full of people just like them; that even in vast, underpopulated Canada there lurked so many kindred car fanatics that a monthly magazine aimed at them would fly off the newsstands while advertisers queued up to buy space in its pages.

This was not, of course, and never would be remotely close to reality. Slick, thick, big-circulation English and American car magazines proliferated on Canadian newsssstands, rendering *CT&T* a puny also-ran and its vaunted unique mission of an all-Canadian outlook a joke. There *was* no all-Canadian automotive outlook. There weren't any Canadian cars. A few amateur airport races and backwoods rallies notwithstanding, there was no Canadian car news. Ergo, few readers and virtually no advertisers for Canada's only automotive monthly.

But its car-crazed proprietors—and, truth to tell, its car-crazed editor—refused to take "no, no, a thousand times no" for an answer. So what if there were few readers and fewer advertisers; we'd put the damn thing out anyway, for ourselves. This helps explain why *Track & Traffic* (soon enough *Trash & Tragic* to connoisseurs) was to other car magazines as Kool-Aid is to Châteuneuf-du-Pape. There being no available photographers willing to shoot road-test cars for the promise of five dollars a picture, I dragooned good old Hugh and his ancient Voigtlander camera into service. Service it was; he even paid for the film. The magazine's dearth of readers was matched by the dearth of contributing writers—actually, other than the editor, none. The editorial budget was my salary and a phone bill. Should I take a trip or go out on a road test, I was expected to pick up the costs myself; after all, as Jerry explained, I'd have to eat and sleep and drive anyway, so why should *Track & Traffic* underwrite my high living?

Because the magazine was never more than a filament's breadth away from financial collapse, Jerry scrounged up ads wherever he could to pay the bills, under whatever conditions he had to. Thus, the magazine's monthly list of car advertisers became the magazine's monthly list of road tests, readers invited to pretend along with us that the Skoda Octavia ad on page 22 had nothing to do with the Skoda Octavia rave review on page 23.

Only somebody with my employment history could call this journalistic Augean stable the best job he'd ever had, but for a while, it was. I loved driving different cars and writing about them; I loved the monthly thrill of putting together a magazine—even this anemic imitation of a magazine—perhaps all the more so because of the Sisyphean task involved.

But the thrill inevitably began to fade and my energy to ebb. What *Track & Traffic* never would be began chafing, as did the growing realization that mine was a dead-end job. Not to mention the pains of leprosy. The last straw came when Jerry decided to bestow *CT&T*'s Car of the Year award for 1962 on a hideously mis-styled little English crapcan already panned by the world automotive press—but also the product of a company with a large ad budget. Maybe the company could be persuaded to buy a few pages in the one magazine willing to call its swine a pearl. Jerry and I duly trooped out to their main offices to present the coveted plaque. After we'd spent an hour or so in an anteroom, a secretary to the marketing honcho appeared to announce that Mister Big was going to be busy more or less forever and to ask, What was the purpose of our visit again?

Jerry handed over the plaque with a few mumbled words, and we departed.

Part V

AMERICA

TO THE RESCUE

DELIVERANCE

For reasons best known to its marketing and P.R. solons, the Canadian branch of the Shell Oil Company decided to stage a cross-country competitive sporting event called the Shell 4000 Trans-Canada Rally in the spring of 1961 and again in 1962. It was the biggest thing in Canadian motorsport's admittedly unspectacular history, an interminable slog from Montreal to Vancouver that drew professional factory entries and virtually every serious weekend rallyist in the northern half of the continent.

Jerry might fume and wail about the cost—and he did, until I came to see my trip expenses almost as embezzlement of company funds—but as editor of Canada's only consumer automotive publication, I was obliged to go.

The Shell caravan had slogged west through northern Ontario, Manitoba, and Alberta and arrived in Saskatoon late one night almost a week later for a twelve-hour stopover. In the parking lot, where the cars would be impounded overnight, a gaggle of drivers, mechanics, rally officials, and journalists stood about exchanging end-of-the-day small talk, and it was there that I met a lanky American in his early thirties, David E. Davis, Jr.

A sign reading TURNING POINT did not immediately light up in the skies overhead, but by cosmic rights it should have. Davis made a joke. I made a joke. Davis said something outrageous, and everybody laughed. This guy was a character. As it happened, we were headed for the same hotel. Come on up later to my room for a drink, Davis said, and have some laughs.

I had some laughs. I left Davis's room an hour or so later with that sure, buoyant feeling that I had just made a friend for life. But David E. Davis, Jr., was from the very first moment a friend apart and above. He was the first sophisticated adult who had ever given me the time of day. He was smart, quick, wickedly funny, and good enough to laugh at my jokes. He was high-spirited; he didn't just like a good time, he demanded a good time—even in Saskatoon, Saskatchewan, after midnight. Davis, it was already obvious, harbored a voracious appetite for interesting people and a withering contempt for phonies, dolts, and bores. From the unpromising makings of the Shell 4000 rally he had somehow collected and nightly convened a kind of movable salon of the craziest, funniest, most interesting people he could recruit. And now I had a pass, good for the balance of the trip through Alberta and the Rockies to Vancouver.

David E. Davis, Jr., wrote articles for *Road & Track* as a minor sideline. His real job was guiding the advertising programs for Chevrolet's sporty Corvette, Corvair, and the Chevy II's running in this rally for his agency back in Detroit, Campbell-Ewald.

By the time the rally ended and after a farewell party at a Chinese restaurant in Vancouver—more belly laughs, more outrage, more hilarious anecdotes—I was in Dave Davis's thrall, one of the acolytes-cum-admiring-protégés he seemed to attract so effortlessly.

The Davis encounter made returning to Toronto and the *Track & Traffic* life a comedown. It had shown, by blazing contrast, a glimpse of what I was missing. I was missing almost everything. It wasn't only that I had managed to find one of the few jobs on earth actually capable of lowering my self-esteem and was corroding into a hack. Life outside the office had become as stagnant and empty as it ever was in Windsor. Chris was now living with me in an *Odd Couple* sort of domestic situation while finishing high school at nearby Forest Hill Collegiate, and we had our own McCall kind of fun, if also the McCall kind of household shabbiness and social isolation.

But after twenty-seven years of it, the hand-to-mouth mode of existence was finally beginning to pall. I was still living like an adolescent abandoned by his parents, still lingering in that limbo of pre-responsibility where you weren't expected to keep an ordered household, eat proper food, or otherwise submit to the rules of the adult world.

This fresh perspective, thanks to that brief exposure to the David E. Davis example. Its effect was profound. Dissatisfaction with my current plight was only stage one; the upward jog in self-regard that followed from Davis's interest and approval fertilized the first tiny seedlings of something like ambition, and they were already beginning to sprout. If they were ever going to blossom, it wouldn't be in this arid environment.

The mounting desire to flee my job and my stagnant life into the bargain was stymied, however, by a keen awareness of the paucity of places to flee to. Every new issue of *Track & Traffic* with my name on it lessened the chances of being considered for hiring by any reputable publication; and this being Canada in 1962, there were few enough of those to begin with. My résumé was thin and checkered with awkward gaps. My creative imagination didn't extend to employment ideas. I seemed destined to view the highway to success and happiness from a cul-de-sac.

It was during these dour deliberations that David E. Davis, Jr., swept into town. He was ensconced for the weekend at the Four Seasons on Jarvis Street, a veritable palace of swank in the Toronto of the time, and on a Saturday afternoon in July I found myself lounging on a balcony overlooking the swimming pool, belting back gin-and-tonics, and exchanging droll urbanities with a clutch of Davisian chums as if I did it every day. Davis was driving somebody's race-trim Ferrari coupe and invited me along on a demonstration run, 100 MPH up the Don Valley Expressway. He still laughed at my jokes, and roped me in later for a gala dinner in the Franz Josef room at Walker

House. And before the caravansary departed the following day, he offered me a job.

I lived off the flattery of the idea—bolting Toronto and Canada and going to work with Dave in advertising in Detroit—for weeks without quite daring to consider it real. The implications were too overpowering. In late August he repeated the offer, this time more concretely, and suggested a visit to the agency in Detroit for an interview. Things were moving almost more quickly than felt comfortable. I needed time to mull them. What I mostly mulled was that nobody could be this lucky. Exchange seedy obscurity for the ad biz big-time, put dowdy Canada behind me for life in the USA, make good money while hobnobbing with David E. Davis, Jr., and his peers? Revolutionize my life in a single, swift bound? If the offer was real, it was the original no-brainer.

My interview in late September served to brush away any timid Canadian self-doubt. Campbell-Ewald needed no samples, no questionnaire to be completed. It was ready to take Dave's word and hire me, at more than double current wages, to write Corvette and Corvair ads.

David E. Davis, Jr., had by now been awarded the supplemental honors of being not just my friend but also my big brother, surrogate father, and mentor. He had changed everything. It was now almost more than I could bear to put up with the squalid world of *Track & Traffic*. I now saw myself—because Dave so saw me—not as a loser but as a comer, who belonged at the center of things, who could have an effect, a secret weapon of talent brought out of mothballs at last. I didn't know what I'd done to deserve all this, but I was half-crazed to start cashing in.

I was at least equally raring to cash out of Toronto and my home and native land. Whatever qualms may have been stirred by the prospect of emigrating had evaporated the moment the decision was made, whereupon I devoted most of the waning weeks until the move amassing corroboration and justification.

They were everywhere. Now that I'd declared Detroit the New

Jerusalem, Toronto was shrinking down into a tank town where the streets were paved with cement, denying me Lebensraum. The best the place had ever made of my blazing talents was to keep me scrambling down near the bottom of the heap; I remembered, from my jobless period two years before, taking a copywriting test at one of the city's bigger advertising agencies and being advised by the haughty jerk in charge to forget it—I didn't have what it took for the ad game. Not your second-rate version of the ad game, bozo.

Final conclusions could wait—and as a matter of fact are still waiting—but my own sorry fault or not, I had been a failure as a Canadian. I had never, ever responded to the tone of the place. The patience, the mildness, the taste for conformity that seemed prerequisites for a tolerable life were beyond me. Canadians so flinched from giving offense, much less seizing the initiative, that it had seeped into the way they talked. For half the population, every utterance ended in a . . . question? Even declarative statements ended up wheedling . . . agreement? And the famous, pathetic Canadian "eh?" was usually tacked on, to further soften it . . . eh? This was not a nation poised to shake the world.

Nobody seemed to have big dreams. Nobody wanted to stand out. Save for annual wheat-bushel quotas and snowfall records, excess might as well be legally outlawed. There wasn't a glamorous public figure in the entire dominion, and "Canadian style" was an oxymoron. At one point in my high school years, as fervent with patriotic zeal as I'd ever be, I decided to bring the saga of Canada's history alive in punchy, fast-moving comic strip form. What ensued was scene after scene of bewhiskered elderly gentlemen in stovepipe hats standing around one conference hall or other and making declarations on the order of "So it is settled, gentlemen. The Cod Tax shall be repealed!" The project yawned to a premature stop.

Hockey aside, rare was the world-class Canadian talent content to stay in Canada. The Americans grabbed off many of the best and the brightest to feed their voracious appetite for excellence.

The immediate question attached to almost any halfway famous Canadian was "Not good enough to make it in the States, eh?" Lesser talent cast a milder glow; seen from space, a culture dominated by Canadians appeared dim and wan. Too dim, too wan for me.

How presumptuous. What gave me the idea that my wares would be any more prized south of the border than they were at home? If Canada was so inherently mediocre, so lax of standards, how come all my huffing and puffing hadn't raised me beyond obscurity and penury? Fair question, I had to admit, and I vowed to figure it out eventually. But for the moment, faith would have to substitute for reason, logic, and hard evidence.

In the end, I could find no reason to think of Canada as any different from what it had been in school geography books since time immemorial: a giant wheat-farming, cod-fishing, timber-felling, ore-smelting, paper-milling, ore-mining enterprise perched on the cusp of greatness since confederation almost a hundred years before, but in no particular rush to arrive there. As far as I was concerned, the sleeping giant had slept in. And it was time I tiptoed away.

Say this for a marginal existence—it's a snap to wrap up. A word to the landlady, the closing out of my bank account, a couple of hours' packing, and I was unplugged and free to leave. The Americans had a charming bureaucratic term, "settler's effects," apparently coined in frontier days. It covered the furniture and other goods every incoming alien resident was permitted to drag across the border and into his new life. My settler's effects were a radio, a portable typewriter, a few books, and some papers. My entire ensemble of homemade and handed-down furnishings I chucked as unworthy of occupying American space.

Given that my circle of friends had never grown beyond a pinhead, it would have been difficult to assemble half a dozen Toronto acquaintances interested enough to be called well-wishers for a farewell party; and in any case the idea never occurred—to me or to anyone else. Jerry and the *Track & Traffic* staff bade their goodbye from the top of the office stairs. Bags stowed in the backseat of my Volvo, I lunched with Chris, now living in a freshman dormitory at the University of Toronto. By mid-afternoon of a gray December Thursday I was on the road, America-bound, singing all the way.

EPILOGUE

It was golden high summer when I took my memoirist's tour of Simcoe in 1995. The mile-long section of Highway #3 where my defection to America began fifty years ago had itself become American, a strip of Dairy Queens and Burger Kings and a Best Western motel with a bar (closing time 10:00 P.M.; it was still Ontario, after all).

Otherwise, it still felt a lot like Simcoe to me. Indeed, the nostalgist's secret suspicion that memory can control time seemed, at first, to be confirmed. The carillon bells still pealed the hours. Individual buildings, whole blocks, entire neighborhoods conspired in the seductive illusion that time had suspended itself that day I left in 1947 and considerately held its breath until the minute the prodigal son was spotted back in town.

The orange-brick house at 209 West Street where we lived from 1940 to 1942, where I remember glimpsing my first airliner as it sailed across my bedroom window against a Maxfield Parrish summer evening sky, could have been preserved under a glass bell for all it had aged. The North Public School had entered a time warp; I could have slipped back into my fifth grade classroom and there would be Mrs. Coombs, barking, "Bruce McCall, you've been marked absent for forty-nine years. Where is your note?" One evening I stood at the corner of Union and Talbot streets, where any moment now Larry and Gary and all the other neighborhood kids would be gathering, as they always did in the after-supper summer dusk under the moth-thronged streetlight nights while the cicadas chirruped and nighthawks caromed overhead.

And then, in an unsummoned rush, the hollowness of it all. I might as well be pressing my nose against the plate-glass window of a diorama. The stream of time had carried away everything alive in that long-ago world. The kids had apparently tired of waiting under the streetlight and hopped the shuttle to the irretrievable past. I was alone among the army of strangers who had taken over and who now slept under the eaves of Aunt May's house, lolled in Aunt Eva's bathtub, trooped into the medical clinic (take that, T.C.!) at 101 Union Street, where our crumbling old stucco house once stood.

Remembrance couldn't compete with reality. Simcoe was now another place under the same name, and so determined to unmoor itself from everything it had once been that a statute of limitations now seemed to govern even ancient ancestral rights; complacent absentee seigneur that I had been, I now had to face the fact that those of the Norfolk County McCalls had expired. The family dynasty that had flourished there for a century and a half had, within one generation—my generation—vanished forever. Even the old family cemetery ten miles south of town near the hamlet of Vittoria, where lie the bones of the earliest Norfolk County McCalls, is now overgrown and lost in an impenetrable copse backing up to somebody's suburban lot among the ginseng crops that are fast replacing King Tobacco. Nearby, the once imposing stone residence built by Simpson McCall in the mid-1800s is only one of the more exhausted looking of a motley of anonymous roadside houses on Vittoria's fringes.

What had seemed a birthright, the sense of permanence and belonging evoked by the word "Simcoe" for as long as I could remember, exists today only in the names—West, Gilbertson, Cameron, Whitside, McCall, McCall, McCall—on the headstones in Oakwood Cemetery. Even a Simcoe afterlife has been foreclosed to me; the McCall family plot where I'd always assumed I'd spend eternity is full up. I poked about halfheartedly for a day while the sentimental fiction of Simcoe as abiding spiritual hearth steadily drained away, and left me feeling dispossessed and diminished, a reduced version of myself.

Toronto's explosive post-fifties growth roared straight on past Danforth Avenue, marooning places like the block of flats at Danforth Court in the asphalt wastes, apparently forever. Even the charmlessness endures; I park my car to stroll that scruffy central quadrangle again and test the atmosphere for afterpangs, but a third-floor window instantly shoots open and the sentinel inside snarls, "What the fuck you looking for?" Good question.

Save for the front-yard 1953 sapling turned 1996 spreading maple tree, the bungalow at 1793 Byng Road in Windsor could be waiting for T.C. to come roaring home from the office in his three-tone eighteen-foot-long Chrysler and plow to his usual crash stop in the seventeen-foot-long driveway, heralding the start of dinnertime festivities. Time has been less kind to downtown, where the synthetic joy of a gambling casino is the only sign of life in an urban graveyard as forlorn and desolate as downtown Detroit, across the river. Windsor and I had our differences, but I never wished for things to come to this.

The Windsor Women's Dance Project—even the sign radiates militancy—occupies the former Windsor Advertising Artists suite at Pelissier and University. I chicken out of my plan to knock on the door and ask indulgence for a ruminative look around, and instead stand on the sidewalk across the street and gaze up at the second-story window on the world where I daydreamed away most of my late adolescence and early adulthood.

Several minutes later and I'm growing tired of waiting for time's mellow perspective to kick in and revelations to start flowing. As with all other such confrontations in this experiment in time travel, no new meaning is revealed. Nothing is revealed except the folly of hoping—and I realize I had nurtured just such a mystical hope for most of my life—that the act of passing my eyes over the physical surfaces of the past could restore it to life for an instant or two, long enough to reenter and, by my applying all the wisdom of the intervening years, resolve its mysteries at last. Those windows across the street become just windows again. An hour later I'm at Detroit Metro, waiting for the plane back to New York and home.

All six of us, my siblings and me, are now older than either of our parents lived to be. In a combined life span of 350 and counting, in fact, we have spent a grand total of perhaps three weeks in hospitals and have proven immune to all serious illness and disease except for that deadly duo spawned by genes and early environment: alcoholism in a couple of cases; depression in varying degrees of severity across the board. All of us married. If they were alive today, T.C. and Peg would find themselves burdened by sixteen grandchildren and six great-grandchildren.

Mike married within months of joining the Navy in 1952 and sired six offspring of his own. He retired from the service, divorced, and with his companion, Jo, now lives in the Annapolis Valley in Nova Scotia, a bushy-bearded elder whose walk and mannerisms increasingly suggest the living reincarnation of Grandfather Walt.

Hugh found fortune elusive. He too would stub his toe in commercial art, leave Windsor for Toronto, and one day even man what was left of the rickety editor's chair at *Track & Traffic*. The idea that I had stolen part of his soul, along with his clothes and his half share in our cars, haunted me and still does. But adversity never soured Hugh's sweet nature, and after too many bleak years, Hugh married the sister of my first love, Jane, and the two found happiness together that neither had experienced alone.

Tom, like Mike, married almost immediately after leaving home for the Navy and fathered five children. He later divorced, and continues to keep a wary distance from his brothers and sister that has stretched into bouts of estrangement lasting for years.

Walt triumphed. He graduated from his cub-reporter days at the *St. Thomas Times-Journal* to become a national award-winning reporter for the *Windsor Star* (he dashed into the building he happened to be driving by when it exploded, helped rescue the injured, then dashed to the office to write his account), an automotive columnist, author of dense and factually incontestable reference volumes on fire apparatus, Cadillacs, the cars of General Motors, and the history of the hearse. He became a husband and father and a man who—like the boy—has never met an hour he couldn't fill with fun and stimulation. In his late fifties, he is pink-faced, unwrinkled, and by a factor of about a hundred to one the jolliest of the bunch. Walt drives his own personal fire truck, has long since paid off the mortgage on a Tudor pile in Windsor that would leave his father adrool with envy, and— uncanny, delicious, exquisite irony of ironies—was until his recent retirement a public relations executive at Chrysler of Canada, daily thrombosing the shade of T. C. McCall.

Chris left university, joined Walt as a reporter at the *Windsor Star*, moved to New York, and became managing editor of David E. Davis's magazine *Car and Driver* before marrying my best friend, John Jerome, and decamping to northern New Hampshire. She avoids New York and wider civilization like the plague but remains confidante, confessor, chum, and conscience. Our baby sister is the steadiest and most grown-up of us all, freelance editor and recent author of a marvelous book on the Adirondacks.

My siblings and I never outgrew the mutual-defense mentality fostered in the years of our joint and individual travails. Our shared experience will probably bind us forever in a kind of survivors' club. I'm sometimes unsure if we like one another so much as we're simply unable to pull free of the habit of needing one another.

Videotaped by a social anthropologist, our occasional reunions would yield vital clinical material. We reflexively revert, within minutes, to our hierarchal roles of forty years ago: Mike the wise if reluctant leader, Hugh the listener and archivist and fall guy, Walt the junior partner and still the brat, Chris the revered kid sister, me the moody one, as likely to retreat into a surly funk as to jabber and jape. Decades after they ceased being risky, physical or even verbal expressions of affection still terrify us. Maybe we should join the circus, because you could stuff all five of us into a phone booth and we'd find a way not to touch.

Beyond the fact that Larry Leatherdale grew up to be a doctor, I know virtually nothing today of my earliest Simcoe contemporaries.

One ex–North Public School classmate did track Hugh and me down in Windsor in the fifties. He was a drug addict and lowlife, a spectral figure with long black fingernails, bad skin, and strange ferret teeth. The auld lang syne failed to take.

Aside from brother Walt, Windsor today is bereft of even the few intimates I had. Jane, long married, still lives there. Weeks after a lukewarm rapprochement between us in 1963, Alex was killed in a freak accident in the Porsche that I'd recommended he buy. He wasn't yet forty. Mike Barber, the M.G. zealot and debater-goad, died in his forties of kidney disease. The young New York editor upon whom I imposed myself in search of guidance at the start of my writing career was Eliot Fremont-Smith, who went on to become the daily book reviewer for *The New York Times* in the seventies. Many years later, when I published my first book, he gave it a glowing review.

I was determined not to look back once I left Toronto in 1962, and was as good as my vow. I avoided the place for years. The few familiar names from the Toronto era faded into the past—all except my Danforth Tech art class friend and maternal substitute April and my erstwhile publishing partner Eric. Eric returned to Toronto from self-exile in the mid-sixties, made a fortune as a dashing entrepreneur, and ended up in Kingston Penitentiary after a mob of fleeced investors exposed just what all that dashing had involved. He called me in New York a few years later, proposing a get-together. He had important business there imminently with some Egyptian gentlemen and would call. I'm still waiting.

The United States of America gave me no cause to regret having forsaken the land of my ancestors, and in fact proved those fevered boyish imaginings of life under the Stars and Stripes to be almost prescient. I was no longer a slipping cogwheel in an obsolete machine. The Americans had plenty of room, and lots for me to do. The sense of being near the epicenter was tonic. It awoke the energy and focused the ambition to push even nearer. Within two years of arriving in America I had rendezvoused with what I'd always felt to be my destiny and was living in New York. The blandishments of a career in the advertising big leagues brought sweet redemption to the high school dropout and lifelong underachiever—too much, perhaps; I clung to advertising long after it had lost its allure, denying my true vocation as a freelance writer and illustrator. But I finally did break away, and the journey that had begun in that closet at 101 Union Street led to the day I was handed the keys to my very own office at *The New Yorker.* The man who claimed that there are no second acts in American life was wrong.

New York City has now been my home for longer than Canada was. Late at night sometimes as I stare at the bedroom ceiling of our apartment on Central Park West, my American wife asleep beside me, it still seems unreal: I let a childish vision, a self-created fairy tale, be my guide. And damned if it didn't work.

I intend finally to make the obvious official and exchange my longtime resident alien status for U.S. citizenship. It's been thirty-four years since I crossed the border, for heaven's sake. Of course there are endless bureaucratic procedures involved—forms to fill out, appointments to make, and on any given day in any given week, wouldn't you know it, something always seems to come up. But mark my words: Any day now. Next week is looking good, in fact. Certainly the end of the year. Absolute latest.

BLACK ICE

by Lorene Cary

The story of a bright, ambitious black teenager from Philadelphia, who, when transplanted to an elite school in New Hampshire, becomes a scholarship student determined to succeed without selling out. In recounting her journey into selfhood, Lorene Cary creates a universally recognizable document of a woman's adolescence.

"Probably the most beautifully written and the most moving African-American autobiographical narrative since Maya Angelou's *I Know Why the Caged Bird Sings*."
—Arnold Rampersad
Autobiography/African-American Studies/0-679-73745-6

THE ROAD FROM COORAIN

by Jill Ker Conway

A remarkable woman's clear-sighted memoir of growing up Australian: from the vastness of a sheep station in the outback to the stifling propriety of postwar Sidney; from an untutored childhood to a life in academia; and from the shelter of a protective family to the lessons of independence.

"A small masterpiece of scene, memory and very stylish English. I've been several times to Australia; this book was the most rewarding journey of all." —John Kenneth Galbraith
Autobiography/0-679-72436-2

TRUE NORTH

by Jill Ker Conway

In this second volume of her memoirs, Jill Ker Conway leaves Australia for America, where she becomes a renowned historian and, later, the first woman president of Smith College. She enters a lively community of women scholars and examines the challenges that confront all women who seek to establish public selves and reconcile them with their private passions.

"A thinking woman's memoir . . . it resounds with ideas about nature, culture, and education. . . . *True North* shines with the lasting luster of hard marble." —*Philadelphia Inquirer*
Memoir/Women's Studies/0-679-74461-4

THE SHADOW MAN
A Daughter's Search for Her Father
by Mary Gordon

This is the memoir of a woman who, after thirty years of unflinching love for a memory, sets out to discover who her father really was. Gordon finds an immigrant who lied about his origins; a Jew who became a virulent anti-Semite; and a devout Catholic who was also a pornographer.

"Stunning . . . a painful and luminous book . . . that somehow, amazingly, reconciles Ms. Gordon's feelings of love and horror, guilt and forgiveness, and transforms them into art."
—*The New York Times*

Memoir/0-679-74931-4

AN UNQUIET MIND
A Memoir of Moods and Madness
by Kay Redfield Jamison

Kay Redfield Jamison is one of the world's most renowned authorities on manic-depressive illness; she is also one of its survivors. It is this dual perspective—as healer and healed—that makes her bestselling memoir so lucid, learned and profoundly affecting.

"Written with poetic and moving sensitivity . . . a rare and insightful view of mental illness from inside the mind of a trained specialist."
—*Time*

Psychology/Memoir/0-679-76330-9

RIDING THE WHITE HORSE HOME
A Western Family Album
by Teresa Jordan

A haunting memoir about the generations of women who learned to cope with physical hardship and loneliness in the beautiful yet grim landscape of the West. *Riding the White Horse Home* is at once Teresa Jordan's family chronicle and a eulogy for the West her people helped shape.

"Spellbinding. . . . the emotional scope of Jordan's prose is as vast as the ranch she grew up on—succoring one moment, shattering the next."
—*Seattle Times*

Memoir/Travel/0-679-75135-1

GIRL, INTERRUPTED
by Susanna Kaysen

Set in the exclusive grounds of McLean Hospital, Kaysen's memoir encompasses horror and razor-edged perception while providing vivid portraits of her fellow patients and their keepers. In this brilliant evocation of a "parallel universe," Kaysen gives a clear-sighted depiction of various definitions of sane and insane, mental illness and recovery.

"Poignant, honest and triumphantly funny . . . [a] compelling and heartbreaking story."
—Susan Cheever, *The New York Times Book Review*
Autobiography/Psychology/0-679-74604-8

REFUGE
An Unnatural History of Family and Place
by Terry Tempest Williams

Through tragedies both personal and environmental, Utah-born naturalist Terry Tempest Williams creates a document of renewal and spiritual grace that is a moving meditation on nature, women, and grieving.

"Moving and loving . . . both a natural history of an ecological phenomenon, along with a Mormon family saga . . . a heroic book." —*Washington Post Book World*
Women's Studies/Nature/0-679-74024-4

Available at your local bookstore, or call toll-free to order:
1-800-793-2665 (credit cards only).